Battleground Europe

WALKING YPRES

Battleground series:

Stamford Bridge & Hastings by Peter Marren
Wars of the Roses - Wakefield/Towton by Philip A. Haigh
Wars of the Roses - Barnet by David Clark
Wars of the Roses - Tewkesbury by Steven Goodchild
Wars of the Roses - The Battles of St Albans by
Peter Burley, Michael Elliott & Harvey Wilson
English Civil War - Naseby by Martin Marix Evans, Peter Burton
and Michael Westaway
English Civil War - Marston Moor by David Clark
War of the Spanish Succession - Blenheim 1704 by James Falkner
War of the Spanish Succession - Ramillies 1706 by James Falkner
Napoleonic - Hougoumont by Julian Paget and Derek Saunders
Napoleonic - Waterloo by Andrew Uffindell and Michael Corum
Zulu War - Isandlwana by Ian Knight and Ian Castle
Zulu War - Rorkes Drift by Ian Knight and Ian Castle
Boer War - The Relief of Ladysmith by Lewis Childs
Boer War - The Siege of Ladysmith by Lewis Childs
Boer War - Kimberley by Lewis Childs

Mons by Jack Horsfall and Nigel Cave
Néry by Patrick Tackle
Le Cateau by Nigel Cave and Jack Shelden
Walking the Salient by Paul Reed
Ypres - Sanctuary Wood and Hooge by Nigel Cave
Ypres - Hill 60 by Nigel Cave
Ypres - Messines Ridge by Peter Oldham
Ypres - Polygon Wood by Nigel Cave
Ypres - Passchendaele by Nigel Cave
Ypres - Airfields and Airmen by Mike O'Connor
Ypres - St Julien by Graham Keech
Walking the Somme by Paul Reed
Somme - Gommecourt by Nigel Cave
Somme - Serre by Jack Horsfall & Nigel Cave
Somme - Beaumont Hamel by Nigel Cave
Somme - Thiepval by Michael Stedman
Somme - La Boisselle by Michael Stedman
Somme - Fricourt by Michael Stedman
Somme - Carnoy-Montauban by Graham Maddocks
Somme - Pozières by Graham Keech
Somme - Courcelette by Paul Reed
Somme - Boom Ravine by Trevor Pidgeon
Somme - Mametz Wood by Michael Renshaw
Somme - Delville Wood by Nigel Cave
Somme - Advance to Victory (North) 1918 by Michael Stedman
Somme - Flers by Trevor Pidgeon
Somme - Bazentin Ridge by Edward Hancock
Somme - Combles by Paul Reed
Somme - Beaucourt by Michael Renshaw
Somme - Redan Ridge by Michael Renshaw
Somme - Hamel by Peter Pedersen
Somme - Villers-Bretonneux by Peter Pedersen
Somme - Airfields and Airmen by Mike O'Connor
Airfields and Airmen of the Channel Coast by Mike O'Connor
In the Footsteps of the Red Baron by Mike O'Connor
Arras - Airfields and Airmen by Mike O'Connor
Arras - The Battle for Vimy Ridge by Jack Sheldon & Nigel Cave
Arras - Vimy Ridge by Nigel Cave
Arras - Gavrelle by Trevor Tasker and Kyle Tallett
Arras - Oppy Wood by David Bilton
Arras - Bullecourt by Graham Keech
Arras - Monchy le Preux by Colin Fox
Walking Arras by Paul Reed
Hindenburg Line by Peter Oldham
Hindenburg Line - Epehy by Bill Mitchinson
Hindenburg Line - Riqueval by Bill Mitchinson
Hindenburg Line - Villers-Plouich by Bill Mitchinson

Hindenburg Line - Cambrai Right Hook by Jack Horsfall & Nigel Cave
Hindenburg Line - Cambrai Flesquières by Jack Horsfall & Nigel Cave
Hindenburg Line - Saint Quentin by Helen McPhail and Philip Guest
Hindenburg Line - Bourlon Wood by Jack Horsfall & Nigel Cave
Cambrai - Airfields and Airmen by Mike O'Connor
Aubers Ridge by Edward Hancock
La Bassée - Neuve Chapelle by Geoffrey Bridger
Loos - Hohenzollern Redoubt by Andrew Rawson
Loos - Hill 70 by Andrew Rawson
Fromelles by Peter Pedersen
Accrington Pals Trail by William Turner
Poets at War: Wilfred Owen by Helen McPhail and Philip Guest
Poets at War: Edmund Blunden by Helen McPhail and Philip Guest
Poets at War: Graves & Sassoon by Helen McPhail and Philip Guest
Gallipoli by Nigel Steel
Gallipoli - Gully Ravine by Stephen Chambers
Gallipoli - Anzac, The Landing by Stephen Chambers
Gallipoli - Landings at Helles by Huw & Jill Rodge
Gallipoli - Suvla – August Offensive by Stephen Chambers
Walking the Italian Front by Francis Mackay
Italy - Asiago by Francis Mackay
Verdun: Fort Douaumont by Christina Holstein
Zeebrugge & Ostend Raids 1918 by Stephen McGreal

Germans at Beaumont Hamel by Jack Sheldon
Germans at Thiepval by Jack Sheldon

SECOND WORLD WAR

Dunkirk by Patrick Wilson
Calais by Jon Cooksey
Boulogne by Jon Cooksey
Saint-Nazaire by James Dorrian
Normandy - Pegasus Bridge/Merville Battery by Carl Shilleto
Normandy - Utah Beach by Carl Shilleto
Normandy - Omaha Beach by Tim Kilvert-Jones
Normandy - Gold Beach by Christopher Dunphie & Garry Johnson
Normandy - Gold Beach Jig by Tim Saunders
Normandy - Juno Beach by Tim Saunders
Normandy - Sword Beach by Tim Kilvert-Jones
Normandy - Operation Bluecoat by Ian Daglish
Normandy - Operation Goodwood by Ian Daglish
Normandy - Epsom by Tim Saunders
Normandy - Hill 112 by Tim Saunders
Normandy - Mont Pinçon by Eric Hunt
Normandy - Cherbourg by Andrew Rawson
Das Reich – Drive to Normandy by Philip Vickers
Oradour by Philip Beck
Market Garden - Nijmegen by Tim Saunders
Market Garden - Hell's Highway by Tim Saunders
Market Garden - Arnhem, Oosterbeek by Frank Steer
Market Garden - Arnhem, The Bridge by Frank Steer
Market Garden - The Island by Tim Saunders
Rhine Crossing – US 9th Army & 17th US Airborne by Andrew Rawson
British Rhine Crossing – Operation Varsity by Tim Saunders
British Rhine Crossing – Operation Plunder by Tim Saunders
Battle of the Bulge – St Vith by Michael Tolhurst
Battle of the Bulge – Bastogne by Michael Tolhurst
Channel Islands by George Forty
Walcheren by Andrew Rawson
Remagen Bridge by Andrew Rawson
Cassino by Ian Blackwell
Anzio by Ian Blackwell
Dieppe by Tim Saunders
Fort Eben Emael by Tim Saunders
Crete – Operation 'Merkur' by Tim Saunders

With the continued expansion of the Battleground Series a **Battleground Series Club** has been formed to benefit the reader. The purpose of the Club is to keep members informed of new titles and to offer many other reader-benefits. Membership is free and by registering an interest you can help us predict print runs and thus assist us in maintaining the quality and prices at their present levels.

Please call the office on 01226 734555, or send your name and address along with
a request for more information to:
Battleground Series Club Pen & Sword Books Ltd,
47 Church Street, Barnsley, South Yorkshire S70 2AS

Battleground Europe

WALKING YPRES

Paul Reed

Pen & Sword
MILITARY

First published in Great Britain in 2017 by
Pen & Sword Military
An imprint of
Pen & Sword Books Ltd
47 Church Street
Barnsley
South Yorkshire
S70 2AS

ISBN 978 178159 003 4

Typeset in Times New Roman by Chic Graphics

Printed and bound in England by
CPI Group (UK) Ltd., Croydon, CR0 4YY

Pen & Sword Books Ltd incorporates the imprints of
Pen & Sword Archaeology, Atlas, Aviation, Battleground, Discovery,
Family History, History, Maritime, Military, Naval, Politics,
Railways, Select, Social History, Transport, True Crime,
Claymore Press, Frontline Books, Leo Cooper, Praetorian Press,
Remember When, Seaforth Publishing and Wharncliffe.

For a complete list of Pen & Sword titles please contact
PEN & SWORD BOOKS LIMITED
47 Church Street, Barnsley, South Yorkshire, S70 2AS, England
E-mail: enquiries@pen-and-sword.co.uk
Website: www.pen-and-sword.co.uk

Contents

Introduction 6
Visitor Information 7

Chapter One   **Ypres Town Walk** 9
Chapter Two   **Menin Gate – Hellfire Corner – Potijze Walk** 37
Chapter Three   **Yser Canal Walk: Ypres to Boesinghe** 58
Chapter Four   **Sanctuary Wood – Hooge – Bellewaarde Ridge Walk** 78
Chapter Five   **Zillebeke Walk** 103
Chapter Six   **The Bluff – Hill 60 Walk** 117
Chapter Seven   **Langemarck Walk** 138
Chapter Eight   **Passchendaele Walk** 152
Chapter Nine   **Behind the Lines Walk: Brandhoek–Vlamertinghe** 170
Chapter Ten   **Poperinghe Town Walk** 190
Chapter Eleven   **Locre – Kemmel Walk** 208
Chapter Twelve   **'Whitesheet' Walk** 227
Chapter Thirteen   **Messines Ridge Walk** 245
Chapter Fourteen   **'Plugstreet Wood' Walk** 263

Acknowledgements 286
Abbreviations 287
Further Reading.. 289
Index 291

Introduction

The battlefields around Ypres were, for four years of the Great War, the main British and Commonwealth sector on the Western Front. One in four of the British and Commonwealth soldiers who died in the war fell here, and one in three of Britain's casualties on the Western Front died in Flanders Fields. Together with the Somme, it is a place that defines our knowledge of the Great War. When we think of Ypres, or *Wipers* as the troops once called it, we think of those vast wastelands filled with muddy shell holes: a lunar landscape drifting almost into infinity. It was a battlefield that symbolised the war, and came to symbolise Britain's sacrifice too: Ypres became a place of pilgrimage as early as 1919, something that continues to this day as nearly half a million people travelled to Flanders in the opening year of the Great War Centenary in 2014.

For me personally, Ypres has always been the gateway to the Great War, and I suspect for many others it will be the same. I first walked the ground here as a very young man on a school trip and have been returning ever since. Ypres has changed dramatically in those decades and many areas have disappeared with development, but walking the ground proves, as with all battlefields, that getting off the beaten track is where we can reconnect with the Great War and listen to that last witness of the conflict: the landscape, and all it has to tell us.

And even in this changing world there will always be constants, which restore our faith and ensure that contact with events over a century ago remain vivid, and meaningful. The Last Post still sounds each night under the Menin Gate, the huge scale of loss at Tyne Cot and Langemarck still provokes gasps from first-time visitors, and there is still quiet solitude in the Upper Room of Talbot House at Poperinghe. Here we can renew the debt we owe to the generation of the Great War, remembering the survivors as well as the fallen, and vow to return and never forget, long after the centenary period has come to an end.

Paul Reed
Kent, the Somme and Flanders
www.ww1revisited.com
@sommecourt on Twitter

Visitor Information

THE WALKS: The scope of this book is aimed at the most common form of traveller to Flanders: individuals or small groups in a car. Each walk is circular, so that a vehicle can be left in a given location, and returned to (usually) without having to walk back across the same route. However, the walks will also suit anyone visiting the battlefields in coach parties, by foot alone, or by bicycle or mountain bike. Car crime in Belgium is pretty rare but walkers should be aware of the possibility when choosing somewhere to park their vehicle, and it is advisable never to leave valuables on display.

DISTANCE: The length of each walk is shown in miles and kilometres, to give some idea of how much walking is required. All walks can be done at a gentle stroll, taking time to stop and look at the surroundings and discuss the areas you visit, and, as there are few areas of really high ground in Flanders, save Kemmel Hill, then it is not difficult terrain to negotiate.

THE MAPS: The maps are based on field sketches drawn by the author during the research for this book. They have been redrawn and made true-to-scale wherever possible. All maps have been simplified and usually only show roads, tracks and other features directly connected with the walk in question. They are, however, suitable for orientation purposes. Detailed Belgian NGI maps of the Ypres area can be purchased in local bookshops and the In Flanders Fields Museum.

GETTING THERE: The area around Ypres can easily be reached by car from the Eurotunnel, and from ports at Calais, Dunkirk and Zeebrugge in around an hour in most cases. By train you can take the Eurostar to Lille or Brussels and then take a local train to Ypres. For more information see the Visit Flanders website (www.visitflanders. com).

ACCOMMODATION: There are many places to stay in Ypres and the surrounding area, from hotels in the city to bed and breakfast accommodation, some of them on local farms. The Ypres Tourist Office (www.toerismeieper.be) has full details of all available accommodation.

WHAT TO TAKE: As always with Flanders, the weather can be mixed and waterproofs, a spare jumper and strong shoes are never wasted on a trip to the battlefields. In the summer, extra water, sun lotion and a hat are equally useful. Good walking boots are recommended for all walkers. Although there are many inexpensive models currently on the market, the more money you spend on a pair of boots, the longer they are likely to last. Ones that are already waterproof, or can be easily made so, are essential. A small walker's rucksack is useful for carrying supplies, camera and other gear; again a waterproofed one would be a wise choice.

THE IRON HARVEST: Even a century after the battles around Ypres, ploughing in Flanders each year unearths a vast arsenal of live ammunition, shells, grenades and mortar bombs. All should be regarded as dangerous and not touched under any circumstances. Every year these deadly relics cause casualties, many of them fatal. Safe souvenirs can be bought in many locations on the battlefield.

WESTERN FRONT ASSOCIATION: For those with more than a passing interest in the Great War, membership of the WFA is essential. One year's subscription includes three copies of both *Stand To!* (the WFA's glossy magazine) and the *Bulletin* (the in-house newsletter). There are dozens of local branches throughout the UK and abroad. It is good for making useful contacts, exchanging information and ideas. For further information see the WFA website (www.westernfront association.com).

NOTE: The author and publishers bear no responsibility for any events or injuries which arise through the walking of these routes, nor the interpretation or misinterpretation of any directions or maps. All walks are conducted at the walker's own risk and responsibility, and vehicles and property are left at the owner's risk.

Chapter One

Ypres Town Walk

STARTING POINT: Cloth Hall, Ypres
GPS: 50°51′03.8″N, 2°53′07.9″E
DISTANCE: 6.4km/3.9 miles

WALK SUMMARY: *A fairly short walk around picturesque Ypres exploring many of the places in the town associated with its occupation by British troops during the Great War. Particularly suitable for inexperienced walkers. The walk can also be combined with the one in Chapter 2 for a full day on the battlefields.*

Ypres has been known by many names over the centuries and now, being within the Flemish region of Belgium, it is called Ieper. By the fourteenth century Ypres was the centre of the European cloth trade, the material being bought and sold in the magnificent building of the Cloth Hall, which dates from 1260. The population of the town at this time was over 40,000. Fortified by Vauban in the late 1600s, Ypres was besieged on

Ypres on the eve of the Great War.

9

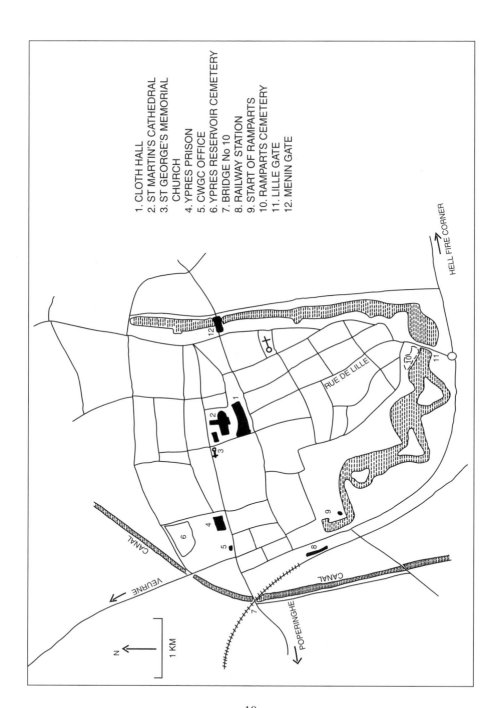

1. CLOTH HALL
2. ST MARTIN'S CATHEDRAL
3. ST GEORGE'S MEMORIAL CHURCH
4. YPRES PRISON
5. CWGC OFFICE
6. YPRES RESERVOIR CEMETERY
7. BRIDGE No 10
8. RAILWAY STATION
9. START OF RAMPARTS
10. RAMPARTS CEMETERY
11. LILLE GATE
12. MENIN GATE

HELL FIRE CORNER

RUE DE LILLE

CANAL

VEURNE

CANAL

POPERINGHE

N

1 KM

The Cloth Hall burning, November 1914.

many occasions. British soldiers under the infamous Grand Old Duke of York fought in Flanders in 1793, and at the time of Waterloo the British occupied Ypres itself and its defences were improved by an officer of Engineers. By the time of the Great War the town was very much in decline and its population substantially diminished. However, in October 1914 Ypres stood in the way of the German advance on the channel ports and within a matter of a few months following the fighting here it became a symbol of sacrifice and defence against the German aggressor. As the war progressed it became the cockpit of the British sector of the Western Front. Stories of the town filled the press as the war progressed and many people have left us their impression of it.

By the end of the war Ypres and its many beautiful buildings were in ruins, and a quarter of a million British and Empire soldiers – one in four of those who died in the Great War – had died in its defence. As early as 1919 veterans began to return to the battlefields where they had fought, and relatives came in search of the grave of a loved one or the place of his death if he were among the missing. As the town was slowly rebuilt, a veritable industry grew up around these pilgrimages and many ex-soldiers lived and worked in Ypres. Others stayed on to work in the military cemeteries being made more permanent by the then Imperial War Graves Commission, so by the 1930s there was a substantial British community in the city.

Battlefield tours continued up until just before the Second World War, there being a revival of interest in the war during the 1930s – and also following the unveiling of the Menin Gate in 1927 and its moving Last Post ceremony (see below). Ypres fell after a short but decisive battle in May 1940, and four years of occupation followed before it was liberated by the Polish Armoured Brigade in September 1944. The events of an even greater war put Ypres and the trenches of the Western Front into shadow for many years, and there were few visitors to the old Salient. A further revival took place in the late 1970s and early 1980s, just as the men who fought here began to 'fade away', like all old soldiers. With an increasing interest in family history in the approach to the Great War Centenary and widespread coverage in the media, in 2014 the city of Ypres had close on half a million battlefield visitors and the interest continues to grow, clearly testified to by the huge numbers of people who attend the Last Post ceremony at the Menin Gate each evening.

Aerial photo of the ruins of Ypres in the snow, 1916.

The huge square of the GRANDE PLACE, or *Grote Markt* as it is today, was the main thoroughfare through this part of Ypres. Many battalions crossed its cobbled surface to go up to the trenches via the Menin Gate. On one occasion in September 1915 men of the 10th Battalion West Riding Regiment were caught by shell-fire in the square on their way up to Hooge, suffering many casualties. The graves of those who died that day are buried in Ypres Reservoir Cemetery (visited later in the walk).

Hugh Pollard gives a typical account of a journey into Ypres:

Entering Ypres in wartime was like entering a tomb; streets and houses were alike obliterated and rough paths cut through the ruins towards the Grande Place and the ruin of the Halles, and along where streets had once been, were the only roads. There was utter silence but for the guns and the whole air was heavy with the indescribable scent of war – a blend of chemicals, chloride of lime, and the vague plaster smell of crushed old buildings. Ypres was not a town, but a desert.[1]

The last shell to fall in the square was on 14th October 1918; two soldiers were killed by the explosion.

The CLOTH HALL has been restored to its former glory, but the work was not finished until as late as 1962. It was first struck by shells and seriously damaged in November 1914, resulting in a fire which gutted much of the upper floor. Gradually shells reduced the building to ruins, but its familiar structure became a landmark to the British soldiers who came through Ypres in the war years. Huntley Gordon records one such visit in July 1917, while serving with 112th Brigade RFA:

Presently we reached the Square, where stands the famous Cloth Hall. I've heard of the Taj Mahal by moonlight – but for me it could never be so impressive as this ruin. The stones and masonry gleamed snowy white and the massive tower stood there, raising its jagged turrets against the dark sky like some huge iceberg. Its base emerged from a vast heap of fallen masonry that had been brought down from above, and levelled off into a sea of brick and stone rubble all around the cobbled square. There it stood, the shattered but invincible emblem of all that the Ypres Salient means – awe-inspiring and unforgettable.[2]

Many soldiers were so inspired by the spectacle they souvenired pieces

British battlefield pilgrims at the ruins of the Cloth Hall in Ypres, 1920s.

The centre of Ypres rebuilt around the ruined Cloth Hall, 1930s.

of it and took them home. Two officers of the Royal Naval Air Service were caught doing this in 1915, and, as many of the townspeople of Ypres were still living in the area at this time, the subsequent courts martial felt the act bordered on looting. However, the two officers survived their brush with military law. Others were never caught, and hundreds of pieces of the old Cloth Hall, the Cathedral and indeed many other buildings are preserved in the collection of the In Flanders Fields Museum, having been returned many years later by the men who took them.

14

Inside the Cloth Hall today are many of the town council offices which are not open to the public, but on the ground floor is the excellent TOURIST OFFICE (see Visitor Information) which has a wealth of useful information on the local area and staff who speak fluent English. Nearby is the entrance to the IN FLANDERS FIELDS MUSEUM (www. inflandersfields.be). In Flanders Fields opened in 1998, taking over from the old Ypres Salient Museum which had existed for many years, and changed the approach from objects to interpretation. The museum was substantially updated and expanded in 2012 and reopened once more. Visitors now take a poppy bracelet around the exhibits, which enables them to access more information. It offers an excellent background to a wider visit to the Ypres battlefield and has many unique features such as the touch-screen aerial photographs showing the battlefield in the war and today. Allow two to three hours to see the museum properly. If you can make it up the many stairs, take the tour to the top of the Cloth Hall tower from which on a clear day the whole tour area and much of the battlefields can be seen.

Back in the main square, go under the Cloth Hall end archway into a cobbled parking area in front of ST MARTIN'S CATHEDRAL. The original St Martin's dated from the thirteenth century, although a place of worship had existed on this site since 1073. Before the war the spire was much shorter than today, although plans had been made to change this. These were eventually realised in the post-war reconstruction as by 1918 the Cathedral was almost completely destroyed by shelling.

The Cathedral was often used by troops billeted in or passing through Ypres and a tragic episode took place here in August 1915 when the 6th Battalion Duke of Cornwall's Light Infantry (DCLI) of 14th (Light) Division was in the town before moving up the line. Coming up from Vlamertinghe on 10th August, the battalion made use of the many cellars in Ypres then allocated for billeting purposes. These deep brick-lined natural dugouts usually offered good protection against German shelling. On the same occasion it was discovered by a DCLI officer that the cloisters of St Martin's were still in good condition, as yet untouched by shell-fire, and C and D companies were detailed to rest there. The battalion *War Diary* tells what happened two days later, on 12th August 1915:

Enemy commences to shell cloisters and Place at 6.15am. The men in the cloister thinking they were safe did not move. Enemy guns or gun fire every quarter of an hour and after a few shots got the exact range of the cloisters. The first direct hit brought down

The ruins of St Martin's Cathedral, Ypres.

most of the W. end of cloister ceiling and buried several men. The enemy continued to fire for five hours, putting in 17-inch shells at first every quarter and later every half hour, with smaller shells and shrapnel in between. Many of the men who went to rescue their comrades were themselves buried. The warning was first conveyed to Bn HQ whereupon Major Barnett and the adjutant Lt R.C. Blagrove ran over to the cloisters to endeavour to get the men out. Both were instantly killed by the explosion of a very large shell which apparently fell in [the] open square just north of the cloisters.[3]

The remaining officers of 6th DCLI put out a warning for men to keep away from this shelled area, fearing further casualties, but the non-conformist chaplain, Captain Harris, went back with four volunteers from the battalion to try to get the injured out. Harris himself was wounded on this occasion, but rescue attempts continued when soldiers from the 11th Battalion King's Liverpool Regiment, the divisional pioneer battalion, arrived to assist. Some men were pulled from the rubble but casualties that morning amounted to two officers and eighteen other ranks killed, two officers and nineteen other ranks wounded. Later it was discovered that the gun which had shelled the cathedral was firing from Houthoulst Forest, over 10 miles away, and had been directed by a German aeroplane which had spotted an observation post in the tower of St Martin's. The sad conclusion to this episode came during the reconstruction of the cathedral after the war when several bodies of 6th DCLI men were found in the ruins. Some accounts claim the number to have been as many as forty, others more than a hundred, but graves in Ypres Reservoir Cemetery do not bear this out.

Go inside the Cathedral by the door visible on the other side of the parking area. There are several memorials and commemorative windows connected with the Great War around the interior. Coming back outside and turning left, follow the Cathedral round to a small green with a Celtic cross set on it. This is a memorial to the men from Munster, in particular the Royal Munster Fusiliers, who fell at Ypres between 1914 and 1918. From here continue to follow the Cathedral round in an anti-clockwise direction. Eventually you will come out into an area of rubble and broken statues. These are all from the original cathedral, and were so damaged that they could not be set in place again. From here continue towards the west door but join the road that runs in front and turn right, crossing another area of parking to a church with a Cross of Sacrifice on the roof and located on the corner of Elverdingestraat.

ST GEORGE'S MEMORIAL CHURCH was once symbolic of the very large English community in Ypres, which existed between the wars. The church was designed by Sir Reginald Blomfield, who had also designed the Menin Gate, and was built between 1928 and 1929. The idea was to provide a typical English church for pilgrims to the battlefields and cemeteries. Regiments, divisions and units, as well as individual families, were invited to place memorial plaques within the church and each pew was given in memory of a soldier who died at Ypres. Today St George's is a quiet place of peace and meditation, a welcome break from the busy streets of Ypres. With its many memorials, which continue to be added to each year, it is a museum in its own right and services are held here regularly. The British settlement is much diminished, the school to the rear of the church closing after the Second World War and now only open by appointment with the staff of the church. A memorial in the entrance to the school buildings commemorates every Etonian who fell at Ypres – Eton College donated a great deal of money towards the construction of the settlement in the 1920s. The upkeep of the church is managed by the Friends of St George's, who welcome donations or offers of help.

Leaving the church, turn left and continue down Elverdingestraat. This was a busy route into Ypres and the main square during the war. Soon a turning to the right appears and opposite is the entrance to the large Ypres prison building. Stop here.

The PRISON was one of the strongest buildings in Ypres; Rudyard Kipling remarked that it was 'a fine example of the resistance to shell-

Ypres prison, 1919.

fire of thick walls if they are thick enough'. Because of this an advanced dressing station (ADS) was established here in late 1915, and many other units used the rooms within, among them the Town Major of Ypres. A telephone exchange linked the prison to all the major sites between here and Poperinghe.

If you wish to visit the offices of the Commonwealth War Graves Commission, where enquiries about war graves can be made, and maps showing the location of cemeteries and memorials purchased, continue along Elverdingestraat. The office is a little further up on the right at Number 82. Otherwise turn right here down Minneplein and follow the wall of the prison until a military cemetery appears on the left. Follow the road left and the entrance is seen a little further along.

YPRES RESERVOIR CEMETERY

Originally known as Ypres Prison Cemetery, as it backed onto the prison which served as an ADS, the name was changed after the war so that the relatives of the men buried here did not think their loved ones had died in prison. It was by no means the only cemetery in Ypres, and there were many isolated graves and small graveyards throughout the town. Those from the western area of Ypres were brought into this cemetery after the war. Others were moved out of Ypres to cemeteries further afield, such as Bedford House and Tyne Cot.

This cemetery was started in October 1915, about the time the ADS opened, on a field that was known locally as the 'plaine d'amour' – the field of love. It remained in use until October 1918, and a few burials were also added after the Armistice. The cemetery was used largely as a burial place for men killed in the line just outside Ypres, or for those killed in the town itself either by shell-fire or accidents. In total there are 2,248

Ypres Reservoir Cemetery, 1919.

British graves, along with 151 Canadian, 142 Australian, twenty-eight New Zealand, twelve South African, six British West Indies, four Newfoundland, two Royal Guernsey Light Infantry, one Indian and one German. Seven additional burials are men whose nationality or unit is not known, and of the overall total 1,035 are unidentified. There are twelve Special Memorials.

In Plot V Row AA are the graves of men from 6th Battalion DCLI who died when the cloister of St Martin's Cathedral was shelled (see above). Major C. Barnett and Lieutenant & Adjutant R.C. Blagrove, who died in the rescue attempt, are both found here. Elsewhere, Second Lieutenant Hugh Cholmeley's grave (I-D-82) is most unusual. It bears an inscription showing that he died on 7th April 1916 whilst serving with the 1st Battalion Grenadier Guards on the Canal Bank sector. A second inscription commemorates his brother, Lieutenant Harry L. Cholmeley, who was killed at Beaumont-Hamel (Somme) on 1st July 1916; he has no known grave and is listed by name on the Thiepval Memorial. Not far away headstones commemorate two other brothers, one of whom was brought into this cemetery under unusual circumstances. Captain H.B. Knott (V-B-16) died of wounds with the 9th Battalion Northumberland Fusiliers on 7th September 1915. His brother, Major J.L. Knott DSO (V-B-15), was killed at Fricourt on the Somme on 1st July 1916, whilst second in command of 10th Battalion West Yorkshire Regiment. Although originally buried on the Somme, Major Knott's body was brought to Ypres Reservoir Cemetery after the war on the express wishes of the brothers' parents – a most rare, if not unique, occurrence.

Major John Leadbitter Knott.

Four gunners from the headquarters of A Battery 296th Brigade Royal Field Artillery are buried side by side. Major F. Devonport DSO MC (I-F-39), Captain A.A. Parker (I-F-38), Lieutenant H.P. Jackson (I-F-40) and Battery Sergeant Major F.R. Heath (I-F-41) all died at Wieltje on 25th September 1917 when an 8-inch shell scored a direct hit on their battery mess. All four had long war service, and were brought back here for burial by their men: Wieltje was then under continuous shell-fire.[4]

A highly decorated senior officer lies in Ypres Reservoir Cemetery, close to the Stone of Remembrance. Brigadier General Francis Aylmer Maxwell VC CSI DSO and bar (I-A-37) was mortally wounded by a sniper in the Battle of the Menin Road Ridge, dying on 21st September 1917, aged forty-six. Maxwell was an Indian Army officer of the 18th

**Brigadier General
Francis Aylmer
Maxwell VC.**

Lancers, who had won the VC on 31st March 1900 for saving the guns of a RHA battery whilst attached to Lord Robert's Horse at Korn Spruit in the Boer War. The inscription on his headstone reads, 'An ideal soldier and a very perfect gentleman. Beloved by all his men.'

The cemetery also contains the graves of men serving with the many support units operating in the Ypres Salient. There are gunners from Siege Batteries who had their gun sites in the town; Engineers from Field Companies, Tunnelling Companies, electrical units, road construction companies and light railways; Military Policemen, much feared and disliked, rest here – one can only contemplate their fate, although many were killed on road traffic duty, a dangerous job when shelling was heavy. It is a cemetery which reflects well the myriad of units that came to Ypres, in a quiet location with good views of the Cloth Hall and St Martin's Cathedral.

Leaving the cemetery by the main gate, turn left and continue up the street that runs alongside. Where it joins a main road (going north to Dixmude), turn left and walk down to a small roundabout, keeping to the path. During the war the famous Ypres Water Tower stood near this junction. Here turn right and again staying on the pavement follow this road until it reaches a railway line. Cross the line to a small bridge over the Comines canal.

This was known as Bridge Number Ten on British maps and was the

21

main route into the town from the billeting areas between Ypres and Poperinghe. Just beyond where you are, at the Ypres Asylum – an ADS manned by RAMC Field Ambulances – was a notice which read 'Tin hats must be worn from here onward'. Hugh Pollard came into Ypres via this junction along,

> shell-pitted roads to the deep cut of the Ypres Canal, to halt awhile along the bank, which is trenched and seamed with shrapnel-proof dugouts. At intervals of a hundred yards are bridges of planks across pontoons – men are fishing and bathing in the water.[5]

From Bridge Number Ten turn left into Tuipenlaan, following the line of the Ypres–Comines canal. There are British bunkers built into sections of the canal here, used by personnel based around the station and Bridge Number Ten; they are visible when the undergrowth is low. Half-way down this street take a path to the left at a pedestrian crossing, which goes across the canal into an area of housing. Here turn right and follow this to the main road, *Dikkebusseweg*, and turn left, recrossing the railway and immediately turning left again; continue to the railway station.

Ypres railway station was once on the line to Roulers to the north-east and Hazebrouck in France, but today trains only run to Kortrijk and Poperinghe. It remained open for much of the war, with branch lines made off it to the many camps and dumps west of Ypres, but came under heavy shell-fire when the Germans took the high ground around Ypres in 1915. Ammunition and supplies were also brought up here, along with tanks during Third Ypres. However, in April 1918, when the German

Ypres station, 1919.

A soldier of the Army Service Corps in the ruins of Ypres station in 1915.

offensive got as far as Hellfire Corner, the station could not be used as the town was too heavily shelled. In ruins by the Armistice, it was totally rebuilt in a modern style unlikely to attract the present-day visitor.

Outside the station, cross the main road by the traffic lights and follow Stationstraat, then take the first right into Rene Colaertplein. Ahead is a path in the trees leading onto the Ramparts. Before that look to your left where there is now a car park. This area and the modern buildings beyond were the site of the famous Ypres Infantry Barracks, the strongest and safest billets in the town. A pre-war Belgian army complex, the Barracks

The Infantry Barracks in 1914.

The Infantry Barracks in 1919.

had very thick walls and could house thousands of men at one time. At the war's end it was one of the few buildings still standing, although badly damaged. Men slept in barrack rooms designed for a fraction of their number, but parts of the place were lit by an electric generator. Men could safely light fires and cook here, although it came under increased fire in April 1918 when the front lines were so close to Ypres. Also known as 'The Esplanade', the Barracks contained a small military cemetery consisting of fourteen graves dating from April 1915 to July 1916 – ten of them from 6th Siege Battery who had their gun sites here. These were later removed to Ypres Reservoir Cemetery.

From here follow the path onto the Ramparts. The Ramparts, originally dating from the seventeenth century, were used extensively by the British during the Great War. Casemates inside housed billets, stores and headquarters. In several places they were loop-holed for extra defence and machine-gun positions established. Observation officers used the Ramparts to look down on the battlefield immediately around the town. When the Germans got to Hellfire Corner in April 1918 the Ramparts became part of the defence line and men of the Royal Engineers added a number of pillboxes. These may be seen as you walk along the next section of the Ramparts leading up to the Lille Gate. From here stay on the path which takes you along the Ramparts at this point and eventually leads to a military cemetery.

RAMPARTS CEMETERY (LILLE GATE)

The French were the first to bury their dead on the Ramparts in 1914, during First Ypres. British burials began in February 1915 and continued until April 1918. The French crosses have long gone and now there are 153 British, fourteen New Zealand, eleven Australian, and ten Canadian graves. The cemetery register unusually records:

> This is one of the smallest of the Ypres cemeteries, but in some ways the most interesting. It is the only one which commands a view of the country round; and by its position it brings together the wars of the eighteenth and twentieth centuries.

The first burials are in Rows B and C, and are from a mix of units holding the Salient in early 1915 – regulars and territorials. Members of the RAMC are numerous: men from Field Ambulances which used the Ramparts. Also seen are soldiers from RE units, particularly Tunnelling Companies. The most senior officer is Major G.H. Walford (F-1) of the Suffolk Regiment, who was Brigade Major of 84th Brigade and was killed at Zonnebeke on 19th April 1915 – just prior to the gas attack of Second Ypres. This picturesque and quiet spot is often a welcome change from the busy town centre, and was a favourite of the late author, Rose Coombs. Nearby a walk along the Ramparts is named in her honour. Speculation also suggests that her ashes are scattered here.

From the cemetery follow the Rose Coombs walk down to the main road. On the left here is a café which makes an excellent stop for a drink, and opposite is an old wooden door which was once the entrance to a

Old soldiers visiting Ypres Reservoir Cemetery, 1920s.

The Ramparts casemates where *The Wiper's Times* was printed in 1916.

The Lille Gate, Ypres.

Looking through the Lille Gate from Ypres, 1919.

1920s Ypres War Museum. Under the Lille Gate itself are a number of Imperial War Graves Commission signs attached to the wall.

The Lille Gate was a major route out of Ypres, perhaps more so than the more famous Menin Gate further along the Ramparts. For most of the war years battalions could leave the town from here largely unobserved by the Germans and were therefore less likely to be shelled going to and from the trenches. Marching south they could turn off at Shrapnel Corner (visible from here) for the line at Zillebeke, or on the way to Hill 60 or the Bluff. There is a door on the Ypres side of the gate, which between the wars housed a museum. During the war it contained one of the most luxurious dugouts in the Salient, built and manned by men of the Canadian Tunnelling Companies who rested here while undertaking mining operations on the Messines Ridge in 1917. It has also been claimed that General Plumer had his headquarters in this dugout during Third Ypres, but this is unlikely. What is well known is that a trench newspaper, *The Wipers Times*, was started here in 1916 by an officer of the 24th Division. Close to the door, on the wall of the gate, are a number of the original Imperial War Graves Commission cast-iron cemetery signs, now very rare.

The street going north from the Lille Gate is Rijselsestraat (Rue de Lille during the war) and further along on the right was the site of Little Talbot House, an outpost of the more famous one in Poperinghe (see Poperinghe walk). The Rev. P.B. 'Tubby' Clayton, and his helpers, opened this one nearer the front line for the many men garrisoned in Ypres, but it often had to close due to shell-fire and damage. A plaque on the wall of the modern building records its former use. It can be walked to from here but it may be better to see it as a follow-up visit after the walk.

Return to the Ramparts path and follow it across the bridge over the Lille Gate. **Once across the bridge**, continue on the path as it follows the line of the Ramparts. The moat is more visible here, but take care along the edge as the bricks are uneven and it is a long drop into the moat! In the last decade the city of Ypres has renovated and opened up several sections of the Ramparts, which can be visited on this section of the walk.

You are soon on the eastern edge of Ypres, and the spire of St Jacques church will be visible to the left. There were many dugouts in this section of the Ramparts. H.S. Clapham was here with the Honourable Artillery Company in June 1915 and recorded in his diary:

> I am now on guard in a miniature trench on top of the ramparts of Ypres. The wall in front goes sheer down fifty feet or more into a moat, one hundred yards broad. At my back the ramparts slope

British graves on the Ramparts during the war, now removed.

upwards dotted with big trees . . . The sun is shining, the birds are singing but beneath all other sounds there is one deep undertone, the buzzing of innumerable flies.

On the other side of the moat there is a brickyard, some three hundred yards long. Broken beams stick out of the piles of bricks at intervals, but there is nothing else to show that the brickyard was once a row of cottages. A dead cow lies half in the water of the moat. Spurts of flame, every now and then, disclose the position of a British battery . . . as I watch, a huge shell bursts in the moat, raising a column of mud and water, and two others find the brickfield amid clouds of red dust. Each time a shell bursts, I duck while the debris patters among the surrounding trees.[6]

From here Clapham could look back into the town and see what was left of the nearby St Jacques church.

The interior, seen from all sides through the broken walls, is a pink heap of brick and plaster. The other walls have gone, but I can see a processional cross leaning against a corner of the inner wall, and in another stands the lamp which is carried before the Host.

In the city the roofs which remained are stripped of tiles. Not

28

a house seems to remain undamaged, and through the broken walls of those least damaged one can see all the household goods. Everything seems to have been abandoned . . . Above the town two towers still keep watch. Half of the one has gone, but two pinnacles are still intact. The other, that of the cathedral, still remains, a square mass, all its decoration gone, but its bulk untouched. For how long? Some fifty shells fell into the town last night, disturbing the rubbish and bringing down a few more walls. It is the strangest sight I have ever seen, but the worst thing about it is that buzzing undertone.[7]

Continue along the path. It will eventually bring you to the Menin Gate.

The Menin Gate was one of several breaches in the Ramparts when they were originally constructed, allowing access to and from Ypres. A bridge crossed the moat here and the entrance was guarded by two huge stone lions – the symbol of Flanders. In October 1914 German cavalry entered Ypres for a brief time via this route, and the same year British troops left the town via the gate for the first time as they proceeded along the Menin Road towards the battlefront. In later years the closeness of the front lines at Hooge and Bellewaarde Ridge made it a dangerous exit from Ypres. Huntley Gordon recalled in July 1917:

For sheer concentrated shelling the Menin Gate stands alone. There is of course no gate there, merely a gap in the stone ramparts of the town, and a causeway crossing the wide moat beyond. Most of the traffic supplying the line in front of Ypres must pass through here, and the Boche takes heavy toll of it – night and day. The bridge, whether originally arched or not, is now a solid mass of

The Menin Gate in 1913.

stonework, supplemented, indeed cemented, by the remains of smashed vehicles and the fragmented bodies of horses and men. In fact everything that passes over it has contributed to its upkeep. During lulls in the shelling, men dash out from their shelters on the massive ramparts, and patch the holes in the road as best they can.[8]

A war-time saying was 'Tell the last man through to bolt the Menin Gate' and there can have been few soldiers who served at Ypres who did not know of or had not travelled through this important landmark. It therefore seemed a most appropriate place to locate the proposed memorial to the missing of the Ypres Salient when the Imperial War Graves Commission began to consider sites in the early 1920s. The Menin Gate was completed

Inside the Menin Gate, 1920s.

The ruins of the Menin Gate during the war.

German soldiers at the Menin Gate during the Second World War.

by July 1927, and the following summer the Last Post ceremony became a regular feature each evening at dusk – the only gap in its playing being the years of German occupation (1940–44). The memorial suffered some damage in May 1940 when it was being used as an observation post by Royal Artillery officers, to watch the advancing German Blitzkrieg as it approached Ypres. British Engineers blew the moat bridge, the resulting explosion and fragments of cobble and brick taking chunks out of the Portland stone pillars. Evidence of this is still visible today on the moat side of the archway. The Last Post ceremony, now timed at 8pm each evening, is an essential part of any visit to the battlefields of Ypres, and no matter how many times one hears it, the tones of the bugles as they echo round the archway are as moving as the first time you attended the Menin Gate. Many people now feel moved to clap at the conclusion of the ceremony, while others might feel this a wholly inappropriate gesture.

MENIN GATE MEMORIAL

The Imperial War Graves Commission (IWGC) was founded under a Royal Charter in 1917, and as the war progressed it soon became apparent that many thousands of men would either remain missing, or be buried in unmarked graves or under a wooden cross simply marked 'unknown soldier'. The Commission therefore decided to erect a number of memorials to the missing at major points along the old Western Front, and the Menin Gate was chosen a suitable site to commemorate those from the fighting at Ypres. However, the number of men who died in the Salient but have no known grave was so vast that the IWGC ran out of space on the Menin Gate when the figure reached 55,000 and an extension for a further 35,000 names was constructed at Tyne Cot. For no particular reason the cut-off date between the two memorials is midnight on 15th August 1917, when the Battle of Langemarck began. The Menin Gate therefore commemorates men who died on or before that date, many of the names being soldiers who fell at First Ypres in 1914. The only exceptions are the Australians, Canadians and South Africans; all their missing from the Salient are listed on these panels.

The following commemorations are those made on the Menin Gate:

British – 40,244
Canadian – 6,983
Australian – 6,198
South African – 564
Indian – 421
West Indian – 6

The poet Siegfried Sassoon felt the Menin Gate was a 'sepulchre of crime', but Field Marshal Lord Plumer appealed to the many families of those honoured here when he said at the unveiling in July 1927, 'They are not missing – they are here'. Like other memorials to the missing, the Menin Gate recalls so many lives that it is difficult at times to come to terms with the sheer numbers of men whose names line these walls. Among them are eight Victoria Cross winners:

	VC	Killed
L/Cpl F. Fisher, 13th Canadians	23.4.15	24.4.15
Brig-Gen C. Fitzclarence, Irish Guards	1899	12.11.14
CSM F.W. Hall, 8th Canadians	24.4.15	25.4.15
2/Lt D.G.W. Hewitt, 14th Hampshires	31.7.17	31.7.17
Lt H. McKenzie DCM, 7th Coy CMGC	30.10.17	30.10.17
Capt J.F. Vallentin, 1st South Staffs	7.11.14	7.11.14
Pte E. Warner, 1st Bedfords	1.5.15	2.5.15
2/Lt S.C. Woodroffe, 8th Rifle Brigade	30.7.15	30.7.15

While each name on the memorial has its own story, to serve as some examples these are a few of those commemorated here:

BROTHERS IN ARMS: There are several pairs of brothers commemorated on the Menin Gate, bearing testimony to the tragedy suffered by many families during the Great War; when brothers joined up together, they all too often died together as well. At Ypres, perhaps most tragic of all was the triple loss which befell the Rachiel family in May 1915. From Holme Road, East Ham, London, three brothers had enlisted together as regular soldiers in the 3rd Battalion Royal Fusiliers before the war. In August 1914 the 3rd Royal Fusiliers were stationed at Lucknow in India and returned to England in December, becoming part of 28th Division – one of the last regular army formations to arrive in France, in January 1915. They served initially on the Messines Ridge and during the Second Battle of Ypres were brought up to the fighting north-east of Ypres. The three Rachiel brothers – Arthur, aged twenty-one, Frank aged eighteen and Fred aged twenty-four – were all killed on 24th May 1915 on the Bellewaarde Ridge. A terrible loss under any circumstances, but for none of them to have a grave for the family to visit must have made it even harder to bear.

FUTURE CANADIAN PRIME MINISTER? Talbot Mercier Papineau was a French-Canadian whose grandfather had fought against the British.

Well educated, and from the Canadian upper classes, Papineau practised law before 1914. When war broke out he obtained a commission in Princess Patricia's Canadian Light Infantry (PPCLI), a regiment formed almost entirely from ex-regular British army veterans who had emigrated to Canada. On the voyage out Papineau gave French lessons to his men, and after a brief spell in England his regiment was the first Canadian unit to reach the front line. Papineau was awarded the Military Cross for bravery at St Eloi in March 1915. In 1916 he became a Staff Officer and during the fighting on the Somme accompanied the Canadian Official Photographer around the battlefield at Courcelette. Frustrated with a desk job, he continually put in requests for a transfer back to

Talbot Papineau.

the PPCLI but did not rejoin his old unit until September 1917 – just prior to the attack on Passchendaele. Promoted Major, he was killed leading his men forward on 30th October 1917, but his body was not retrieved from the battlefield for several weeks. He was buried close to the Passchendaele road, but the white cross marking his last resting place could not be found when his mother wrote to the IWGC after the war. Despite further explorations, Papineau's body was never found. Prior to the Great War he had been a protégé of the then Canadian Prime Minister, and it is widely considered that, if he had survived, Papineau would himself have eventually taken up this office. Given his French-Canadian background, the whole social history of Canada in the twentieth century could have been changed.

GOC MENIN ROAD: Noted in the list of VCs above, Brigadier General Charles Fitzclarence was a charismatic, brave and well liked senior officer who was far from the 'lions led by donkeys' image of many Great War commanders. Born in 1865, the son of a naval Captain who was also Earl of Munster, he was educated at Eton and Wellington College, and joined the Royal Fusiliers in 1886. Promoted Captain in 1898, Fitzclarence transferred to the Irish Guards and was awarded the VC for three distinct acts of bravery during the Siege of Mafeking in the Boer War. At this time he earned his first nickname, 'The Demon', for his daring in the face of often impossible odds. Rapid promotion followed and he was commanding 1st Irish Guards by 1913, and then a Brigade by the outbreak of war.

Brigadier General Charles Fitzclarence VC.

Just prior to First Ypres he was posted to command 1st Guards Brigade, 1st Division, and was instrumental in organising a brilliant counter-attack near Gheluvelt on 31st October 1914, and as the fighting moved back towards Ypres along the old Roman road he earned another sobriquet, 'GOC Menin Road': indeed several observers noted that he appeared at times to be running the whole battle. It was this gallant front-line leadership which eventually cost him his life on 12th November 1914, whilst advancing at the head of his old regiment near Glencorse Wood.

FROM THE RANKS: 'Gentleman Rankers', well educated men from moneyed families who served in the ranks, were often the stuff of fiction but one is commemorated here – Frederick Charles Jennens Marillier. Born at Fairlight near Hastings, Sussex, in 1888, Marillier was educated at a local minor public school. His father was an artist and his grandfather had been a master at Harrow for fifty years. For a reason that even today remains a mystery, he left the comforts of a well-heeled Edwardian family and joined the Royal Sussex Regiment as a Private in 1912. The life somehow suited him and by 1914 he was a Sergeant. During the fighting on the Aisne in September 1914 he was awarded the Distinguished Conduct Medal for bravery in capturing a German trench during a night attack. Eventually persuaded to take a commission, he was promoted

Second Lieutenant in the field. But his service as an officer only lasted a few weeks until his death at Ypres on 30th October 1914.

STRETCHER-BEARER WANTED: The work of the Royal Army Medical Corps is well known, but regimental stretcher-bearers are often forgotten. These were the first port of call for wounded troops in the field.

British soldiers in Ypres during the war.

In peacetime these men would make up the battalion band, and as the war went on soldiers with enough technical skill and common sense to administer basic medical help replaced them. From the battlefield 'SBs' would carry a wounded soldier back to the Regimental Aid Post to be treated by the battalion Medical Officer. One such stretcher-bearer was Lance Corporal Harry West MM of the 13th Battalion Royal Sussex Regiment (3rd South Downs). West was born in Eastbourne, and enlisted with his brother in 1914. He trained as a stretcher-bearer, proceeded overseas in March 1916 and was awarded the Military Medal for bringing in wounded comrades under fire at Richebourg on 30th June – he himself was badly wounded in the process. Returning to his battalion, he served on the Somme, where his brother was killed, and came to Ypres in December 1916. On 31st July 1917, the opening day of Third Ypres, he accompanied the Medical Officer during the attack on St Julien, and the next day was killed by the same shell which wounded the M.O. An officer in the 13th Royal Sussex later wrote, 'his untiring efforts for the sick and wounded in the battles in which this battalion has been engaged has simply been beyond praise'.

From the Menin Gate take the road back into the town centre, Meenstraat, which will soon bring you out into the Grote Markt, Cloth Hall and your vehicle.

Notes

1. Anon. *The Pilgrims Guide to the Ypres Salient* (For Talbot House c.1920s) p.10.
2. Gordon, H. *The Unreturning Army* (J.M.Dent 1967) p.54.
3. 6th Battalion DCLI *War Diary*, 12.8.15, TNA WO95/1908.
4. A/296th Brigade RFA *War Diary*, 25.9.17, TNA WO95/3016.
5. *The Pilgrims Guide to the Ypres Salient* op cit. p.10.
6. Clapham, H.S. *Mud and Khaki* (Hutchinson n.d.) pp.130–1.
7. ibid. pp.131–2.
8. Gordon op cit. p.54.

Chapter Two

Menin Gate – Hellfire Corner – Potijze Walk

STARTING POINT: Menin Gate, Ypres
GPS: 50°51.121′N, 2°53.459′E
DISTANCE: 11km/6.8 miles

WALK SUMMARY: *A long but rewarding walk that could be linked with the previous Ypres Town Walk as it starts in central Ypres and then takes in some of the battlefields close to the city.*

Park your vehicle in central Ypres – there are plenty of parking areas in the main square – and then walk down to the Menin Gate (more information on this in the Ypres Town Walk).

This route was one taken by many soldiers during the war, from the centre of Ypres and out to the front line by passing through the Menin Gate. There was never a gate here although during the war soldiers joked 'tell the last man through to bolt the Menin Gate'. From mid-1915 onwards this route was in view from the German positions on the high ground around the city, meaning that movement through it could only ever be done at night in the darkness. It was regularly shelled and some recent road works here exposed the bodies of several horses killed passing through and buried close by.

The Menin Gate in the 1930s.

37

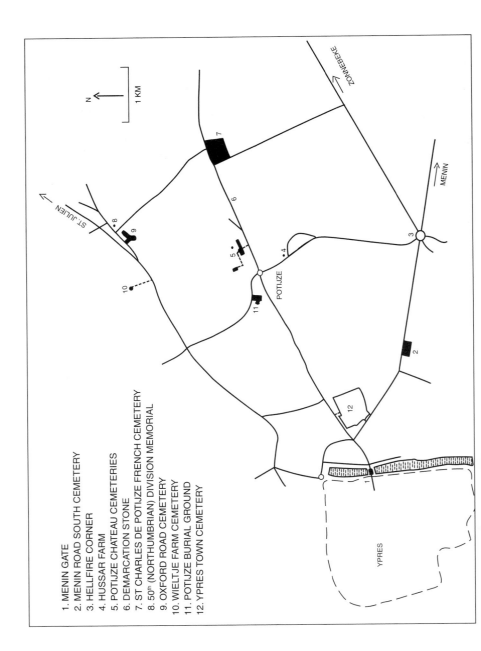

1. MENIN GATE
2. MENIN ROAD SOUTH CEMETERY
3. HELLFIRE CORNER
4. HUSSAR FARM
5. POTIJZE CHATEAU CEMETERIES
6. DEMARCATION STONE
7. ST CHARLES DE POTIJZE FRENCH CEMETERY
8. 50th (NORTHUMBRIAN) DIVISION MEMORIAL
9. OXFORD ROAD CEMETERY
10. WIELTJE FARM CEMETERY
11. POTIJZE BURIAL GROUND
12. YPRES TOWN CEMETERY

The Menin Gate, 1919.

Leaving the Menin Gate walk up the road to the next main junction using the pavement, and there **turn right** onto the Menin Road. Follow this out of town until a British cemetery is reached.

MENIN ROAD SOUTH CEMETERY

The Menin Road ran east and a little south from Ypres to a front-line area which varied very little during the greater part of the war. The position of this cemetery was always just within the Allied lines, although the front line was located at Hellfire Corner in April 1918. It was first used in January 1916 by the 8th Battalion South Staffordshire Regiment and the 9th Battalion East Surrey Regiment, and it continued to be used by units and Field Ambulances untl the summer of 1918. The cemetery was enlarged after the Armistice when graves were brought in from Menin Road North Military Cemetery and from isolated positions on the battlefields to the east. There are now 1,657 servicemen of the First World War buried or commemorated in this cemetery. 119 of the burials are unidentified but special memorials are erected to twenty-four casualties known or believed to be buried among them. In addition, there are special memorials to fifty-four casualties who were buried in Menin Road North

Menin Road South Cemetery, 1919.

Menin Road South Cemetery, 1930s.

Military Cemetery, whose graves were probably destroyed by shell-fire and could not be found. The cemetery was designed by Sir Reginald Blomfield, who was also the architect of the Menin Gate, making this walk very much 'Blomfield' themed in terms of cemetery and memorial design as several sites connected to his work with the Commission will be visited. Blomfield was a Victorian architect who was famous for his work on grand houses such as Chequers and Heathfield Park in Sussex. He had also worked on the Quadrant in Regent Street in London, and his work on cemeteries and memorials began in 1921 when he was 65 years old. Aside from the many sites he worked on, the Cross of Sacrifice which appears in all main cemeteries was also his design. He died in 1942.

Throughout the war there were gun sites in this area and this is reflected in the burials here with more than 250 gunners buried in the cemetery – perhaps the greatest concentration for an original wartime cemetery. Australians from the fighting along the Menin Road and at Polygon Wood are also found here and three men from the British West Indies in Plot II Rows I and J. These Black soldiers were part of a regiment that worked in a labour role on the Western Front and in September and October 1917 were supporting the Australian gunners in this area, carrying shells up to the forward gun sites. Captain Thomas Riversdale Colyer-Ferguson VC (II-E-1) was a twenty-one year old company commander in 2nd Battalion Northamptonshire Regiment who died in the fighting on the Bellewaarde Ridge during the opening stage of the Third Battle of Ypres. He came from a family with strong Kent connections,

Captain Thomas Riversdale Colyer-Ferguson VC.

and his family home Ightham Mote is now a National Trust property. His citation reads:

For most conspicuous bravery, skillful leading and determination in attack. The tactical situation having developed contrary to expectation, it was not possible for his company to adhere to the original plan of deployments and owing to the difficulties of the ground and enemy wire, Captain Colyer-Ferguson found himself with a Serjeant and five men only. He carried out the attack nevertheless, and succeeded in capturing the enemy trench and disposing of the garrison. His party was then threatened by a heavy counter-attack from the left front, but this attack he successfully resisted. During this operation, assisted by his Orderly only, he attacked and captured an enemy machine gun and turned it on the assailants, many of whom were killed and a large number driven into the hands of an adjoining British unit. Later, assisted only by his Serjeant, he again attacked and captured a second enemy machine gun, by which time he had been joined by other portions of his company, and was enabled to consolidate his position. The conduct of this officer throughout forms an amazing record of dash, gallantry and skill, for which no reward can be too great, having regard to the importance of the position won. This gallant officer was shortly afterwards killed by a sniper.[1]

Cross the road here to the north side and then continue along the pavement following the Menin Road, passing two side roads on the left; stop at the wooded entrance to a chateau.

This was the site of the White Chateau, a large house in its own grounds which was used as a headquarters during the First Battle of Ypres. Douglas Haig, then commanding I Corps, placed his HQ here at that time, directing the fighting along the Menin Road. The chateau was rebuilt in the 1920s and today it is a private residence.

White Chateau, Ypres.

Again continue along the Menin Road to the main roundabout, staying on the north side of the road. On the left a British memorial is seen. **Stop.**

This was once one of the most feared spots on the Western Front: Hellfire Corner. A road and railway junction, it was first used by British troops to get to the front line in October 1914. Throughout the war it was a main hub of troop movements but from 1915 this was always done at night to avoid casualties: Hellfire Corner for two years could be seen from the high ground around Ypres. Military Foot Police controlled movement as even at night the area was heavily shelled. Canvas screens were erected at one point to screen activity but these did not last long. A Newfoundlander remembered Hellfire Corner in 1917:

Where the track, which had once been the Menin Road, crossed the remains of the Ypres-Roulers railway was the notorious

Hellfire Corner, 1917.

Memorial at Hellfire Corner in the 1920s.

Hellfire Corner – heartily loathed by the ration limbers, the carrying parties and the ammunition-laden mule trains that nightly had to negotiate the heavily-shelled crossing. Probably the most dangerous spot on the Flemish front, Hellfire Corner was under constant observation by German watchers, and any movement was sure to provoke a flurry of shells. An abandoned gun riddled with bullet and shrapnel holes bore the grim plea: 'Do not stand about here. Even if you are not hit, someone else will be.'[2]

There is a British Demarcation Stone on the left of the roundabout and there are also plans to erect a memorial to the horses and mules killed in this area during the war.

Turn left at the roundabout onto the N345 in the direction of Potijze. Further along a minor road, *Kruiskalsijdestraat*, goes off to the right. Take this road and stop a little way further up and look to your right.

In the distance is the rising ground of the Frezenberg and Bellewaarde Ridges. This high ground was heavily contested during the Second Battle of Ypres in May 1915 when there were often astonishing casualties amongst the infantry units; on one day for example the 2nd Battalion King's Own Royal Lancaster Regiment suffered more than 900 casualties, of which 340 were men killed in action: one of the highest figures for any regiment on a single day in the entire war. The losses amongst the infantry forced the commanders here to move up men from cavalry formations, being used in a dismounted role. These cavalry regiments also took substantial losses and many of the locations in this area had wartime names connected with them: such as Dragoon and Lancer Farms. These ridges remained in German hands after this battle for two years, enabling them to dominate the battlefield. In July 1917 they were captured in the early stages of Third Ypres and then retaken by the Germans in April 1918, who were eventually stopped at Hellfire Corner.

Continue to the end of this minor road until you reach a farm complex on the right. **Stop**.

This was known as Hussar Farm on trench maps, named after the Hussar cavalry regiments who served in this area during the Second Battle of Ypres. In July 1916 the Royal Monmouthshire Royal Engineers, a territorial engineer unit recruited in Wales, was detailed to build an Observation Post into the ruins of the farm buildings. The remains gave

Hussar Farm, 1919.

the OP tower some cover and it was then used by Royal Artillery units who had gun sites close to Ypres. It gave them a clear view of the front-line area around Potijze and was one of ten such structures completed at this time; this is the only example which survives.

The ruins of Potijze Chateau, 1919.

Return to the main road and continue to the roundabout in Potijze. Here **turn right** and follow the N332. Just up on the left follow the CWGC signs and go down a path between the houses.

Potijze was within the Allied lines during practically the whole of the First World War and, although subject to incessant shell-fire, Potijze Chateau contained an advanced dressing station in use from the early period of the conflict. In 1914/15 it was also used as a forward headquarters and Major General Sir Thomas D'Oyly Snow, then commanding the 27th Division, recorded taking his morning tea in the chateau just prior to Second Ypres and watching huge German naval shells pass through the air over the chateau and impact the Cloth Hall in central Ypres behind them in the distance. The village was crisscrossed by trenches and dugouts, and was the location of a large camp by the end of 1917. War poet Edmund Blunden served with the 11th Battalion Royal Sussex Regiment here in 1917 and later recalled:

> The new year was yet very young when the battalion filed through Ypres to take over the trenches at Potijze, which we came to know very well. It was not the worst place in the Salient. I had seen it

already, and its arrangement was simple – a breastwork front line, running from Zonnebeke road to a railway bank on the south; a support line; two good (or not too bad) communication trenches – Haymarket and Piccadilly; Battalion headquarters dugout was near Potijze Château, beside the road. It boasted a handsome cheval-glass and a harmonium, but not a satisfactory roof. This headquarters also enjoyed a kind of Arcadian environment, for the late owner had constructed two or three ponds in the grounds with white airy bridges spanning them, weeping willows at their marges, and there were even statues of Venus and other handsome deities on little eminences, although I did not examine them closely. The château itself, much injured as it was, was not destroyed, and in the upper storey my observers gazed through a telescope on a dubious landscape; lucky these, whose day could not begin before eight, and ended at four with the thickening of what little light there had been. Littered on the damp floor beside them were maps of parts of the estate, some of a great age, and log-books of the number of woodcock, hares, rabbits and I forget what, formerly laid low by shooting parties of this fine house.[3]

At the end of the war little was left of the chateau except the cellars and it was never rebuilt. There are three cemeteries here, all of which will be visited and all three were again designed by Sir Reginald Blomfield. Entering via the path, the Chateau Grounds Cemetery is on the right, Chateau Lawn on the left, and Chateau Wood down a path beyond these two.

POTIJZE CHATEAU GROUNDS CEMETERY

Potijze Chateau Grounds Cemetery was used from May 1915 to September 1918 and at the end of the war consisted of Plot I. Plot II was formed after the Armistice when graves were brought in from isolated sites and small burial grounds to the north-east. A path separates the cemetery from Potijze Chateau Lawn Cemetery, used from May to December 1915, in July 1917 and October 1918. Potijze Chateau Grounds Cemetery contains 476 Commonwealth burials of the First World War, 111 of which are unidentified. The Lawn Cemetery contains 226 burials.

Among the burials here is one from Second Ypres, Captain George Martin Chapman (I-A-12), who was the son of the Judge of the Supreme Court of New Zealand. Born and educated in New Zealand, he went to Cambridge and then studied medicine in London, where he joined the Special Reserve of Officers to serve in the Royal Army Medical Corps.

He was mobilised in 1914, initially serving at Base Hospitals in Le Havre and Boulogne; at Boulogne the French decorated him for bravery when he swam out to a sinking ship and rescued the skipper in heavy storms in December 1914. He then became the Regimental Medical Officer to the 2nd Dragoon Guards and was killed on 13th May 1915 by a shell when he and some of his stretcher bearers went to help a wounded machine-gun team. An officer wrote to his parents:

Captain George Martin Chapman.

We were in the trenches under a very severe shell-fire. Your son was most gallantly attending to the wounded when a shell killed him instantly, as well as two men who were standing by him. We took his body back and buried him in the grounds of a chateau just east of Potijze crossroads, a small village east of Ypres. I cannot tell you what a loss he is to this regiment; he had only been with us two months, but was most popular with officers and men. Please accept the sympathy of the entire regiment with your great loss, and you have the great consolation that he died doing his duty very gallantly as a soldier should.[4]

A young soldier is buried here. Private Fred Lyons (II-F-5) was only seventeen when he was killed with the 15th Battalion Hampshire Regiment (Portsmouth Pals) on 16th May 1918. He had been born in India, where his father was Assistant Engineer to the public works department.

POTIJZE CHATEAU LAWN CEMETERY
Potijze Chateau Lawn Cemetery was used from May to December 1915 and then in July 1917 and finally in October 1918. A path separates this cemetery from Potijze Chateau Grounds Cemetery, which was used from May 1915 to September 1918. At the end of the war it consisted of Plot I, and Plot II was formed after the Armistice when graves were brought in from isolated sites and small burial grounds to the north-east. Potijze Chateau Lawn Cemetery contains 226 Commonwealth burials of the First World War. The Grounds Cemetery contains 476 burials, 111 of which are unidentified.

In Plot A are some men from the 1/8th Battalion Middlesex Regiment who died defending this area in May 1915. These were pre-war Territorials who had come to France via Gibraltar, where they had been

Potijze Chateau Lawn Cemetery, 1919.

on garrison duty in 1914. They lost heavily in the Second Battle of Ypres. The cemetery also reflects the use of the surrounding ground by the artillery with many burials from the Royal Field Artillery and also the Royal Garrison Artillery.

POTIJZE CHATEAU WOOD CEMETERY

Potijze Chateau Wood Cemetery was used from April 1915 to June 1917, and then again three times in 1918. The cemetery contains 157 Commonwealth burials of the First World War.

Among those buried in the cemetery are forty-six officers and men of the 2nd Battalion Hampshire Regiment (Row A) and nineteen of the 1st Battalion Royal Inniskilling Fusiliers (Rows E and F) who died in a gas attack in August 1916. The regimental history records that the Hampshires had moved to Ypres, then considered a 'quiet' sector, from the Somme and that there had indeed been ten quiet days in the trenches at Potijze prior to the German gas attack on 9th August 1916.

A gas cloud was seen approaching slowly from the NE. The wind was light and the gas, moving slowly, was the more efficacious, and between it and the German barrage the battalion suffered terribly, having nearly 240 casualties, more than half fatal . . . the gas, which was phosgene and particularly deadly, killing birds and rats for some distance in the rear and corroding metal, had been sufficiently effective.[5]

Retrace your steps back through the cemeteries. Return to the road and **turn left**, taking the path.

A little further up on the right is a Demarcation Stone. This stone marks the front line at the end of April 1918 but in many respects denotes the fact that Potijze stood on the front line for much of the Great War. It is one of a handful that has the design of a British helmet on the top; most have French or Belgian helmets as the stones were paid for by touring clubs in those countries.

Continue along the road until the French cemetery is reached on the right.

ST CHARLES DE POTIJZE FRENCH CEMETERY

The role of French troops in the fighting at Ypres is a forgotten aspect of the war in Flanders. The French army was heavily involved in both the First and Second Battles of Ypres, but returned to take part in Third Ypres, and again in helping to stop the German advance in April 1918. There were numerous French burial grounds around Ypres by the end of the war but the decision was made to close the majority of them and move the graves to here at Potijze or repatriate them home to France, to be buried in a family grave. It is not known how many were taken home but this cemetery has 3,547 graves, of which 609 are buried in an ossuary, or mass grave. They cover all aspects of the French experience in Flanders, but burials from 1914/15 are most obvious. Muslim graves from some of France's numerous Colonial regiments are also found here.

Leaving the cemetery, cross the road and take *Wieltjestraat* almost opposite. This was known as Oxford Road during the war and was very close to the front-line positions between Potijze and neighbouring Wieltje.

Potijze French Cemetery.

In fact the British front line, from where troops of the 55th (West Lancs) Division made their attack on 31st July 1917, was just 300 metres out towards the fields on your right, about halfway between where you are and the embankment of the A19 motorway which straddles the German front-line positions here.

Continue up *Wieltjestraat* to the end and **turn right**. Walk to the British memorial on your right.

The 50th (Northumbrian) Division was a pre-war Territorial division formed from regiments who recruited locally in the North-East of England. It was dominated by battalions of the Northumberland Fusiliers and Durham Light Infantry, as well as the Yorkshire Regiment (Green Howards). The division arrived in France in April 1915 just as the Second Battle of Ypres started and it was thrown straight into battle, despite many of the men having never before even been in the trenches, let alone in action. In some cases the men had been on active service just a matter of hours before they were in battle. Captain B.M.R. Sharp of the 1/4th Battalion East Yorkshire Regiment, a unit of the division, recalled what was a common experience:

> The march to our line was a queer one. We knew not where we were going, nor what to do; the men's anticipations were not brightened by seeing a dressing station in a very busy state.[6]

Sharp and his men watched sunrise on 24th April 1915, two days into Second Ypres, and suddenly found themselves at war. A month of heavy fighting followed and by the close of it very few men of the pre-war battalions remained, with some battalions losing upwards of eighty per cent casualties. The memorial was designed by Captain Robert Mauchlen MC, who was a decorated officer of the 9th Battalion Durham Light Infantry and had fought with the division. It was unveiled on 1st September 1929 by Field Marshal Lord Plumer, and many old soldiers were present for the ceremony, as well as the families of those who had died.

Retrace your steps and follow the road to the British Cemetery.

OXFORD ROAD CEMETERY

Oxford Road was the name given to a road running behind the support trenches, from a point west of the village of Wieltje south-eastwards to the Potijze–Zonnebeke road. Plot 1 is the original Oxford Road Cemetery and was used by the units fighting on this front from August 1917 to April 1918. In October 1917 another cemetery, known as Oxford Road

Oxford Road Cemetery, 1930s.

Cemetery Number 2, was started close by and now forms Plot V of the cemetery as it appears today. After the Armistice, Plots II, III and IV were added when scattered graves from the battlefields east and south-east of Ypres were brought into the cemetery. There are now 851 Commonwealth casualties of the First World War buried or commemorated in this cemetery. 297 of the burials are unidentified and special memorials commemorate three casualties known to have been buried in the cemetery but whose graves could not be located. The cemetery was again designed by Sir Reginald Blomfield.

Among the burials here is an officer of the Tank Corps who was awarded the Victoria Cross. The Tank Corps was formed in July 1917 from the Heavy Branch Machine Gun Corps and found operating in the fighting at Ypres very difficult due to the boggy nature of the ground and the fact that it had been devastated by shell-fire. Captain Clement Robertson VC (III-F-7) was from an Anglo-Irish family and had been commissioned into the Queen's Regiment. He was later attached to A Battalion Tank Corps, taking part in the fighting at Messines and then Third Ypres. On 4th October 1917 four tanks from his unit, including his own, took part in one of the last tank engagements at Ypres, when they assaulted a German bunker line between the Polygonbeek and Reutelbeek streams just east of Polygon Wood. The citation for his Victoria Cross reads:

For most conspicuous bravery in leading his Tanks in attack under heavy shell, machine-gun and rifle fire. Capt Robertson, knowing the risk of the Tanks missing the way, continued to lead them on foot, guiding them carefully and patiently towards their objective although he must have known that his action would almost inevitably cost him his life. This gallant officer was killed after his objective had been reached, but his skilful leading had already ensured successful action. His utter disregard of danger and devotion to duty afford an example of outstanding valour.[7]

A keen golfer, Clement Robertson was a founder of Delgany Golf Club. There is a memorial to him here and his name appears first on the Captain's Prize Trophy.

Also buried here is one of England's most famous cricketers of the Great War generation: Colin Blythe. Blythe was born in 1879 and played his first game of cricket for Kent when he was only twenty. He quickly became one of the finest and best known cricketers of his generation, achieving record scores. Despite suffering from epilepsy, he had joined the Royal Engineers as a Territorial soldier and when war broke out was mobilised for service. He was later posted to the 12th Battalion King's Own Yorkshire Light Infantry, a Pioneer battalion, and was killed by shell-fire near Passchendaele on 8th November

Colin Blythe.

1917 while his unit was working on trench railway systems in the area. In recent years a period cricket ball has often been left on his grave.

Leave the cemetery and **turn left**. Join the main road and follow it until a CWGC sign is seen on the right. Follow the path through the houses.

WIELTJE FARM CEMETERY

Wieltje Farm Cemetery was made and used by fighting units between July and October 1917. There are some 115 Commonwealth servicemen of the First World War buried or commemorated in this cemetery. Ten of the burials are unidentified and there are special memorials to twenty casualties whose graves were later destroyed by shell-fire. There is also one German grave. The cemetery was designed by A.J.S. Hutton.

This is very much a Third Ypres cemetery with burials from the first day of operations on 31st July 1917 in Rows A and B. Most of these are men from the 55th (West Lancs) Division who attacked the German positions near Wieltje that day. It was then used by burial parties during the Steenbeek River operations in August and September 1917 and there are burials from the 36th (Ulster) and 59th (North Midland) Divisions. The final burials here were in October 1917 as the fighting moved towards Passchendaele.

Return down the path to the main road and **turn right**. Stay on this road into St Jan and then **turn left** at the church onto the N345 towards Potijze. Follow this to the British cemetery.

POTIJZE BURIAL GROUND

Potijze Burial Ground Cemetery was used from April 1915 to October 1918. There are 584 Commonwealth burials of the First World War within the cemetery. This is another of the cemeteries on this walk which was designed by Sir Reginald Blomfield.

This is an interesting cemetery in that it reflects the history of Ypres during the so-called 'quiet' period between the end of Second Ypres in May 1915 and the start of Third Ypres in July 1917. The men buried here did not die in the big battles of the Great War but in the day to day activities of trench warfare. Beyond the Cross of Sacrifice part of the cemetery juts out in rows Q, R and S, and this is a separate section of the ground used by the 11th Battalion King's Royal Rifle Corps in 1916 to bury their dead. It is one of the few examples of a separate battalion plot remaining in any cemetery around Ypres. Rows T and U have more men from the Hampshire Regiment who died in the phosgene gas attack on 9th August 1916. The final burials here were in October 1918 when men from an artillery unit were buried in one row.

Men of the 11th KRRC in Flanders.

Returning to the N345, **go right** and follow the road to the roundabout. Here **turn right** onto the N332 following signs for Ieper and Centrum. Follow this in the direction of Ypres until CWGC signs for Ypres Town Cemetery are seen on the left. Follow the path into the cemetery.

YPRES TOWN CEMETERY AND EXTENSION

Ypres Town Cemetery, close to the Menin Gate, was used from October 1914 to May 1915, and once in 1918. The cemetery contains 145 Commonwealth burials of the First World War, grouped in plots among the civil graves. The Extension, on the east side of the town cemetery, was also begun in October 1914 and was used until April 1915, and on two further occasions in 1918. The extension was much increased after the Armistice when 367 graves were brought in from small cemeteries and isolated positions east and north of Ypres. There are now 598 Commonwealth casualties of the First World War buried or commemorated in the extension. 137 of the burials are unidentified and there are special memorials to 16 servicemen known or believed to be buried among them. Second World War burials number 43, of which 13 are unidentified. The extension was designed by Sir Reginald Blomfield.

Entering from the N332, follow the path into the cemetery Extension. Just ahead on your left is Plot III, Row AA. Buried here are staff officers who were killed in Hooge Chateau on 31st October 1914 when a staff conference was interrupted by a German bombardment. There are two Colonels, two Majors, a Captain and a Gunner signaller in the row, who were killed at Hooge during this incident. Over at the far wall on the left

Ypres Town Cemetery.

is a row of Second World War graves of men who died at Ypres in May 1940 and of aircrew who were shot down and died during the occupation, including a free Czech pilot. On the right, along the hedge, is a row of burials of war grave gardeners. These were family graves that were once elsewhere in the cemetery and moved to the Extension following a redevelopment of the civilian plot where they were. Many of the gardeners were Great War veterans, such as Bill Dunn, who was a churchwarden at St George's in Ypres as well as a gardener.

Walk to the rear of this section and stop at the grave of Lord Worsley (Plot II Row D). Charles Sackville Pelham Worsley was the machine-gun officer of the Royal Horse Guards and was killed defending Zandvoorde on 30th October 1914, aged twenty-seven. Posted as missing, he had been buried by the Germans who had taken this ground and, as it was noted he was an 'English Lord', a plan showing where he was buried was eventually passed down diplomatic channels, his burial site being found just after the war. His wife purchased the ground and eventually his body was moved to this cemetery in 1921 and a memorial placed where he fell, listing all those from the Household Cavalry who had fallen in that area. Lord Worsley's wife published a moving memoir of her husband, which included photographs of her seeing him off at the railway station as his regiment went to war: she would never see him again.

In the far right-hand corner are some steps. Follow these into the main civilian cemetery and immediately stop and **look to your left**. This is the grave of Prince Maurice of Battenberg. A grandson of Queen Victoria, Maurice Victor Donald of Battenberg retained his German name as he died before it was changed to Mountbatten in 1915. Commissioned from Wellington College, he served with the 1st Battalion King's Royal Rifle Corps. He had taken part in the fighting on the Aisne in September 1914 and was killed near Zonnebeke on 27th October 1914. His body was brought here for burial and during the war was visited by many dignitaries. Her Majesty the Queen is related to the young Prince and has visited his grave several times; the last occasion was on 11th November 1998.

Prince Maurice of Battenberg.

As you enter the main cemetery there are more war graves on the left; most of these are from 1914, with some more war grave gardeners buried behind them. Follow the main path straight ahead into an older civilian plot, and then follow this path until it runs parallel to the wall alongside the Menin Road. The graves in this area show signs of extensive damage from shell-fire. Among those buried in this section is Pierre Henri Van den Braembussche. He was the Chief of Police in Ypres and one of those responsible for the formation of the Last Post Association and the playing of the Last Post at the Menin Gate from 1928. Follow the path to the final plot of British graves in what is Ypres Town Cemetery.

This plot includes the graves of some interesting officers of the old pre-war British army and in some respects gives as good a cross-section of the aristocratic nature of the officer class as Zillebeke churchyard. Major Arundell Neave (G-1) served with the 16th Lancers, the family regiment as his great uncle had once commanded it. Educated at Eton, he joined the Lancers just before the Boer War and served with them in India and South Africa. He went to France in 1914 and was Mentioned in Despatches and awarded the French Legion of Honour for bravery. He died of wounds received in the trenches at Hooge. He is related to soldier, spy

Major Arundell Neave.

and politician Airey Neave. Captain Hon. Andrew Mulholland (E2-3) was killed by a bullet while rallying his men in the trenches on 1st November 1914 while serving with the 1st Irish Guards. His father had been a Member of Parliament for North Londonderry. There are three other Honourables buried in the cemetery and also a Lord. Many of the officers had parents who had titles and would have inherited them if they had survived the war. It is in cemeteries like this that you appreciate how the Great War killed the British aristocracy.

There is an original grave marker behind the grave of Captain Graham Percival Shedden (E2-14). The son of a Justice of the Peace from the Isle of Wight, he joined the Artillery in 1904 and served in Hong Kong, where he learnt Cantonese and served on the Legation Guard in Pekin. He was at the staff meeting in Hooge Chateau on 31st October 1914 and was mortally wounded when German shell-fire interrupted it. The cross is his original grave marker. Honorary Captain Edmund Wilkinson (E2-11) was an old sweat who had been commissioned from the ranks. He

Captain Graham Percival Shedden.

had served twenty-six years as an ordinary soldier, taking part in many of Queen Victoria's 'small wars', and had then been commissioned as a Quartermaster in the 1st Loyal North Lancs. While in the ranks he had been decorated with the Distinguished Conduct Medal. He was killed in a key point of the First Battle of Ypres on 31st October 1914, along the Menin Road, aged forty-three. As a Quartermaster his role was not really in the fighting, but as an experienced soldier and one of the few officers left he had stepped up to the mark. Many witnesses describe him 'fighting like a lion' and that he had been recommended for a Victoria Cross. This was never awarded but he was posthumously Mentioned in Despatches.

Exiting the cemetery, you are back on the Menin Road. Here go right and follow the road back to the Menin Gate and central Ypres.

Notes

1. *London Gazette* 4th September 1917. TNA ZJ1.
2. Nicholson, G.W.L. *The Fighting Newfoundlander* (Canada 1964) pp.292–3.
3. Blunden, E. *Undertones of War* (Cobdean Sanderson 1935) pp.171–2.
4. Anon. *Bond of Sacrifice Volume 2* (London 1915) p.84.
5. Atkinson, C.T. *The Royal Hampshire Regiment: Volume Two* (Maclehose & Company, Glasgow 1952) pp.177–8.
6. Wyrall, E. *The Fiftieth Division 1914–1919* (1939) p.14.
7. *London Gazette* 14th December 1917. TNA ZJ1.

A shell damaged farm near Ypres, 1916.

Chapter Three

Yser Canal Walk: Ypres to Boesinghe

STARTING POINT: Yser Canal Basin, Ypres
GPS: 50°51′29.1″N, 2°53′05.2″E
DISTANCE: 14km/8.7 miles

WALK SUMMARY: *This walk follows the line of the Yser canal north from Ypres, an area where the front line remained virtually unchanged for over two years. Many small cemeteries are visited en-route along with the dugouts where poet John McCrae wrote 'In Flanders Fields' in 1915. Although long, it is a gradual and easy walk, and would suit inexperienced walkers.*

Leave your vehicle close to the Yser canal basin; there is a large tarmac area where vehicles can be parked. Alternatively, this walk could be started from the Grote Markt in Ypres. In this case, leave the Grote Markt by Diksmuidsestraat. Where this meets the junction with the N379, turn left and follow the road right – just round the corner is the canal basin area.

In the fourteenth century, when Ypres was centre of the European cloth trade, the Yser canal was the means by which cloth was carried to

The Yser canal, 1919.

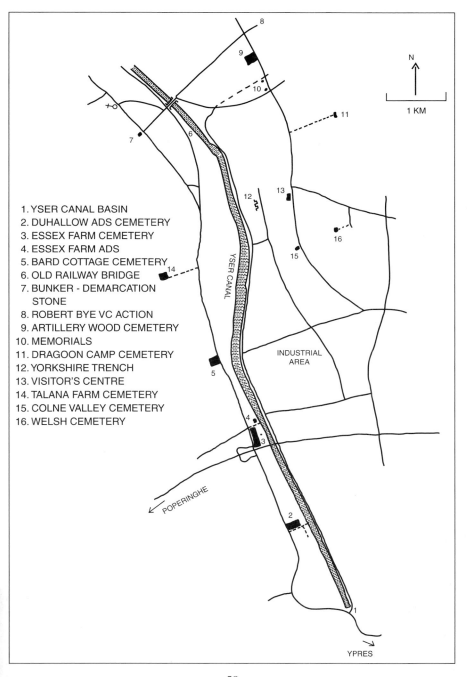

1. YSER CANAL BASIN
2. DUHALLOW ADS CEMETERY
3. ESSEX FARM CEMETERY
4. ESSEX FARM ADS
5. BARD COTTAGE CEMETERY
6. OLD RAILWAY BRIDGE
7. BUNKER - DEMARCATION
   STONE
8. ROBERT BYE VC ACTION
9. ARTILLERY WOOD CEMETERY
10. MEMORIALS
11. DRAGOON CAMP CEMETERY
12. YORKSHIRE TRENCH
13. VISITOR'S CENTRE
14. TALANA FARM CEMETERY
15. COLNE VALLEY CEMETERY
16. WELSH CEMETERY

N

1 KM

YSER CANAL

INDUSTRIAL
AREA

POPERINGHE

YPRES

and from Ypres by boat. During the Great War it formed, at various points, part of the front line and a multitude of constructions were built into the spoil on the west bank. Makeshift bridges, often destroyed and reconstructed on a daily basis, were placed across the canal where it was behind the British lines. One, made prior to the Passchendaele offensive of July 1917, was strong enough to carry the tanks of the 7th Battalion Tank Corps for their attack on St Julien. Today there is no sign of any of these bridges.

From the basin area follow the left edge of the canal basin along Westkaai, past some old factory buildings and warehouses. During the war there were many dumps of equipment and shells around here. At the end of the quay follow a minor tarmac road until it reaches a wooden footbridge; cross and turn right, following the line of the canal. The canal bank at this point was a major billeting area during the fighting for Ypres. H.S. Clapham described a typical scene when he came to this position with the Honourable Artillery Company in 1915:

> We . . . took up our residence in some crazy dugouts on the Yser canal, which we crossed by a pontoon bridge. The dugouts were not even splinter proof, mere shelters from the sun, and along the top of the bank ran a trench, into which we were ordered for shelter whenever shelling started . . . There is plenty of water in the canal, although it is more or less stagnant. It breeds clouds of mosquitoes, which bite like fun, and though it is nice to be able to get a wash when one likes, there are too many floating carcasses of various sorts.[1]

As the war went on, and it became clear that the front line east of the canal bank was not going to change, these 'crazy dugouts' became more and more permanent in appearance, many being shored up with concrete supports and thick timbers.

Continue along the path and further up, opposite a small concrete quay on the other side of the canal, a small access road appears on the left. Follow this to where it crosses a stream. **Stop.**

This is the Yserlee, a minor stream that follows the canal. Looking to the left, past a new house, you can see a grassed embankment. This was the site of Duhallow Advanced Dressing Station (ADS). Constructed in June 1917 by RAMC Field Ambulances of the 39th Division during the period leading up to Third Ypres, it was

> . . . a hive of industry at this time. Dumps of various kinds of shells had been established, whilst battery positions jostled one another

the whole way along. It was inevitable that the enemy should succeed in finding some of these positions. On one such occasion our men were called upon to clear up the gunners. The guns and teams were alike knocked out, one poor youth of eighteen having been blown across the road into a ditch opposite. He was badly wounded and died on the way to the ADS.[2]

During the twenty-four hour period from 31st July 1917 – the opening day of Third Ypres – Duhallow ADS was manned by five medical officers from RAMC units in the 39th Division. The number of casualties treated at this time alone amounted to ninety-four officers and 2,586 other ranks.

Continue along the access road; the nearby military cemetery is soon reached on the right.

DUHALLOW ADS CEMETERY

The cemetery was started just prior to the Third Battle of Ypres in July 1917, as the ADS was established on the canal bank, and was used throughout that offensive, and again until the close of the war. Plots I–IV mark these original graves, some 875 in number; after the war burials from the surrounding area were brought into the cemetery. Among the 1,560 or so soldiers buried here are 1,442 British, twenty-six Canadian, thirteen Australian, twelve Newfoundland, six New Zealand, three South African, two British West Indies, two Indian, two French and one Belgian. There are also fifty-four Germans, and Special Memorials to ten British soldiers originally buried in Malakoff Farm Cemetery at Brielen, whose graves were destroyed by shell-fire. Other Special Memorials exist to

Duhallow ADS Cemetery in the 1930s.

twenty-nine men from Fusilier Wood Cemetery at Hollebeke, in the southern sector of the Salient.

The graves reflect the units involved in the opening phase of Third Ypres, in particular those from the 39th Division, and the fighting around Kitchener's Wood and St Julien. The Guards and 38th (Welsh) Divisions are also well represented, from their actions at Boesinghe and the Pilckem Ridge. 'A most gallant soldier' – according to the headstone inscription – is buried here. Lieutenant O. Brown (VII-C-20) was a typical cavalry officer; educated at a public school, commissioned from Sandhurst into the 7th Hariana Lancers, Indian Army, he died on the Frezenberg Ridge on 24th April 1915 attached to the 4th Dragoon Guards; his grave was moved to Duhallow after the war. Lieutenant F.M. Drury (III-E-9) of the 1/1st Hertfordshires had first come to Flanders as a private in the Honourable Artillery Company in September 1914, and was wounded three times before being killed on 7th January 1918, still aged only twenty-four.

In Plot II Row F is a mass grave of forty-one men from the 13th Company Labour Corps who were killed on 9th January 1918 when a truck-load of salvaged ammunition from the surrounding area was detonated by a bomb dropped from a German aircraft. Many of the men were attached from other units and the headstones show a variety of cap badges, particularly the Seaforth Highlanders.

From the cemetery return along the access road to the Yser canal towpath. Turn left and continue north. Later on the route passes under a modern road bridge and beyond this the spoil bank that lined the canal is clearly in evidence. The front line was over to the right about 2 kilometres distant, beyond the area of the modern factory units. This area of the canal bank was under almost constant shell-fire. Further along on the left another access road appears. Here was a main bridge across the Yser, Number 4 Bridge, which also carried a light railway line known on trench maps as La Belle Alliance Tramway. This ran all the way to Buffs Road, north of Wieltje.

Now follow the access road, which becomes cobbled. Just past where the cutting in the spoil bank ends, there is a line of concrete bunkers and sandbags to the right. This is the site of Essex Farm ADS. The cemetery is reached by the same access road, a little further up on the left.

ESSEX FARM CEMETERY AND BUNKERS

Arguably one of the most famous and frequently visited sites in the Ypres Salient, Essex Farm was named after a small cottage that stood beside the Boesinghe road at the entrance to the canal access track. When the 4th Division took over this sector in mid-1915 an ADS was established

Essex Farm ADS Bunkers, 1918.

by their RAMC units, and as this division included the 2nd Battalion Essex Regiment, the site was probably named by them. The ADS was dug into the canal bank, and at this stage was a primitive timber and elephant-iron affair similar to the 'crazy dugouts' near the canal basin described by Clapham. During Second Ypres it was manned by officers and men from the Canadian Army Medical Corps of 1st (Canadian) Division, who treated many gas cases. One of the officers was Captain John McCrae, an amateur Canadian-born poet who, after the death of a friend, and coming out of the ADS one morning to see the ever-growing number of wooden crosses, was moved to write the now immortal poem, *In Flanders Fields*:

In Flanders fields the poppies blow
Between the crosses, row on row
That mark our place; and in the sky
The larks, still bravely singing, fly
Scarce heard amid the guns below.

We are the Dead. Short days ago
We lived, felt dawn, saw sunset glow,
Loved and were loved, and now we lie
In Flanders fields.

Take up our quarrel with the foe:
To you from failing hands we throw
The torch; be yours to hold it high.
If ye break faith with us who die
We shall not sleep, though poppies grow
In Flanders fields.

John McCrae submitted the poem to *Punch* magazine, which subsequently published it, and it soon became world famous. In recognition of this location's importance, the Belgian regional government erected a memorial to McCrae just outside the cemetery and its design has led many people to believe the poet is buried here. However, John McCrae was later promoted and by 1918 was a Lieutenant Colonel at a base hospital near Boulogne. Having worn himself out, he died of pneumonia in January that year and was buried in Wimereux Cemetery. He now also has a second memorial here, where the full text of the poem can be read.

The concrete bunker visible today was built on the site of the original ADS used by McCrae in 1915. Dating from 1916, the ADS was made permanent for the forthcoming Third Ypres offensive, although nearby Duhallow became the main ADS for this sector at that time. Each chamber in the bunker had its own use (see plan), and the thick concrete must have afforded a great deal of protection from shell-fire. Wounded

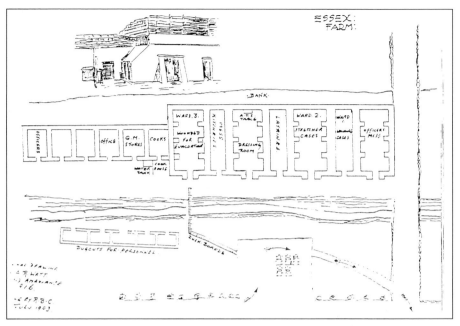

Wartime plan of Essex Farm. (*Reg Barrett-Cross*)

were brought here via communication trenches on the opposite bank of the canal to Number 4 Bridge, and often on the light railway. Once assessed, more serious cases could be evacuated further back via motor ambulances which waited on the Boesinghe road by the ruins of Essex Farm cottage. Graffiti, largely attributable to veterans returning to the area after the war, can be found in the last few chambers. Flooded and inaccessible for many years, the bunkers were purchased and restored by the town of Ypres in the early 1990s. The whole site was later expanded upon and now a path beyond the final bunker can be followed to visit further bunker remains, where interpretation panels explain the layout of the site.

Harry Kendall was serving as a Trooper in 1st King Edward's Horse during Third Ypres and left a graphic description of this area at that time:

I . . . [was] stationed for some time on these crossroads near the Essex Farm graveyard. Fritz had a bad habit of sending shells over and ploughing up the graves. For many weeks there was little peace at that end of Essex Farm road – even for the 'glorious' dead. Often a dozen times a day we were smothered over with mud from the graves torn up by Fritz's exhuming shells . . . Possibly the worst phase of this post by number four bridge was the eternal review of dead men before one's tiring eyes. Slaughtered men lying about in all shapes and forms around this unholy post of ours. Sometimes these immolated human beings . . . would be wrapped in Army blankets, tied around the head and feet. At other times, nothing but War's frightful disfigurements or mutilations were to be seen on the faces of the bodies of these 'glorious' corpses.[3]

A Great War veteran returns to Essex Farm in the 1930s.

The Essex Farm Cemetery has 1,088 British, nine Canadian, five German and nineteen unnamed graves. Of these eighty-three are unknown and there are nineteen Special Memorials. Plot I is very much a 'comrades cemetery' with distinctive unit plots, in particular from battalions of the 49th (West Riding) Division, whose memorial obelisk is to the rear of the cemetery. This Territorial formation from the West Riding of Yorkshire had the distinction of serving along the canal bank sector for the longest continual period. The graves of their men who died here during that time are scattered among the cemeteries south of Boesinghe, many of which will be visited on this walk. Among their casualties in Plot I is a soldier from the West Riding Field Ambulance RAMC who has an interesting inscription on his headstone. The parents of Corporal D. Normington (I-M-17), who died on 12th November 1915, aged twenty-two, chose 'For the love of his wounded comrade he bravely gave his life.'

In another regimental plot, belonging to the Rifle Brigade, the often visited grave of Private Valentine Joe Strudwick (I-U-8) can be found. From Dorking, Surrey, and part of a large family, Strudwick was born on Valentine's Day 1900 and died a month short of his sixteenth birthday when his battalion was shelled in the front line. His body and those of his comrades were brought back to Essex Farm for burial. Although he is not the youngest soldier to die in the war, and possibly not the youngest to die in Flanders, his grave attracts the attention of many school parties as he is the same age as many of the students who now visit. Strudwick was one of those young men who had lied about his age to enlist; his size and appearance got him through the cursory checks made by recruiting sergeants and he was one of thousands of 'boy soldiers' who served. Also nearby is the grave of Private Thomas Barrett VC (I-Z-8) of the 7th Battalion South Staffordshire Regiment who died on 27th July 1917. A veteran of Gallipoli and the Somme, Barrett was awarded his VC posthumously for patrol work in No Man's Land against German snipers. His citation reads:

> For most conspicuous bravery when as Scout to a patrol he worked his way towards the enemy line with the greatest gallantry and determination, in spite of continuous fire from hostile snipers at close range. These snipers he stalked and killed. Later his patrol was similarly held up, and again he disposed of the snipers. When during the subsequent withdrawal of the patrol it was observed that a party of the enemy were endeavouring to outflank them, Pte Barratt at once volunteered to cover the retirement, and this he succeeded in accomplishing. His accurate shooting caused many casualties to the enemy, and prevented their advance. Throughout the enterprise he was under heavy machine gun and rifle fire, and his splendid example of coolness and daring was beyond all praise. After safely regaining our lines, this very gallant soldier was killed by a shell.[4]

Return to the canal via the access road and continue north along the towpath. Just before the canal bends, there is another access road on the left which leads you out onto the main Ypres–Boesinghe road. During the war another trench railway crossed Number 6 Bridge at this point and was known as Lancashire Farm Tramway. It ran from Spahi Farm just behind the British front line. Carefully cross this busy road and turn right, along a footpath to the nearby military cemetery.

BARD COTTAGE CEMETERY

Bard Cottage was a small dwelling between the Ypres road and the Yser canal, and close to a bridge bearing the same name. The cemetery was made beyond the spoil bank, which gave it protection from German observation in the line some distance away. The first burials were made in June 1915, and the cemetery remained in use until the fighting had moved out of the Salient by October 1918. In particular the graves here

Canal bank bunkers at Ypres, 1916.

reflect the trench service of 38th (Welsh) and 49th (West Riding) Divisions, which held the canal bank sector between 1915 and 1917. By Third Ypres there was a large concentration of artillery batteries in the area, and graves from these units are also particularly noticeable. After the war forty-six isolated burials were brought into the cemetery and buried in what is now Plot VI Row C. Of these some thirty-two were from Marengo Farm Cemetery, which was situated just opposite the access road you used to reach the main road. The majority of the soldiers laid to rest at Marengo Farm were men of the 2nd Battalion Seaforth Highlanders and the 1st Battalion East Lancashire Regiment, who were killed in June 1915. Like many farms in the area, it acquired its name during the period when French troops were on the Yser canal in 1914/15. Today Bard Cottage Cemetery contains the graves of 1,616 British, nine Canadian, six Newfoundland, three British West Indian and two South African soldiers. In addition there are also the graves of three German prisoners who died of wounds, and three Special Memorials.

Retrace your route back to the canal and turn left, following the towpath north. This next section of the canal which continues to an area of lock-gates was still behind the British trenches, although the further north you travel, the nearer the front line was. Again there were footbridges across the canal, built and rebuilt daily, and dugouts in the spoil bank to the left. Continue until you reach the lock keeper's cottage on the left. There is a British bunker in the grass area on the left. This appears to have been an observation bunker built into a British trench close to where the front line crossed from the east to the west bank of the canal, affording good observation of the German trenches and No Man's Land.

Continue along the towpath until you reach a bridge across the canal. This was the old railway bridge, destroyed in the war and later rebuilt but decommissioned many decades ago. The bridge is safe. Standing on it looking north, you are looking right down No Man's Land, with the British trenches on the left and Germans on the right. The flooding of the Yser plain further north dropped the level of the water during the war, but it was impassable to patrols so both sides were deadlocked here for more than two years. The close proximity of the trenches here meant that the front line was only held by small numbers of men, otherwise they presented too great a target to the enemy.

British troops in the trenches, Boesinghe sector, 1917.

Return to the towpath and continue north until the path meets the main road. Here **go left** and follow the pedestrian crossing across the N369 towards the village. Take the **first right** into Doktor Dekemelelaan and follow this to the end, **walking across the road to the church**.

The Boesinghe sector was taken over from the French in mid-1915 by units of the 4th Division; thereafter it remained the left flank of the British army on the Western Front. The small village of the same name was just west of the Yser canal, and boasted a large ornate chateau which was used thereafter as brigade headquarters for units in the line here. Field Ambulances also set up an ADS in the chateau grounds, and several military cemeteries were established around the village, one in the chateau park itself. From the church (whose churchyard contains British graves from May 1940) go past this chateau, where bunker remains can be seen at certain times of the year to a much larger bunker next to a modern house.

Boesinghe in ruins, 1916.

70

This large blockhouse was used as an observation post, and as all the surrounding houses at that time had been knocked flat by shell-fire, it afforded good views towards the German trenches across the canal. Today it is surmounted by a German Minenwerfer trench mortar, which fired the larger version of the much-feared 'Minnies' known to all British soldiers. In front is a Demarcation Stone, one of several in the Ypres Salient marking the limit of the German advance in April 1918. This one bears a Belgian helmet, as it was men from the Belgian army who defended the village at that time. Although the Germans crossed the Yser canal, Boesinghe itself did not fall but became part of the front line until September 1918.

Take the road directly opposite the bunker, Brugstraat, and follow it back to the main road (N369). At the end cross via the pedestrian crossing opposite an old mill. This will lead you via a footpath onto the Boesinghe canal road bridge. Stop on the footpath on the bridge.

The front line ran through this area from 1915 until just prior to the Third Ypres offensive. Looking north, for some time the allied trenches were again on the left bank and the Germans on the right. British divisions which served in this sector suffered many casualties from the day to day activities of trench warfare, the more so as the lines were so close at this point. In the weeks leading up to the 31st July 1917 attack a plan was made to move the front line eastwards across the canal, and thus make it a more favourable position from which to advance. Units from the Guards Division were selected for this operation, and in the days leading up to it the German front line was saturated with gas shells fired from 4,000 Livens projectors of the Special Companies Royal Engineers. In the final phase this bombardment was increased when 4.5-inch howitzers fired further gas shells onto strongpoints and woods along the banks of the Steenbeek river to the rear of the German lines. The 49th (Reserve) Division holding the German outposts was driven to breaking point by the gas and by 24th July 1917 realised its position was no longer tenable and withdrew to trenches nearer Artillery Wood. British patrols confirmed this the day after and the line moved forward, across the canal, with few casualties. By 27th July over 3,000 yards length and 500 yards depth of former German positions were now in British hands, enabling the Guards Division to launch its attack on 31st July without having to cross the canal first and thereby no doubt saving many lives.

Continue across the canal bridge and, as the road bends right, take a minor road, Molenstraat, directly opposite. Follow it. Further ahead the road turns right and becomes *Poezelstraat*. Continue for a hundred yards down the minor road ahead and then **stop**.

The ground ahead of this road was where the Guards Division

assaulted Pilckem Ridge on 31st July 1917. Among them were the 1st Welsh Guards. Sergeant Robert James Bye of this battalion was awarded a Victoria Cross for his bravery here on that day; when pushing forward, he captured several strongpoints during the attack on Artillery Wood and killed, wounded or captured over seventy Germans. Bye's VC was gazetted some weeks later, and he survived the war. His citation reads:

Sergeant Robert James Bye VC.

> For most conspicuous bravery. Sjt Bye displayed the utmost courage and devotion to duty during an attack on the enemy's position. Seeing that the leading waves were being troubled by two enemy blockhouses, he, on his own initiative, rushed at one of them and put the garrison out of action. He then rejoined his company and went forward to the assault of the second objective. When the troops had gone forward to the attack on the third objective, a party was detailed to clear up a line of blockhouses which had been passed. Sjt Bye volunteered to take charge of this party, accomplished his object, and took many prisoners. He subsequently advanced to the third objective, capturing a number of prisoners, thus rendering invaluable assistance to the assaulting companies. He displayed throughout the most remarkable initiative.[5]

Return to Poezelstraat, which leads you to the military cemetery further up on the right.

ARTILLERY WOOD CEMETERY

On a site just north of Artillery Wood (which was never replanted), this ground was attacked and captured by the 2nd Guards Brigade on 31st July 1917. The Guards established a small 'comrades' graveyard here at that time, and it was then used by other units as a front-line cemetery for the operations across Pilckem Ridge. Burials continued until March 1918, and by the conclusion of the war there were 141 graves, of which forty-two are men from artillery units who had their gun sites nearby as the fighting moved forward. In the 1920s the cemetery was enlarged by the inclusion of 1,154 burials from the Boesinghe–Pilckem Ridge battlefield; many of them came from the cemetery located in the grounds of

Boesinghe Chateau. Today the graves number 1,243 British, thirty Canadian, ten Newfoundland, five Australian, two New Zealand and one South African. There are twelve Special Memorials and of the total number 506 are unknown.

Every regiment of Foot Guards is represented in this cemetery, giving it very much a Guards Division feel. Among them are comrades from Robert Bye's 1st Welsh Guards. The second most represented unit is the 38th (Welsh) Division, which attacked on the right flank of the Guards on 31st July. The most famous of these burials is Private Elas Evans (II-F-11) of 15th Battalion Royal Welsh Fusiliers, who died of wounds in a regimental aid post on the Pilckem Ridge that day, aged thirty. Better known by his pen name 'Hedd Wyn', Evans was arguably the most famous and important twentieth-century poet who wrote in Welsh, and his grave continues to attract many visitors.

Nearby is another Great War poet, Francis Ledwidge (II-B-5), who was one of Ireland's most important twentieth-century poets. Ledwidge was born at Slane, County Meath, in August 1887 into a large Irish family. His father died when he was five and they lived in poverty for many years. Leaving school at fourteen, he worked first as a farm labourer and then on the roads. In his spare time he wrote poetry; his first published poem appeared in 1910, leading to a collection in book form. Ledwidge joined the 5th Battalion Royal Inniskilling Fusiliers in October 1914 and served at Gallipoli the following year. After being evacuated back to England with sickness in 1916, he transferred to the 1st Battalion and fought at Arras and then at Ypres. Like Evans, he also died on 31st July 1917, when his battalion was on working parties near Boesinghe. In the pouring rain Francis Ledwidge had stopped to have a welcome cup of tea. Almost immediately a stray shell exploded close by, killing him instantly. Further down from the cemetery is a modern memorial to Ledwidge located on the site of the railway line close to where he died. It is easily spotted as the Irish flag normally flies above it.

Leaving the cemetery, turn right at the end of Poezelstraat, stopping on the right-hand corner.

This is one of several gas attack memorials in the Salient, in this case commemorating men of the 45th (Algerian) and 87th (Territorial) Divisions of the French army who were on the left flank of the British lines when gas was used for the first time on 22nd April 1915. Overwhelmed by the poisonous cloud, the French troops understandably ran – and suffered many casualties. The ancient Breton Calvary, which forms the centre point of the memorial, indicates the Territorial regiments were from Brittany; the surrounding stones were specially brought up from the region after the war. There is also a very good bronze orientation table, but the planting of trees on the site has somewhat obscured the view.

From the memorial **cross the main road** into Kleine Poezelstraat. Continue and take the second path on the left, signposted by a green CWGC sign. Follow the path to the cemetery.

DRAGOON CAMP CEMETERY

Dragoon Camp was a position a little south of the Boesinghe–Pilckem road, named after a ruined building marked on maps as Dragoon House. It was just short of the German line of defence around the hamlet of Pilckem itself and was on the line of the 38th (Welsh) Division advance on 31st July 1917. The burials were started by the 13th Battalion Royal Welsh Fusiliers and at one stage the site was known as the Villa Gretchen Cemetery, after another ruined building nearby. The final burials were made in October 1917 and today the cemetery contains the graves of sixty-six soldiers, ten of whom are unidentified.

A group of men from the 15th Battalion Royal Welsh Fusiliers (London Welsh) killed in the operation which moved the line forward at Boesinghe (see above) are buried in one plot of Row B. Among them is Major Evan Davies (B-1), a Newport man who had fought with his battalion at Mametz Wood on the Somme and was Mentioned in Despatches. A patrol from his battalion was ordered forward when a report from the Royal Flying Corps recorded that the Germans had pulled back in this area. Davies and his men were ambushed by heavy machine gun fire and he was amongst the first to fall. It is likely that his body and those of his men were not recovered until after Third Ypres began. Elsewhere the cemetery contains a large number of artillerymen from units which occupied the area as the battle moved on towards Langemarck. Air Mechanic E.T. Rose (A-3) was among the final burials here but he was serving as an attached signaller to an artillery unit rather than in any capacity with his parent unit, 9th Squadron Royal Flying Corps. Rose was one of hundreds of RFC men doing this vital work in 1917.

Return via the path to the main road and **turn left**. Then take the **first path on the right**, marked with wooden posts. This leads into an industrial area which in 2012 was still under development and the layout may change. Follow the path to the end and **turn left** into Bargiestraat. Continue until an area of preserved trenches is reached on the right.

This is Yorkshire Trench and Dugout. In the late 1990s the industrial estate around this site was under development. It was being constructed on ground untouched since the Great War and a local archaeological group, called The Diggers, was granted a licence to work one step ahead

German trench at Pilckem Ridge, 1916.

of the bulldozers. At this time work on Great War sites did not attract the
attention of professional archaeologists and The Diggers were amateurs,
but they carried out an extensive classic rescue archaeology project which
resulted in the recovery of not just a huge amount of material, but the
remains of more than 200 soldiers of all nations involved in the fighting.
Part of their work was filmed for the BBC documentary *The Forgotten
Battlefield* and some of the artefacts they recovered are now on display

in the new In Flanders Fields Museum and also at the Hooge Crater Museum. The work of The Diggers ended some time ago and today archaeology in Flanders is highly regulated but projects continue, most recently at Messines in 2012 and Langemarck in 2016.

The Yorkshire Trench and Dugout site was an attempt to at least try to preserve some of the rich archaeological remains found by The Diggers. A section of trench constructed originally by units of the 49th (West Riding) Division was reconstructed and preserved using semi-concreted sandbags. The line of an original French trench was marked with wooden walkways and the location of the Yorkshire Dugout, most likely from 1917, was indicated with a gravel layout. The entrances to the dugout can still be seen, but it is flooded and access is not possible. Information panels support the site and it gives a good impression of just how confined Great War trenches were.

Yorkshire Trench and Dugout site.

Walk to the end of Bargiestraat and **follow it right** until it meets Oostkaai. A bus picks up close to this junction but otherwise here **turn left** and follow the canal all the way back to the basin in Ypres. Several of the sites visited earlier in the walk can be seen to your right and it is best to walk on the grass verge.

FOLLOW UP VISIT: TALANA FARM CEMETERY
The cemetery is located south of Boesinghe on the N369. Park on the main road and take a footpath; a green CWGC sign is seen on the opposite side of the road pointing to a grass path on your left, which leads across the fields to the cemetery.

Two divisions are well represented here. The 4th Division held this sector after Second Ypres in May 1915 until the summer of that year, and in particular there are many soldiers of the 1st Rifle Brigade. Among them is CSM W. Halliwell MC (I-E-8), a Warrant Officer who had been awarded a Military Cross for bravery; he was killed on 6th July 1915 during the fighting for Fortin 17. The other division was the 49th (West Riding), which took over this sector in August 1915, after the 4th had gone south to the Somme. Burials from Third Ypres in 1917 include a row of four officers all killed on the same day. These made up the headquarters of 9th Battalion Northumberland Fusiliers; their dugout at Stray Farm on Pilckem Ridge was struck by a single shell, killing the commanding officer, adjutant, medical officer and intelligence officer. They are buried left to right, with Lieutenant Colonel A. Bryant DSO (III-K-1) being the first grave. He was a regular in the Gloucestershire Regiment, attached to the battalion.[6]

Notes

1. Clapham, H.S. *Mud and Khaki* (Hutchinson n.d.) p.186.
2. Jobson, A. *Via Ypres* (Westminster Publishing Co. Ltd 1934) p.98.
3. Kendall, H. *A New York Actor On The Western Front* (Christopher Publishing House 1932) pp.73–4.
4. *London Gazette*, 4 September 1917, TNA ZJ1.
5. ibid.
6. See 9th Battalion Northumberland Fusiliers *War Diary*, 17.10.17, TNA WO95/2466.

Chapter Four

Sanctuary Wood – Hooge – Bellewaarde Ridge Walk

STARTING POINT: Trench Museum, Hill 62, Sanctuary Wood
GPS: 50°50′12.7″N, 2°56′46.4″E
DISTANCE: 8.4km/5.2 miles

WALK SUMMARY: *This route follows some of the most important ground around the Menin Road on the centre 'bulge' of the Salient. Heavy fighting took place here in 1915, and the front lines barely changed for another two years. The area of mining activity on the Bellewaarde Ridge is also visited.*

Park your vehicle in the car park of Sanctuary Wood Trench Museum. It is suggested that you visit the museum first, as it has many photographs and maps relating to the area covered by this walk.

Sanctuary Wood, 1916.

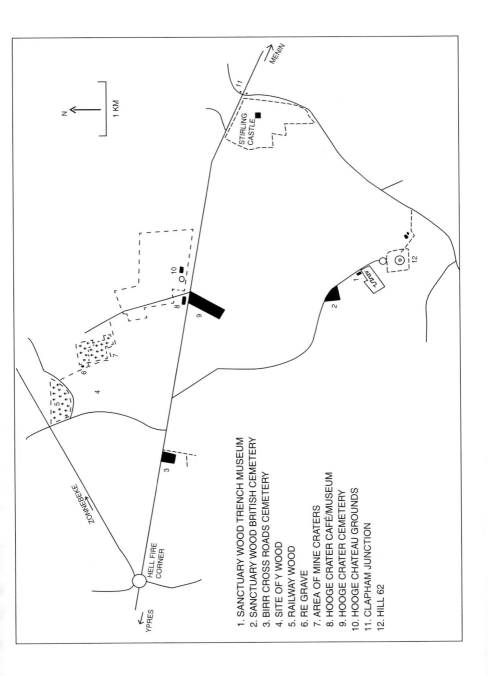

1. SANCTUARY WOOD TRENCH MUSEUM
2. SANCTUARY WOOD BRITISH CEMETERY
3. BIRR CROSS ROADS CEMETERY
4. SITE OF Y WOOD
5. RAILWAY WOOD
6. RE GRAVE
7. AREA OF MINE CRATERS
8. HOOGE CRATER CAFÉ/MUSEUM
9. HOOGE CRATER CEMETERY
10. HOOGE CHATEAU GROUNDS
11. CLAPHAM JUNCTION
12. HILL 62

Sanctuary Wood Trench Museum was started in the early 1920s by a local Belgian family, and was one of a number of such museums in the area where trenches were on display; today it is the only one which survives and went into new ownership following the death of the grandson of the original owner in 2014. The museum reopened and was renovated in 2015 and the unique trench system remains, along with an eclectic collection of relics.

Sanctuary Wood was the name given to a wood south of the Menin Road where, during First Ypres, men isolated from their units gathered together before going back up the line. The area was also used to screen units going up to the front, as it did not directly come into the battle area until the end of First Ypres, being shelled for the first time on the night of 13th/14th November 1914. By 1915 it was part of the front line on the nearest low ridge to Ypres. This high ground from Hill 62 to Hooge and the Bellewaarde Ridge commanded the positions before the town and from 1915 until it was finally taken from the Germans in the opening phase of Third Ypres, there was a great deal of fighting for the possession and repossession of this area. An officer of the 13th Battalion Canadian Infantry (Royal Highlanders of Canada) described the scene here in June 1916:

> Sanctuary Wood was by this time a wood in name only. Such trees as stood were riven and leafless, while their fallen branches added to the maze of wire and trenches beneath. The air was heavy with the sickening odour of decay, so that the whole battered district, even by day, was a place of grisly horror and evil omen.[1]

Inside the main museum building is a wide array of battlefield relics, weapons equipment and uniforms. Photographs of the area are also on display, but perhaps the museum's most unique feature are the stereoscopic viewers dating from the 1920s. These show three-dimensional black and white images, largely from French and German sources, which are among the most harrowing you are ever likely to see. Some are truly gruesome, and those of a nervous disposition might find them too disturbing to look at. They present a side of the war rarely seen in British collections.

Outside, in the wood itself, are the remains of a British second-line trench system dating from around 1915/16. Many visitors and indeed historians remain convinced these trenches are not 'real'. It is certainly true that work on them has been carried out since they were first preserved in 1919, but that is largely to stop them from collapsing. Using new technology[2] it is possible to map the trenches using GPS and they

Sanctuary Wood Trench Museum, 1920s.

compare to two trenches which are visible on 1916 and 1917 trench maps. The main section of trench appears to have been Hill Street trench and the communication trench was Fort Street. One section of short communication trench that comes into Hill Street appears also to be Border Lane. Major R.T. Rees, 8th Battalion Loyal North Lancs, referred to one trench in this area as a 'filthy ditch' in late 1915, and today they often still live up to this reputation. Visitors follow the trench lines through the wood following the zigzagged main second-line trench (Hill Street). Here and there are fire-bays, trench mortar positions, remains of dugouts and funk holes, and about half way along is the entrance to a tunnel. Concrete lining has replaced the wartime wooden shoring, and although it is often wet and muddy, the tunnel is safe to walk through and is lit all the way along. Inside it branches; to the right it joins a communication trench (Fort Street), to the left it once continued all the way to the front line on Hill 62, but now it comes out near some shell holes on the edge of the wood. Duckboards, sandbags and of course the smell and noise of war are missing, but visitors often find this among the most evocative places anywhere in the Ypres Salient today. The museum collection has now spilled into a second building, and there are many battlefield relics on display in the wood. The last of the old trench museums, it is the final link to the post-war battlefield pilgrims who once visited the area in their thousands.

Leaving the museum, **turn left** and follow the road – known as Maple Avenue – to a military cemetery further along on the left.

SANCTUARY WOOD BRITISH CEMETERY

There were three military cemeteries in Sanctuary Wood by 1916, containing fifty-six, fifty-five and one hundred graves respectively from the May–August 1915 period. All of them were virtually obliterated in the fighting for Hill 62 in June 1916 when this ground was swept by shell-fire. Traces of the second cemetery remained after the war when battlefield clearance parties returned, and this became the nucleus of the present cemetery (now Plot I). This original cemetery had been expanded by 1918 to 137 graves, including forty-one Canadians and one German. Due to wartime damage, the exact location of many of these burials could not be ascertained and today eighty-eight of them are commemorated by Special Memorials at the rear of the cemetery. Plots II–V were added between 1927 and 1932, when 1,852 war graves were brought in from a wide area around the Ypres Salient – in some cases from far away as Nieuport on the Belgian coast. The total number of commemorations are therefore: 1,734 British, 142 Canadian, eighty-eight Australian, eighteen New Zealand, three South African, three Newfoundland, and one German. Of these 1,353 are unidentified – nearly eighty per cent.

Lieutenant Gilbert Talbot.

The most frequently visited grave in Sanctuary Wood British Cemetery is that of Lieutenant Gilbert Talbot (I-G-1), who was killed at Hooge with 7th Battalion Rifle Brigade on 30th July 1915. The son of the Lord Bishop of Winchester, Gilbert Talbot's brother, Neville, was a great friend of fellow army chaplain the Rev. P.B. 'Tubby' Clayton, who had been serving in the Salient with 6th Division. In an old town house at Poperinghe the two men established in late 1915 an 'oasis' behind the front line for soldiers out on rest, which they christened 'Talbot House' after Gilbert Talbot. It is still there today; see Poperinghe Town Walk.

Plot I originally contained many graves of units from the 14th (Light) Division, which fought in the Hooge–Sanctuary Wood sector in mid-1915. Among them are five officers from the 6th Battalion Duke of Cornwall's Light Infantry (DCLI), who were killed at Zouave Wood on 30th/31st July 1915 (see below): Captain F.M. Aston (I-C-4), Lieutenant W.E.H. Birch (Sp Mem), Second Lieutenant A.C. Challoner (I-C-9), Lieutenant F.E.B. Hulton-Sams (Sp Mem) and Lieutenant G.M. Paddison (Sp Mem).

Outside the cemetery is a private memorial to Lieutenant Thomas Keith Hedley Rae, who died in the fighting at Hooge on 30th July 1915 with 8th Battalion Rifle Brigade, a sister battalion of Gilbert Talbot's 7th Battalion, and also serving in the 14th (Light) Division. Keith Rae was educated privately due to ill health but later studied at Baillol College, Oxford, and became a teacher at Marlborough. He was last seen, burnt from a flame attack and bleeding from wounds, firing at the advancing Germans. His body was never found and his name is commemorated on the Menin Gate, but after the war his family became one of many who paid for a private memorial to commemorate their loss. This cross was initially erected in the grounds of Hooge chateau, close to the spot where he was last seen. In the 1970s the last direct descendant of the family that owned Hooge chateau asked for the memorial to be moved to a place where it could be properly tended, and it was then that the CWGC took over responsibility and relocated it here.

Return to Maple Avenue and turn left, continuing in the direction of the Menin Road. Further along, as the road bends, there are good views to your right, towards Hooge and Hooge Crater Cemetery, visited later in the walk. **Stop here.**

Zouave Wood once stood in these fields, roughly between the road you are on and Hooge Crater Cemetery; there is a triangular-shaped pasture beneath the cemetery which was approximately the northern peak of the wood. Heavy fighting took place here in July 1915 when the 14th (Light) Division – a formation originally raised during the Peninsular War – fought for the possession of Bellewaarde Ridge, Hooge, and Zouave and Sanctuary Woods. The Germans used flame-throwers in this battle for the first time on the Western Front against British troops, when on 30th July 1915 a number of units in the division came up against several

The Menin Road near Hooge, 1914.

of them. One of those involved was the 6th Battalion DCLI, which advanced on Zouave Wood when it was overrun and despite heavy casualties managed to take the position. Above them the ground sloped up to Hooge, were the Germans were, but the 6th DCLI was ordered to hold on at all costs. For the next two days the men were subjected to bombing attacks, infantry assaults and continuous shell-fire. It was only when flame-throwers were used that men from C Company fell back. Sergeant Silver of the battalion machine-gun section called out 'If you don't get back to your line, I'll open fire on you. The 6th Cornwalls are damned well going to stick it.'[3] At midnight on 31st July what was left of the 6th DCLI handed over the position intact.

Continue along Maple Avenue until it meets the Menin Road.

The Menin Road from Ypres up to Hooge was a busy thoroughfare throughout the war years, and was heavily tunnelled in 1915 by Engineers from the 14th (Light) Division, who were in the Hooge sector at that time. In 1930, when the road was undergoing repairs, and after particularly heavy rain, a whole section collapsed just east of Hellfire Corner and another close to Birr Cross Roads. On the site of a former underground dressing station, the resulting hole was fifty feet across and forty feet deep.

Go left onto the main road and follow in the direction of Ypres. Continue past houses and a café to a cemetery on the left-hand side of the road. The Menin Road is busy, so use the pavements at all times.

BIRR CROSS ROADS CEMETERY

Birr Cross Roads was a position on the Menin Road named by the 1st Battalion Leinster Regiment after its regimental depot. The cemetery was started in August 1917 during the Third Battle of Ypres and as there was an underground Dressing Station close by, the men who died of wounds here were buried on this spot. It continued into use until March 1918 and in April the ground was overrun and once more was close to the front line, then at Hellfire Corner further down the road. By the end of the war the cemetery contained nine irregular rows of graves, now part of Plot I, but was greatly enlarged when graves were brought in from the surrounding battlefields and from several smaller cemeteries, which included:

BELLEWAARDE RIDGE MILITARY CEMETERY, ZONNEBEKE: this was a little way north-east of Bellewaarde Lake, almost on the top of the low hill which rises northwards from the Menin Road between Hooge and Clapham Junction. It contained the graves of seventeen soldiers from Australia and eleven from the United Kingdom, who fell in September and October 1917.

Birr Cross Roads, 1916.

BIRR CROSS ROADS CEMETERY No 2: seventy-five metres south of No 1 (the present cemetery), this contained the graves of eighteen soldiers from the United Kingdom who fell in July and August 1917.

UNION STREET GRAVEYARDS No 1 and No 2, ZILLEBEKE: these lay due north of Zillebeke village, between Gordon House and Hellfire Corner, and contained the graves of nineteen soldiers from the United Kingdom who fell in August and September 1915.

There are now 833 Commonwealth servicemen of the First World War buried or commemorated in this cemetery. 336 of the burials are unidentified, but there are special memorials to nine casualties known or believed to be buried among them. Other special memorials commemorate eighteen casualties buried in Birr Cross Roads Cemetery No 2 and the Union Street Graveyards, whose graves were destroyed by shell-fire, and one Belgian interpreter whose grave cannot now be found.

Among the Special Memorials by the entrance is one to Captain Harold Ackroyd VC MC (Spec Mem 7). A forty year old medical officer attached to the 6th Battalion Royal Berkshire Regiment, Ackroyd had been decorated for bravery with his battalion at Delville Wood on the Somme in 1916 and was awarded a posthumous Victoria Cross in August 1917:

> For most conspicuous bravery. During recent operations Capt. Ackroyd displayed the greatest gallantry and devotion to duty. Utterly regardless of danger, he worked continuously for many

hours up and down and in front of the line tending the wounded and saving the lives of officers and men. In so doing he had to move across the open under heavy machine-gun, rifle and shell fire. He carried a wounded officer to a place of safety under very heavy fire. On another occasion he went some way in front of our advanced line and brought in a wounded man under continuous sniping and machine-gun fire. His heroism was the means of saving many lives, and provided a magnificent example of courage, cheerfulness, and determination to the fighting men in whose midst he was carrying out his splendid work. This gallant officer has since been killed in action.[4]

Among the graves moved into the cemetery is that of Second Lieutenant Raymond Lodge (II-D-5), who was killed by shrapnel at Hooge while serving with the 2nd Battalion South Lancashire Regiment on 14th September 1915. He was the son of Sir Oliver and Lady Lodge; Sir Oliver was a physicist who was a key player in the development in British wireless radio technology. He had a big family, but the loss of his son Raymond hit him hard and he became one of those who turned to spiritualism to try to make contact with his son. Sir Oliver published extensively on it, including transcribed conversations with the dead Raymond. Whatever one believes of this, parents like Sir Oliver and Lady Lodge found it comforting and added a unique inscription to their son's headstone:

Second Lieutenant Raymond Lodge.

Raymond, who has helped many to know that death is not the end.

Leaving the cemetery, **turn right** and walk back up the Menin Road. Further up cross the road carefully and **take the signposted road to the left** where a CWGC sign for RE Grave can be seen. Follow the road uphill to just before some farm buildings on the left. **Stop here.**

Y Wood was located in the fields to the right of this road, and the ground rises up to some woods which are on the crest of Bellewaarde Ridge. The Cross of Sacrifice of RE Grave can also be seen. Y Wood was a position captured by the Germans in early 1915 and assaulted by the 1st Honourable Artillery Company and other units of the 3rd Division on

The German view towards Ypres from Bellewaarde Ridge.

16th June 1915. H.S. Clapham described the fighting that day as 'full of horrors and I feel almost competent to write another story of the descent into Hell'.[5] His battalion had got into the German front line and consolidated its position. Flags were used to indicate progress in the attack and some were seen in the second line. It was then that a whistle blew and Clapham's company was moved out into No Man's Land. He found the forward trenches full of dead, and the order came round to dig in. Clapham and his comrades began the laborious task of moving the barbed wire from the old German parapet onto the parados. Sandbags were filled and new communication trenches dug – but the captured lines were pummelled by German artillery and casualties mounted. A German attack followed a further heavy bombardment, but it was beaten back. Eventually relieved, Clapham noted,

> . . . we have lost half the battalion and nearly all our officers, including the Colonel and Second-in-Command. Those of us who are left look worn and old, and our nerves are in tatters.[6]

Continue on the road uphill until it meets another minor road on the right. Turn right and stop by the wood on your left.

This is Railway Wood. So named since it bordered on the Ypres–Roulers railway line (now a fast road link to Zonnebeke), Railway Wood was part of the front line by 1915 and was fought over several times;

Stretcher bearers of the Liverpool Scottish who served with Noel Chavasse at Hooge.

mining activity was prominent in this part of the Salient. For many years there were several small mine craters in the Railway Wood area, but now only a handful remain as farmers filled them in. Major William 'Billy' Congreve, the son of a Victoria Cross winner who would himself win a posthumous VC on the Somme in 1916, visited the sector just after the 16th June 1915 attack:

> Eventually we worked our way round to Railway Wood. Here the mess was very bad. Also the Germans were very close, only about fifteen yards. A burial party of some sixty men arrived and got to work . . . Everything was quiet while we were up there, hardly any snipers at work in the German lines and no shelling. There is no doubt about the value of the ground gained. Looking back towards Ypres from the trench between Railway Wood and Y Wood, one can see every bit of ground.[7]

From the same position today the view afforded to Billy Congreve is quite apparent and the importance of these low ridges around Ypres and why both sides fought for their possession clearly obvious.

Continue down the minor road which runs alongside Railway Wood. Although there are signs of shell holes inside, it is private property and cannot be entered. Part of the wood now has a house built in it. As the road bends, there is a cart track on the right, with a CWGC signpost for RE Grave. Follow this to the Cross of Sacrifice visible in the fields.

RE GRAVE, RAILWAY WOOD

Located on ground that was the apex of the fighting here, the RE Grave (Royal Engineers Grave) is a unique military cemetery. There are no headstones here – just a Cross of Sacrifice on the base of which are recorded the names of twelve men. All died below ground in tunnelling operations on the Bellewaarde Ridge and at Hooge between 14th December 1915 and 22nd July 1917, their bodies lost or buried in the maze of tunnels and galleries below where you are now. Some of these men were Royal Engineers, others transferred or on loan from infantry units, a common practice. The main inscription reads:

> Beneath this spot lie the bodies of an officer, three NCOs and eight men of, or attached to, the 177th Tunnelling Company RE who were killed in action underground during the defence of Ypres.

Around the RE Grave is evidence of these mining operations; small craters, often filled with water, lie only a short distance away but are usually wired off and are on private ground. A whole range of them existed across the fields towards Railway Wood but gradually they have disappeared.

From RE Grave return to the track and turn left and follow the path round the corner to another memorial. This is a recent memorial to the 1/10th Battalion King's Liverpool Regiment (Liverpool Scottish). This unit took part in the attack here on 16th June 1915, coming up the slopes which the memorial now overlooks. The medical officer of the unit was

Royal Engineers Grave in the 1930s.

Hooge. Memorial 177th Company Royal Engineers and Railway Wood Cemetery.

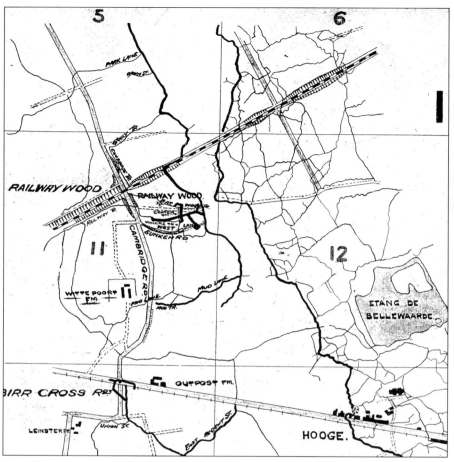

Battlefield map of the Bellewaarde Ridge.

Wartime aerial view of the Bellewaarde Ridge to Hooge in 1917, but showing the earlier mine craters.

Modern aerial image of the Bellewaarde Ridge. (*John Giles archive*)

Noel Chavasse. The son of the Bishop of Liverpool, he was awarded a Military Cross here for bravery in this action while recovering the wounded. He would go on to be awarded a Victoria Cross on the Somme in 1916 and a posthumous bar at Ypres in August 1917; he was one of only three men who achieved this distinction.

From the memorial follow the track and **then immediately turn right** following a new path round the edge of the woodland. This area has been renovated as part of the Great War Centenary and the wooded area purchased, enabling public access. All of the mine craters here are now accessible and while the private farm buildings beyond must be respected, this fascinating part of the Western Front showing the intensity of the underground war here can now be visited in a way not previously possible. The mine craters all date from 1915 and 1916, during the long period of static warfare in this sector. Stay on this path until it reaches a minor road and then **turn right** and go downhill. Just before the Menin Road, **stop**.

In the trees on the left was the site of the famous Hooge Crater. Many people have speculated where this crater was but modern mapping software can accurately plot that this was the location of the large mine blown at 7pm on 19th July 1915. The charge, placed by 175th Tunnelling Company Royal Engineers, formed a crater 20 feet deep and 120 feet wide. An assault by the 4th Battalion Middlesex Regiment took it, but it was lost in the flame-thrower counter-attack later that month. The crater

Hooge Crater, 1916.

was retaken by the 2nd Battalion Durham Light Infantry, which assaulted by the hill from Sanctuary Wood, and remained in British hands until the ground was lost in the assault on the Canadian positions here in June 1916. No trace of the crater exists today.

Continue and **turn immediately right**, towards the front entrance of the Hooge Crater Café and Museum.

HOOGE CRATER CAFÉ AND MUSEUM
This superb museum is situated on the former battlefield at Hooge, where several large mine craters obliterated this section of the Menin Road during the war. The scene here was one of utter desolation, a morass of shell holes and craters, and a typical account is that of the 2nd Leinsters in August 1915:

> The Leinsters lay astride the Menin Road round the lips of the crater with both flanks in the air. The inside of this vast crater presented a terrible appearance; the enemy had turned it into a honeycomb of dugouts during the period when they held it. Tier upon tier of dugouts made from lines of railway sleepers – yet this cover did not save them from our guns: it became a veritable death trap. Fully 200 mangled German corpses lay in the crater, and after the Leinsters had completely consolidated the new line they had

92

The battlefield at Hooge, 1917.

the task of filling in this crater with lime and earth. Not a blade of grass was visible on this shell-pitted and bleached-up terrain of the Hooge Ridge.[8]

The museum is located inside an old school and chapel, and entrance is gained via the café. The exhibits are arranged around a series of life-size dioramas depicting various aspects of the Ypres Salient, with extensions showing battlefield archaeology and a film about the fighting along the Menin Road. Maps and photographs abound, and near the old entrance is an amazing collection of shells and ordnance from all nations and of all calibres. The weight alone must be staggering and the combined

'This was Hooge' – Hooge rises from the ashes, early 1920s.

explosive effect of these pieces when live unimaginable. Thankfully they are now all deactivated and safe. Outside are field guns and other large pieces. Run by a friendly and knowledgeable Belgian family, the museum sells books and souvenirs, and is a good place for lunch and has clean toilets. Not only is it one of the best museums near Ypres, it is a great place to eat and rest while walking the battlefields.

Leaving the museum, carefully cross the Menin Road to the military cemetery opposite.

HOOGE CRATER CEMETERY

Another of the larger cemeteries in the Salient, burials were started here during Third Ypres by the 7th Division in October 1917. The area was then still littered with mine craters, and a small plot of seventy-six graves existed by 1918. These are now in Plot I, Rows A to D. After the war it was selected as a site for one of the main concentration cemeteries and 5,800 graves were moved to it. These and the originals now total: 5,153 British, 509 Australian, 119 New Zealand, ninety-five Canadian, and two British West Indies Regiment. Of these 3,580 are unknowns – over half. There are also forty-five Special Memorials.

This is one of the largest concentrations of Australian Imperial Force (AIF) graves in the Salient, and an AIF Victoria Cross winner is buried here. Private Patrick Joseph Bugden (VII-C-5), from New South Wales, was serving with the 31st Battalion AIF and was awarded a posthumous

Hooge Crater Cemetery, 1920s.

VC for bravery in Polygon Wood in September 1917. His citation reads:

> For conspicuous bravery and devotion to duty when, on two occasions, our advance was temporarily held up by strongly held pillboxes. Private Bugden, in the face of devastating fire from machine-guns, gallantly led small parties to attack these strong points, and, successfully silencing the machine-guns with bombs, captured the garrison at the point of the bayonet. On another occasion, when a Corporal, who had become detached from his company, had been captured and was taken to the rear by the enemy, Private Bugden, single-handed, rushed to the rescue of his comrade, shot one enemy and bayoneted the remaining two, thus releasing the Corporal. On five occasions he rescued wounded men under intense shell and machine-gun fire, showing an utter contempt and disregard for danger. Always foremost in volunteering for any dangerous mission, it was in the execution of one of these missions that this gallant soldier was killed.[9]

Leaving the cemetery, carefully **recross the road** and **turn right**, going east along the Menin Road, following the path. A few hundred yards further on, still on the left and set back from the road, is Hooge chateau. It is now a hotel-restaurant and can be visited by following the main entrance into the grounds.

Hooge chateau was one of the largest such buildings in the Salient, with extensive grounds that backed onto the Bellewaarde Ridge. It was destroyed by 1918, and the current building is roughly on the site of the original chateau stables. During First Ypres Hooge chateau was used as a headquarters by 1st and 2nd Divisions. Disaster struck at the height of the battle on 31st October 1914 when two shells pitched through the roof dramatically interrupting a staff meeting. Major General S.H. Lomax, commanding 1st Division, was so badly wounded by the blast he never really recovered and died some months later in England. Six senior staff officers were killed instantly, another dying of his wounds, and two others were wounded. NCOs and men attached to the staff and assisting in the conference were also injured. At such a crucial point in the battle it seemed that the situation might be lost with the death and wounding of so many important officers, but Major General Monro, commanding 2nd Division, despite being blown off his feet, went back to command his men and the Germans were held on the Menin Road. Those killed in this incident were taken back to Ypres Town Cemetery and buried together.[10]

Hooge chateau eventually fell to the Germans, but by 1915 it had become part of the front line and mining operations began in the area.

The lines moved to-and-fro in June, July and August 1915, and on 25th September another large-scale attack was launched by the 3rd Division as a diversionary attack for the Battle of Loos, then being fought in northern France. H.S. Clapham described the scene in his diary just prior to the operation:

> The ground all round was in a horrible condition, churned and flung up in small hillocks, overlooking evil-smelling water-holes. It was strewn with bones, broken tools, burst sandbags, and pieces of torn clothing.[11]

The 2nd Battalion Middlesex Regiment was also participating in this attack, and one of its officers, Lieutenant Rupert P. Hallowes, was awarded a posthumous Victoria Cross for his bravery. Hallowes was born in Redhill, Surrey, and educated at Haileybury College. He was an early member of the then fledgeling Boy Scouts movement, shot at Bisley for

Lieutenant Rupert Hallowes was awarded a posthumous VC for his bravery at Hooge, September 1915.

his college, and joined the Artists' Rifles (a Territorial battalion of the London Regiment) in 1909, while working as assistant manager of the Mansel Tin-Plate Works. He proceeded overseas with the Artists' Rifles in December 1914, and was commissioned when the unit became an OTC, being gazetted in April 1915 to the Middlesex Regiment. The area around Hooge was well known to him, and he was awarded the Military Cross for his bravery in the fighting here on 19th July 1915. His citation for the operations of 25th September onwards reads:

> For most conspicuous bravery and devotion to duty during the fighting at Hooge . . . Second Lieutenant Hallowes displayed throughout these days the greatest bravery and untiring energy, and set a magnificent example to his men during four heavy and prolonged bombardments. On more than one occasion he climbed up on to the parapet, utterly regardless of danger, in order to put fresh heart into his men. He made daring reconnaissance of German positions in our lines. When a supply of bombs was running short he went back under very heavy shell-fire and brought up a fresh supply. Even after he was mortally wounded he continued to cheer those around him and to inspire them with fresh courage.[12]

The words of encouragement he shouted to his men echoed those of the Colonel of the 57th Foot (later the Middlesex Regiment) over a hundred years before at Albuera during the Peninsular War, when he urged his men to 'Die Hard', thus earning the regiment the name 'The Die-Hards'. That same call was repeated by Hallowes here at Hooge. Badly wounded, Rupert Hallowes was evacuated back to Ypres where he died of wounds on 30th September 1915, aged thirty-four. After the war his grave was moved to Bedford House Cemetery; see the Bluff Walk.

The Hooge chateau grounds are accessible to the public, and the chateau itself has a good bar serving refreshments. Mine craters are clearly visible here but they are not the famous Hooge Crater, which many visitors believe they are. In fact these are German mines blown underneath the men of the 28th Battalion Canadian Infantry on 6th June 1916. The battalion lost heavily in the explosion of these mines and was thrown back, the positions here being lost and not retaken until 1917. By the side of the larger water-filled crater is a German pillbox dating from late 1916, which was repaired and later used by the British after the ground was captured on 31st July 1917 by units of the 8th Division. Visitors are welcome, and there is a donations box, but the hotel should be respected.

Aerial photo of the 1916 mine craters and battlefield around Hooge Chateau.

Returning to the Menin Road, turn left and continue eastwards, keeping to the footpath/cycle path but beware of cyclists as they have right of way. Soon the Bellewaarde Amusement Park is reached on the left. Just outside, by the road, is a regimental memorial. This

Hooge Chateau, 1914 and 1915.

commemorates the officers and men of the King's Royal Rifle Corps who fought and died in the Ypres Salient, 1914–18. Another of the same design exists on the Somme; they mark the two great killing grounds of the Western Front which claimed the lives of many riflemen. Now dwarfed by the huge car park attached to the Amusement Park, some pilgrims might find it a touch ironic that such a place exists in the middle of an area where so many men fought and died. Others might see it as a good thing that a former battlefield is now a place where young people laugh and play.

Staying on the Menin Road, continue eastwards for another kilometre, past some woodland on the right, until a road junction is reached. Memorials can be seen on both sides of the main road.

This place was known as Clapham Junction on British maps. In 1914 the 1st Battalion Gloucestershire Regiment fought here, and the obelisk on the left of the road commemorates its fallen. The other memorial is to

The KRRC Memorial in the 1970s.

the 18th (Eastern) Division, considered by many military historians as one of the finest British divisions which served on the Western Front. Other divisional memorials exist on the Somme, where it was one of the only divisions to achieve all its objectives on 1st July 1916. The 18th fought here at Ypres in July and August 1917, when Captain Harold Ackroyd MC RAMC, medical officer to the 6th Battalion Royal Berkshires, was awarded a Victoria Cross for bravery in tending the wounded in the opening stage of Third Ypres. He was sniped and killed in Jargon Trench, near Glencorse Wood; his body was brought further back for burial in Birr Cross Roads Cemetery.

Leaving the Menin Road, go south on the road by the 18th Division memorial, Pappotstraat. Although it is private and access cannot be gained, in the woodland on the right of this road was the wartime location of Stirling Castle.

Stirling Castle was the name given to a small chateau set in wooded grounds south of the Menin Road. The area was fought over during First Ypres and then captured by the Germans; the chateau then remained behind their lines until 1917. By the opening stage of Third Ypres, the ruins of the chateau were reinforced with several concrete bunkers. The position was attacked by the 90th Brigade, 30th Division, on 31st July 1917, when men of the Manchester Pals battalions advanced under heavy fire but lost direction. The 17th Battalion King's Liverpool Regiment (Liverpool Pals) then came up, but it was units from the 21st Brigade which finally cleared Stirling Castle that day, and held a new defence line east of it, with their left flank on the Menin Road at Clapham Junction.

Today the chateau has been rebuilt and is a private residence, but at certain times of the year signs of shell holes and trenches can be seen amongst the trees. Sadly one cannot freely wander through them.

Pappotstraat was known as Green Jacket Ride on British trench maps, as it was near here that the King's Royal Rifle Corps, which in Napoleonic times had worn green jackets as uniforms, fought in 1914. The regiment had two battalions in Flanders at this time; the 1st Battalion alone lost 1,037 officers and men by the close of First Ypres.[13]

Continue south on Pappotstraat for about 2 kilometres. Just before a large modern farm ahead to the left, and at a bend in the road, a tarmac track is seen on the right, leading off to a small farmhouse. **Turn right** and follow this to the metal farm gate. At the end **go left** and follow a small footpath going off at an angle. This brings you via a gap in the hedge into the grounds of Hill 62 Canadian Memorial.

The action at Hill 62 in June 1916 was known to the Canadians as the Battle of Mount Sorrel and it became one of the Canadian Expeditionary Force's (CEF) battle honours. Hill 62 was one of the few remaining pieces of high ground on the ridge immediately east of Ypres still in British hands, and the Germans were determined to take it. At just after 6am on 2nd June 1916 an attack on the Canadian positions was launched, part of a large attack from Hooge, through Hill 62, Mount Sorrel to Observatory Ridge. Hill 62 was held by 3rd (Canadian) Division, and an intense artillery bombardment of its lines smashed a hole in the defences through which over 8,000 German soldiers – largely Wurtemberger units – poured

Hill 62 Canadian Memorial site in the 1930s.

Canadian Memorial Hill 62 - Ypres

in and took the high ground. During the fighting Major General Mercer, commanding 3rd Division, was killed and a brigade commander wounded. Casualties were heavy; the 4th Canadian Mounted Rifles alone lost 640 men. A counter-attack was organised the same day using battalions from both 2nd and 3rd (Canadian) Divisions, but it was thrown back with heavy losses. The fighting continued, and on 6th June further positions were taken by the Germans, including the area around Hooge chateau. Sir Julian Byng, commanding the Canadian Corps, then organised a well-planned counter-stroke, which was executed on 13th June. Despite poor weather, the CEF managed to push the Germans back and regain most of their original start line, but positions at Hooge and nearly half of Sanctuary Wood were not retaken until the battles of 1917. The operations cost the Canadians more than 3,000 dead, making it the deadliest 'sideshow' the CEF took part in on the Western Front.

The site on Hill 62 was one of a number selected after the war to commemorate the principal Canadian actions on the Western Front. With the exception of Vancouver Corner, near St Julien, all are of the same design and each stone bears an inscription in English and the local language indicating which action is commemorated. Hill 62 is one of the largest Canadian sites in the Salient, and Maple Avenue, along which you have already walked, was specially constructed after the war to link it with the Menin Road.

From the memorial walk back down to the car park of Sanctuary Wood Trench Museum, and your vehicle.

Notes

1. Featherstonhaugh, R.C. *The 13th Battalion Royal Highlanders of Canada 1914–1919* (By the Regiment 1925) p.109.
2. Among them is Nigel Cave's *Sanctuary Wood & Hooge* (Pen & Sword 1993) which covers the area of this walk in some detail.
3. Brice, B. *The Battle Book of Ypres* (John Murray 1927) p.260.
4. *London Gazette* 4th September 1917.
5. Clapham, H.S. *Mud and Khaki* (Hutchinson n.d.) p.141.
6. ibid. p.157.
7. Norman, T. *Armageddon Road: A VC's Diary 1914–16* (William Kimber 1982) p.152.
8. Brice op cit. p.158.
9. *London Gazette* 23rd November 1917.
10. Brice op cit. p.141 and *War Diary* 2nd Division Headquarters, 31.10.14, PRO WO95/1283.
11. Clapham op cit. p.210.
12. *London Gazette* 16th November 1915.
13. Figures given in Anon. *The King's Royal Rifle Corps Chronicle 1914* (Warren & Son 1915) p.138.

Chapter Five

Zillebeke Walk

STARTING POINT: Transport Farm (Railway Dugouts) Cemetery
GPS: 50°50′07.4″N, 2°54′11.1″E
DISTANCE: 8km/4.9 miles

WALK SUMMARY: *A fairly short walk across easy ground, this route is suitable for novice or first-time walkers. It covers the area around the important village of Zillebeke, close to and part of the front line almost continuously between 1914 and 1918.*

Park your vehicle outside Transport Farm Cemetery. It is easily reached from Ypres either on foot or by car via the Lille Gate, and turning off at Shrapnel Corner on the N336.

TRANSPORT FARM (RAILWAY DUGOUTS) CEMETERY
Transport Farm was the name given to a collection of buildings close to the Ypres–Comines railway line. Its name probably originates from the fact that battalions in the line around Zillebeke or Hill 60 had their

Transport Farm (Railway Dugouts) Cemetery in the 1930s.

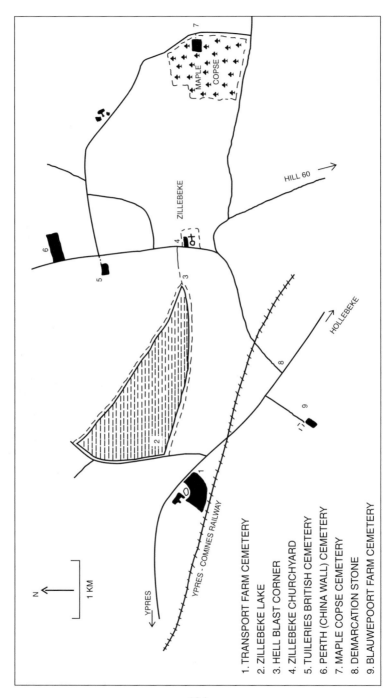

N

1 KM

YPRES

YPRES - COMINES RAILWAY

HILL 60

ZILLEBEKE

HOLLEBEKE

MAPLE COPSE

1. TRANSPORT FARM CEMETERY
2. ZILLEBEKE LAKE
3. HELL BLAST CORNER
4. ZILLEBEKE CHURCHYARD
5. TUILERIES BRITISH CEMETERY
6. PERTH (CHINA WALL) CEMETERY
7. MAPLE COPSE CEMETERY
8. DEMARCATION STONE
9. BLAUWEPOORT FARM CEMETERY

transport lines in the vicinity. At this point the railway line is on a high embankment and British soldiers soon dug into the sides creating dugouts and stores, and an advanced dressing station was established by 1916, marked on British maps as Railway Dugouts ADS. Burials began during Second Ypres in April 1915, and increased once the ADS opened; many graves were damaged by shell-fire during 1917, and again in 1918 when the front line was close by. By the end of the war there were 1,705 burials; 258 of them were destroyed and no longer marked. When the cemetery was made permanent these lost burials were commemorated with Special Memorials. A further 423 graves were brought in from the surrounding area in the 1920s, making the total commemorations: 1,629 British, 594 Canadian, 154 Australian, four Indian, four German prisoners, three New Zealanders, two whose units were unknown, and one British West Indies Regiment. Of the total 430 are unnamed, and including the above mentioned, there are 333 Special Memorials, mostly by the main entrance.

Outside the main cemeteries like Tyne Cot and Lijssenthoek, one of the largest concentrations of Canadian graves in the Salient can be found here, including men from several of the Canadian divisions killed holding the line at St Eloi, and in the Hill 62–Observatory Ridge–Mount Sorrel– Hill 60 sectors during the first half of 1916. Lieutenant A.N.P. Service (VI-J-1) was killed by a shell in Trench 38 at Hill 60 on 18th August 1916. He was the brother of Robert Service, a famous Canadian poet, who himself served with the Canadian Army Medical Corps here in 1916 and later published *Rhymes of a Red Cross Man*. In Plot VI Row I is a battalion burial site of men from the 60th Battalion Canadian Infantry. Nineteen of them died on 12th August 1916 when the battalion was holding trenches 37 to 42 on Hill 60. At one point that day the Germans raided the

***Rhymes of a Red Cross Man* by Robert Service.**

front-line positions and, carrying boxes of dynamite, succeeded in entering trenches 37, 39 and 41. However, men of the 60th soon beat them back and the boxes of dynamite and their fuses were captured and handed over to a RE tunnelling officer who was inspecting Hill 60 at the time. In the defence of these trenches the battalion lost two officers and twenty-six men killed, and two officers and fifty-six men wounded.[1]

A number of other battalion, brigade or divisional burial sites can also be found within Transport Farm, including many soldiers who also died in the fighting around Hill 60. The 1/4th Battalion Yorkshire Regiment buried a number of their men in Plot II Row K in early 1916. Twelve of them died on 14th February when the Germans blew a mine at trenches 37 and 38 south of the Ypres–Comines railway cutting between Hill 60 and Verbrandenmolen. A strong bombardment of the British positions followed, in which many of the front-line trenches and the communication trenches leading up to them were damaged, destroyed or blown in. Contact was lost with the men in the forward positions. As the bombardment slackened, officers and men made their way back into the front line, where 'two men were dug out alive from the trench near the crater and one man picked up alive after having been blown 40 yards . . . he died soon after he had been brought in'.[2] Also in Plot II is a communal grave of men from the 8th Battalion Durham Light Infantry. Fifteen graves in Row D are men who died on 2nd March 1916 when several units in the 17th (Northern) Division attacked the Bluff. 8th DLI was holding positions just north of Verbrandenmolen and so was not directly involved in the attack, but came under tremendous punishment during the day. Apart from a heavy bombardment of shells of all calibres, phosgene gas descended on the Birdcage and a mine was blown.[3]

From the fighting for Hill 60 during 1917 are several graves of interest. One is a group of officers from the 11th Battalion West Yorkshire Regiment. This was the battalion which actually captured the hill during the Battle of Messines on 7th June 1917, and six of its officers are buried in VII-N-5; the inscription on one of the headstones reads: 'To faithful warriors cometh rest.' The last Hill 60 Victoria Cross winner is buried here. Second Lieutenant F. Youens VC (I-O-3) of the 13th Battalion DLI received the award posthumously on 7th July 1917 for bravery in the fighting from Hill 60 to Battle Wood. Lieutenant Colonel J.H. Bowes-Wilson (VII-M-10) is the most senior officer buried at Transport Farm; he was killed commanding the 9th Battalion York and Lancaster Regiment on 7th June 1917, aged thirty-seven. His headstone bears the badge of his original regiment, the Duke of Wellingtons.

Leaving the cemetery by the main entrance, turn right onto the road and continue for a short distance, then take the first turning on the left. This is the signposted entrance to Zillebeke Lake or Zillebeke Vijver. Stay on this and beyond the trees the lake is soon visible. Continue to the first building on the western edge of the lake; there is a good panoramic view from here.

During the war Zillebeke Lake was known by several other names – Etang de Zillebeke or Zillebeke Bund among them. It was the only significant area of water on the battlefield, and as early as 1914 British soldiers bathed in it. The water was never fit to drink, however, and signs

Zillebeke Lake, 1916.

warned soldiers against this obviously tempting idea. The high banks that surround the lake were tunnelled into and dugouts and an advanced dressing station were constructed by 1917. Nearby men of the Royal Field Artillery established their gun sites, and the path that follows the edge of the lake was used as a route to and from the trenches east of Zillebeke village. The 1/5th Battalion Leicestershire Regiment knew this area in mid-1915:

> The lake is triangular and entirely artificial, being surrounded by a broad causeway, 6 feet high, with a pathway along the top. On the western edge the ground falls away, leaving a bank some twenty feet high, in which were built the 'Lake dugouts' – the home of one of the support battalions. From the corner house to the trenches there were two routes, one by the south side of the lake, past Railway dugouts . . . and Manor Farm to Square Wood; the other . . . along the north side of the lake, where a trench cut into the causeway gave us cover from observation from Hill 60.[4]

Stay on the road and at the north-west corner of the lake take a tarmac path on the right which follows the north bank into the village. It takes less than twenty minutes to walk into Zillebeke from here. However, further along **stop at the north-east corner of the lake**.

An officer of the Army Service Corps near Zillebeke Lake in 1915.

This area was known as Hell-blast Corner to the men who served here during the war, as troops and limbers going to and from the forward positions would often be observed by the Germans on the high ground between Hill 62 and Observatory Ridge, or Hill 60, and be shelled. There was also a large headquarters dugout at this point, used variously by gunners, sappers and infantry battalions and brigades. Sir John Glubb, known in later life as 'Glubb Pasha', came to Zillebeke as a young subaltern in the Royal Engineers in December 1915. 151st Brigade had its HQ here at that time, and it was one of Glubb's regular haunts, as related in his memoirs *Into Battle*.

Continue on the path into the village. It brings you out into the main street, Zillebeke Dorp. **Stop**.

Sir John Glubb recalled passing through Zillebeke in December 1915:

Every shattered fragment of a house is full of filth, old clothes, rags and bedding, left behind by the original inhabitants when they fled, and since used for sleeping on or torn up to dress wounds. Everything is soaked with rain, blood and dirt. Strewn around are thousands of half-empty jam or bully-beef tins, the contents putrefying, together with the remains of rations, scraps of bone and meat. There is no living thing visible but rats, big brown rats, who themselves are often mangy, and who barely trouble to get out of your way.[5]

Turn right and go towards the church. The entrance to the churchyard is a little further up, just in front of the church itself. The British graves are in a plot to the left.

ZILLEBEKE CHURCHYARD

There are thirty-two graves in what is very much akin to an English churchyard, constituting a somewhat rare burial ground in the Salient. Although there are several other ranks, the majority of the graves are officers from the British Regular army that went to war in 1914, from newly commissioned subalterns to long-serving lieutenant colonels. During First Ypres in November 1914 cavalry and Guards units were in action around Zillebeke and used the churchyard to bury the officers who fell at that time. A few others were added later and the last burials were from Canadian units in June 1916. The officers buried here give a good cross-section of the type of men who were commissioned into the Regular army before 1914. Many leading public schools are represented. Several of the men are from titled and wealthy families. Among the interesting individuals buried here are:

Major Lord Bernard Charles Gordon-Lennox: The third son of the Duke of Richmond, Bernard was born in London in 1878. He went from Eton into Sandhurst and was first commissioned in 1898 into the Grenadier Guards. He fought in the Boer War and later served in China and went to war with the 2nd Battalion Grenadier Guards, taking part in the retreat from Mons and in the fighting on the Aisne. He was killed near Zillebeke on 10th November 1914. He was married with sons, and his wife tragically died in 1944 when a Doodlebug struck the Guards Chapel in London.

Lord Bernard Charles Gordon-Lennox.

Baron Alexis George de Gunzberg: One of the most fascinating characters buried in Zillebeke Churchyard, who like Steere has his own private grave marker (a huge tomb), is Second Lieutenant Baron Alexis de Gunzburg. He was Russian by birth and his parents had a town house in Paris and a chateau outside the city. Born in Paris, Alexis was educated at Eton and acquired a great love of England. By 1914 he was working in London and following the outbreak of war became a naturalised British citizen so he could join the army. Commissioned into the 11th Hussars in

Baron Alexis de Gunzberg.

109

September 1914, he served during First Ypres attached to the Royal Horse Guards and 7th Cavalry Brigade as an Interpreter. He was killed near Zillebeke on 6th November 1914, aged twenty-seven, while carrying a message from Lord Kavanagh, commanding the brigade, to Colonel Wilson of the Royal Horse Guards, who died the same day and is buried next to him.

Lieutenant Henry Bligh Fortescue Parnell, 5th Baron Congleton: Educated at Eton and Oxford, he inherited his title in 1904. Parnell was a keen sportsman and huntsman, typical of that class, and was master of a hunt. He was also widely travelled and had contemplated an expedition to the Antarctic. Commissioned into the Grenadier Guards in 1912, he went to France in August 1914 and was killed near Zillebeke on 10th November 1914, aged twenty-four. His brother inherited the title and survived the war.

Lieutenant Henry Fortescue Parnell, 5th Baron Congleton.

Major Robert Edward Rising: Born in 1871, Major Rising was an experienced officer who had been educated at Charterhouse and Cambridge. He was commissioned in 1892 and fought in the Boer War. He went to France with the 1st Battalion Gloucestershire Regiment in August 1914 and was awarded a Distinguished Service Order for bravery in the fighting near Langemarck in October 1914. He was mortally wounded in the fighting at Zwarteleen on 7th November 1914 whilst in command of the remnants of his company.

Major Robert Rising.

Second Lieutenant Howard Avenel St George: A young officer in the 1st Life Guards, he trained for action as a cavalryman but by First Ypres he was dismounted and in the trenches. He was killed by a sniper on the Zwarteleen road on 15th November 1914, aged nineteen, after having reported to his commander about the state of the front line. His family helped with the rebuilding of Zillebeke church; his portrait hangs in the church entrance and one of the stained-glass windows is dedicated to him.

Second Lieutenant Howard Avenel St George.

Lieutenant Colonel Arthur de Courcy Scott: One of two older officers in the cemetery, he went from Wellington College into Sandhurst and served extensively in India. He took over command of the 1st Cheshires in November 1914 following the unit's heavy officer casualties since Mons. He fought with them at First Ypres and was then killed in the fighting for Hill 60 on 6th May 1915, aged forty-nine.

Lieutenant Colonel Arthur de Courcy Scott.

Lieutenant John Henry Gordon Lee Steere: another young officer, this nineteen year old platoon commander from Jayes Park, Ockley, Surrey, went from school into the 3rd Battalion Grenadier Guards and was killed near Zillebeke on 17th November 1914. His well connected parents, like the De Gunzbergs, pre-empted the war graves commission and placed their own memorial on his grave and resisted all attempts to have it removed. These two private memorials together are another of Zillebeke Churchyard's unique features.

Lieutenant John Lee Steere.

Lieutenant Colonel Gordon Chesney Wilson: like Colonel Scott, he was forty-nine years old when he died in the fighting for Zwarteleen on 6th November 1914 whilst commanding the Royal Horse Guards. His military career went back to 1887 and during the Boer War had served with Lord Baden-Powell at Mafeking. He married into the Spencer-Churchill family. He took the Royal Horse Guards to war in 1914 and like other cavalrymen here found himself on foot with a rifle in his hand, dug-in in trenches, rather than charging the enemy on horseback. The inscription on his grave reads: 'Life is a city of crooked streets, death the market place where all men meet.'

Lieutenant Colonel Gordon Chesney Wilson.

Return to Zillebeke Dorp and turn right, following Maaldestedestraat north out of the centre of the village. After a short while a CWGC sign appears on the left; follow the path down to the cemetery.

TUILERIES BRITISH CEMETERY

The Tuileries was a tile factory west of the road that ran from Hellfire Corner on the Menin Road into Zillebeke village. The buildings were used widely during the war. Totally destroyed by 1918, the factory was never rebuilt. A small military burial ground was started nearby in 1915, and largely as a result of fighting near Hill 60, 106 British and three French soldiers were buried in what is now the cemetery. Subsequent fighting in this area damaged many of the grave markers and now the only identified graves are those in Plot I, of whom sixteen are unknowns. The remaining eighty are commemorated by Special Memorials which line the walls, creating a huge open lawn in the middle and thereby making it unlike any other cemetery in the Salient.

Three battalions from the 5th Division dominate the burials: 1st Royal West Kents, 1st Cheshires and 2nd Duke of Wellingtons. Each has around twenty casualties buried at the Tuileries from the period leading up to the heavy fighting on Hill 60 in May 1915. Captain J.E.G. Brown (A-2) died with the 1st Battalion Royal West Kent Regiment on 22nd February 1915 while serving as the battalion's scout and bombing officer. Brown joined the army in 1911 and was posted to the 2nd Battalion in India; he became a specialist in Indian languages, hoping to transfer to the Indian Army. But the war intervened and by October 1914 he was in the front line near Zillebeke; by Christmas he was an acting company commander.

Captain J.E.G. Brown.

Return via the path to the road and **turn left** and **then first right** onto Schacteweidestraat. Follow this out of the village, passing a road on the right, to a fork in the road. Take the right-hand fork, a continuation of Schacteweidestraat, and walk gradually downhill. There are good views from here to the northern part of the Ypres battlefield to your left, and the ground around the Menin Road and Hooge. Further along **stop**.

Across the fields to your right was a farm building known as Dormy House, now replaced with a modern farm. Although in ruins during the war, it was reinforced with concrete supports and artillery units used it as an observation post. It had similar views across the ground as you have from this position. This area during the war was very different, of course, and Huntley Gordon recalled one visit to the OP in mid-1917 whilst serving with 112th Brigade Royal Field Artillery:

Here through a concrete slot I had my first long look through binoculars at the enemy trenches. The gunner subaltern on duty pointed out the various landmarks which were not easy to see in that monotonous landscape.

First there was the area of Sanctuary Wood; not really a wood, only a wilderness of splintered tree-stumps, and certainly no place to go for sanctuary . . . Then over to the left more skeleton trees, identified as Glencorse Wood, Inverness Copse and Black Watch Corner . . . But don't think that these places could be identified by anyone but an expert. All I could see was lines and lines of sandbags alternating with hedges of rusty barbed wire, brown earth and grey splintered tree-trunks.[6]

Continue on Schacteweidestraat until it reaches a wooded area on your right: Maple Copse.

MAPLE COPSE CEMETERY
Maple Copse is believed to have acquired its name because of the trees planted here rather than through a Canadian connection, although the Canadians were here in force by 1916. This area was close to the front line during the war, and there are good views from this cemetery towards Hill 62 – the Canadian memorial can usually be seen – and Sanctuary Wood. To the right the ground rises to Observatory Ridge. An officer of the 1/5th Leicesters called Maple Copse in 1915 an 'isolated little wood with several dugouts in it' and burials of men killed in the front line on nearby Hill 62 began about this time. By 1916 there was an advanced

Maple Copse, 1916.

British guns near Zillebeke.

dressing station in Maple Copse, which was particularly well used during the Canadian action in this sector in June. It was also during this period that many of the original graves were destroyed by shell-fire. By 1918 the cemetery was closed due to battle damage and after the war only twenty-six of the 256 graves could be positively identified. The rest are commemorated by Special Memorials: headstones arranged within the cemetery in alphabetical order. Of the total buried here, 114 are British and 142 Canadian; of these forty are unknown.

Many of the Canadian graves are from units in the 4th (Canadian) Division which were posted here after arrival in France in August 1916. There are several 60th Battalion casualties, including Captain Hon. A.T. Shaughnessy (D-11), who was killed on 6th June 1916, aged forty-four. The graves of tunnellers are also in evidence; both men from the 175th Tunnelling Company RE in November 1915, and five miners of the 2nd Canadian Tunnelling Company, all of whom died on 15th February 1917. These men worked on the deep tunnel systems in this area during the so-called 'quiet period' between Second and Third Ypres.

Leaving the cemetery turn right and follow to the next junction. Here turn right again onto Zandvoordsestraat. Further up on the left is a new memorial to the Canadian battle in this area in June 1916, which has an information panel. It overlooks the site of the front lines south of Observatory Ridge overlooking Armagh Wood, the right flank of the Canadian positions in June 1916.

Continue back into the village and at the next junction turn right and follow the road through the village, ignoring the turning to the right back towards the church. Walk out of Zillebeke over the railway line and to the next road junction, where there is a British-helmeted Demarkation Stone marking the extent of the German advance here in April 1918. **Turn right** and then up ahead **go left**, following a minor road down towards a farm and military cemetery.

BLAUWEPOORT FARM CEMETERY

Blauwepoort Farm was the name given to a small farm complex here; literally translated it means 'blue gates' and both the original and the new replacement farm still has them. It was used as a headquarters, largely for artillery units dug in around where the farm was. The cemetery was originally started by French troops, Chausseurs Alpins, who were more used to fighting in mountain snow rather than the flat lands of Flanders. They were among the many French regiments that fought around Zillebeke in 1914. The French graves were later removed, some to the French cemetery at Potijze.

The cemetery was only used by British units for around a year from February 1915 and there are ninety burials, eight of which are unknown. The first identified burial is Private A.W. Cook (A-14), who died serving with the 1st Battalion Dorsetshire Regiment on 26th March 1915. Most

The view to Ypres from Transport Farm.

Ypres from Railway Dugouts   December 1916.

115

of the burials are men killed between Hill 60 and the trenches around Verbrandenmolen on the Bluff. By late 1915 the burials here were men from New Army battalions, not the Regulars of a few months before, and the final identified graves are from February 1916, dating from the fighting on the Bluff at that time.

Return to the main road and **turn left**. Follow the road, recrossing the railway line, until it reaches Transport Farm Cemetery and your vehicle.

Notes

1. 60th Battalion Canadian Infantry *War Diary*, 12.8.16, TNA WO95/3879.
2. 1/4th Battalion Yorkshire Regiment *War Diary*, 14.2.16, TNA WO95/2836.
3. 8th Battalion Durham Light Infantry *War Diary*, 2.3.16, TNA WO95/2841.
4. Hills, J.D. *The Fifth Leicestershire: A Record of the 1/5th Battalion the Leicestershire Regiment TF during the War 1914–1919* (Echo Press 1919) p.41.
5. Glubb, J. *Into Battle: A Soldier's Diary of the Great War* (Cassell 1978) p.28.
6. Gordon, H. *The Unreturning Army* (J.M.Dent 1967) pp.41–2.

Gas casualties from Ypres being treated in April 1915.

116

Chapter Six

The Bluff – Hill 60 Walk

STARTING POINT: Bedford House Cemetery
GPS: 50°49.624′N, 2°53.279′E
DISTANCE: 12.3km/7.6 miles

WALK SUMMARY: *A long but rewarding walk, largely along quiet tracks or minor roads, taking you across the Bluff, now a nature reserve, to the infamous Hill 60. Several front-line cemeteries are visited en-route.*

Either **park your vehicle** in a lay-by outside the entrance to Bedford House Cemetery or you could walk to this point from Ypres, which is only a few kilometres away.

BEDFORD HOUSE CEMETERY
One of the larger cemeteries in the Ypres Salient, it is situated in the grounds of the old Chateau Rosendal, called Bedford House or Woodcote House on British maps. It remained behind the British lines for the whole

Bedford House, 1916.

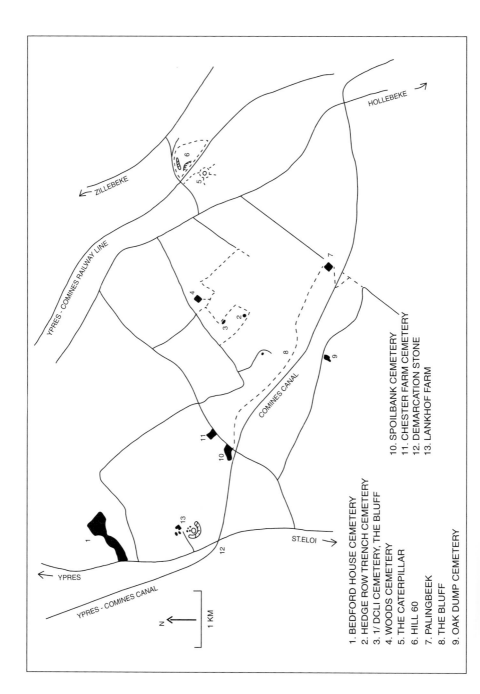

HOLLEBEKE

ZILLEBEKE

YPRES - COMINES RAILWAY LINE

6

5

7

4

3

2

COMINES CANAL

8

9

11

10

13

1

YPRES

12

ST.ELOI

YPRES - COMINES CANAL

N

1 KM

1. BEDFORD HOUSE CEMETERY
2. HEDGE ROW TRENCH CEMETERY
3. 1/ DCLI CEMETERY, THE BLUFF
4. WOODS CEMETERY
5. THE CATERPILLAR
6. HILL 60
7. PALINGBEEK
8. THE BLUFF
9. OAK DUMP CEMETERY
10. SPOILBANK CEMETERY
11. CHESTER FARM CEMETERY
12. DEMARCATION STONE
13. LANKHOF FARM

118

of the war, and the chateau buildings were gradually destroyed by shell-fire. The cellars and outbuildings were used as an advanced dressing station by RAMC Field Ambulances, and the main house sometimes as an advanced brigade headquarters. By the Armistice there were six so-called 'enclosures', Numbers 1 and 5 being removed to other cemeteries in the 1920s. The three remaining ones became Bedford House Cemetery and a sixth, forgotten, enclosure was later discovered and this is now by the main entrance, where there are also a number of Second World War graves. Canon Scot, serving as a chaplain with 1st (Canadian) Division, visited Bedford House in April 1916:

> Bedford House . . . stood in what must have been once very beautiful grounds. The upper part of the house was in ruins, but the cellars were deep and capacious and formed a good billet for the officers and men. At one side there was a dressing station and in the garden were some huts protected by piles of sandbags.[1]

In total there are 5,067 burials at Bedford House, of which some sixty per cent are unknowns. It is best to examine each of the enclosures individually.

Enclosure No 2 was started in December 1915, and remained in use until October 1918. After the war 437 graves were added, the majority of which came from the École de Bienfaisance and Asylum British cemeteries in Ypres. The former was located on the south side of the Menin Road, just north of the railway line, in the grounds of a large school which served as an ADS. By 1918 there were 140 graves. Asylum British Cemetery was the largest to be concentrated into Bedford House, with 283 burials. Located alongside a large mental hospital just outside Ypres on the Poperinghe road, it also served as an advanced dressing station and was used between 1915 and 1917. The total number of graves in Enclosure No 2 is therefore: 672 British, twenty-two Australian, twenty-one Canadian, five New Zealand, five British West Indies and one German flying officer. Of these thirty-three are unknown and there are twenty-four Special Memorials.

Among the soldiers here are a large number of Hooge casualties, particularly from units in the 14th (Light) Division. Elsewhere, Lieutenant Colonel O.M. Croshaw DSO (I-A-21) was an officer in the Glasgow Yeomanry, who died commanding the 53rd Battalion Australian Infantry on 26th September 1917. The Australian official historian, C.E.W. Bean, felt that Croshaw was 'one of the noblest British officers in the AIF' and records that he had a premonition of his death, saying to his fellow officers before the attack on Polygon Wood,

'Gentlemen, your men before yourselves. Look to your flanks. God bless you lads, till we meet again.'[2]

Enclosure No 3 is the smallest at Bedford House, and was used only for a limited time between February 1915 and December 1916. There are fifty-five British and five Canadian graves; of the former, twenty-two are men of the 7th Battalion East Yorkshire Regiment killed between August and October 1915. No additional burials were moved in here after the war.

Enclosure No 4 is the largest, with 3,188 British burials, 309 Canadian, 179 Australian, twenty-five New Zealand, twenty Indian, seventeen South African, three Royal Guernsey Light Infantry, one British West Indies, one Russian and one German. Of these 2,478 are unknown and there are twenty-five Special Memorials. This enclosure was started in June 1916 and continued in use until February 1918. The original graves were largely men from London Regiment battalions of the 47th (London) Division, including a row of London Irish Riflemen in Plot I Row I, who died in a trench raid on the German lines at Verbrandenmolen in April 1917. This raid was one of a handful during the war in Flanders that involved an entire battalion. After the war 3,324 burials were moved in here, many from former German burial grounds that contained British casualties.

Private A.E. Kemp, 1/19th London Regiment.

Captain G.F.H. Charlton (XIII-H-5) was killed on 6th October 1916 with the 10th Battalion South Wales Borderers. The register records that 'his only brother fell near Warlencourt, Somme, 26th August 1918'. A senior officer is Lieutenant Colonel G.S. Tulloch (XI-C-11), a Boer War veteran who died commanding the 2nd Battalion Gloucestershire Regiment at Sanctuary Wood

Original battlefield grave of Private A.E. Kemp, 1/19th London Regiment, at Bedford House.

on 9th May 1915, aged forty-eight. Two brothers are buried here. Privates G. Hamilton (I-P-3) and S. Hamilton (I-K-12) were both serving with the

21st Battalion Canadian Infantry near Mount Sorrel when they died on 14th June 1916. One of the most visited graves is that of Second Lieutenant R.P. Hallowes VC MC (XIV-B-36), of the 4th Battalion Middlesex Regiment, who was mortally wounded at Hooge and died on 30th September 1915 (see Hooge – Bellewaarde Ridge Walk).

Enclosure No 6 by the main entrance has 534 burials, of which 499 are unknowns. Records seem to indicate that after the war it was planned to move these graves elsewhere, as it was not included in the original cemetery register. A group of Second World War graves can also be found here, of men who largely died in the fighting near Hollebeke in May 1940.

Leave the cemetery by the driveway and gate, then turn left on the footpath by the main road and follow it for a short distance. Take the next turning on the left, Waastenstraat, and follow it right then left to reach a farm. Continue until the road bends to the right, and stop.

Ahead of you is a clear view of the ground known to British troops as the Bluff. The Ypres–Comines canal runs south from Ypres and at this

Battlefield visitors on the Ypres–Comines canal, 1930s.

point a large cutting was made across ground that is part of the Messines Ridge. During the nineteenth century the spoil from the excavations was thrown up on either side of where the canal was being constructed, and during the war it was this that was known as the Bluff, and further along, as the Spoilbank. To your extreme left the modern wind propeller close to Hill 60 can be seen on clear days; ahead of you several Crosses of Sacrifice from military cemeteries can also be seen: this is Verbrandenmolen, and the wooded area on the right is the Bluff itself.

Trench lines were established by French troops in the area between Verbrandenmolen and the Bluff at the end of 1914. The front-line positions here when the British took over were all numbered, rather than named, trenches, and fighting continued for almost four years, the positions only moving a matter of a few yards here and there. Many units passed through this sector; the 2nd Battalion Manchester Regiment holds the record for the longest tour of duty, holding the Bluff for eighty-seven consecutive days from April to July 1915. In February 1916 the Germans launched a series of attacks on the line then held by 14th (Light) Division, capturing at one point part of the British front line. Units of 3rd Division were called up and retook the trenches on 2nd March. A good account of the type of fighting during this action is given by Lieutenant Colonel H. d'Arch Smith of the 2nd Battalion Suffolk Regiment:

Zero hour was 4.30 and no preliminary bombardment warned the enemy; the advance moved silently forward and took them unaware. At 4.35 the Boche rockets went up, and a triple barrage fell across our line of attack; but he was too late; his first line trenches were in our hands before his gunners received the SOS. Our men advanced as the sticky ground would allow, and the objective was reached without much resistance except for a stubborn defence on the left which held up our men and caused many casualties before . . . they reached their aim. On the right the line of attack had to go round the lip of an enormous crater at the eastern end of the Bluff . . . As the day broke large streams of fleeing Huns could be seen inside our lines anxious to give themselves up, and striving to get under cover from the terrible rifle fire and bombardment from their own guns, which had now reached such a point of frenzy that you could not hear a word shouted close to your ear . . . The brilliant success of the attack was followed by the fearful work of consolidating, which in this case meant that you crouched behind a half blown away parapet and endeavoured to make it higher by filling sandbags with mud from under your own feet, piling these on top, and incidentally

Mine craters on the Bluff, 1916.

making a pond for your own feet to stand in . . . When finally the
battalion was relieved, it took a whole long night, owing to the
havoc of the ground.[3]

Mine warfare then became a very prominent feature of day to day life
here, and many craters scarred the ridge between Verbrandenmolen and
the Bluff. During the Battle of Messines in June 1917 this ground was
captured. Passing back to the Germans in April 1918, the final battle for
the Bluff took place on 28th September 1918 when 14th (Light) Division,
which had been here in 1916, returned and swept up the position.

Continue on this road. Pass another farm, and the road eventually
meets another. Go straight across up a minor road, Verbrandenmolen-
straat, also signposted with a CWGC board. This area has been planted
with woodland in recent years as part of turning it into a nature reserve.
This has obscured some of the views and it is worth remembering that
the landscape here did not look like this prior to 1914. Stay on this minor
road and follow it left further up. Go past a turning to the right – which
leads to a farm known as Pear Tree Farm on trench maps – and a few
hundred yards further on take the first track on the right. Follow this
through the trees until you reach the military cemetery.

HEDGE ROW TRENCH CEMETERY

This cemetery, located close to the front line, was started in March 1915 when Private W. Drury (Sp Mem C-13) of the 2nd Duke of Wellingtons was killed and buried here on 24th March. It took its name from a nearby communication trench which ran up to the front line at Trench 32. Occasionally it was also known as Ravine Wood Cemetery. Graves were added later, although they often suffered from shell-fire, until August 1917. The burials consist of ninety-four British, two Canadian, and two whose names and units are unknown. Private W.A. Stokes (Sp Mem E-3) of the 3rd Battalion Rifle Brigade is the youngest soldier here; he was only seventeen when he died on 29th October 1915. There is a significant representation of men from the 8th Buffs, who died in November 1915, and from the London Regiment from 1917; among the latter Captain H.W. Joel (Sp Mem D-3) of the First Surrey Rifles, who was killed in the Battle of Messines on 7th June 1917, aged only twenty.

Leave by the gate and follow the path to your left that then takes you slightly downhill to the next military cemetery.

1/DCLI CEMETERY, THE BLUFF

This cemetery was started by, and named after, the 1st Battalion Duke of Cornwall's Light Infantry in April 1915, and the unit buried their dead here until July. Fifty-one officers and men from this battalion rest here, and a few from other regiments were added afterwards. In 1919 twenty-three graves were moved in from the area between Hill 60 and the Bluff, and now form Row D.

When the first edition of this book was published in 1999 an interesting headstone was noted among the unknown graves in Row D. It read 'A Captain of the Great War, Queen Victoria's Rifles'. In April 1915 the Queen Victoria's Rifles (9th Battalion London Regiment) saw action on Hill 60. This grave and other unknowns from the QVRs buried here must relate to this action as the battalion was never in this part of Flanders again for the rest of the war. Research later showed that only one Captain from the QVRs died at this time and had no known grave, his name being recorded on the Menin Gate. He was Captain Gilbert Fazakerley-Westby, who was killed on 21st April 1915. He was born at Grosvenor Square in 1881, and his parents lived in Mowbreck Hall, Kirkham; he joined the QVRs in 1911, crossing to France with them in November 1914. After his death at Hill 60 the QVRs' commanding officer wrote, 'I cannot speak too highly of your son; all ranks loved and respected him. His fortitude and forbearance during that terrible week [at Hill 60] was an example to the whole regiment and never to be forgotten.' After a number of researchers contacted the CWGC about this grave, it was accepted that it was his and in the early 2000s the headstone was changed and now bears his name.

Leaving the cemetery, turn left and follow the cut grass path prepared by the CWGC, which leads to the next cemetery.

WOODS CEMETERY

This cemetery was started by the 1st Dorsets and the 1st East Surreys in April 1915, and remained in use by many different units until September 1917. It was close to the trenches, and men killed in the front line were brought back here for burial by those serving in this sector. Canadian and London Regiment graves are particularly numerous. There are 212 British burials, 111 Canadian and three Australian. Of these thirty-two are unknown.

The Canadian graves largely date from April 1916, and are men from units in the 1st (Canadian) Division. Private F.E. Calderon (II-G-11) of the 2nd Battalion Canadian Infantry was killed on 3rd April 1916, aged forty-two. His father was a member of the Royal Academy, and Calderon himself was born in London, educated at Rugby and worked in the Maritime department of Canada between 1907 and 1914. Elsewhere, London Regiment graves are from battalions in the 47th (London) Division which occupied this sector from late 1916 onwards, when they arrived here after several engagements on the Somme (most notably High Wood), until after the Battle of Messines. The first of their burials are found in Plots IV and V; among the early casualties was S.H. Moxon (V-B-2), who has the unusual rank of Sergeant-Bugler. An accomplished musician, he was a King's Trumpeter and member of the Royal Society of Musicians; he died on 25th October 1916, aged thirty-eight. A unique aspect of this cemetery is a field grave that forms a promontory on the western wall (II-Z-1). Possibly in a shell hole or gun pit, these three men of the Royal Artillery lie where they were buried by their comrades in 1917. The date of death is recorded as 12th November; two are shown as belonging to 124th Brigade RFA and the other to Y/37 Trench Mortar Battery. It is likely all three died while manning a 2-inch heavy trench mortar, better known as a 'Toffee Apple' or 'Plum Pudding', as these weapons operated very close to the front line.

Leave the cemetery by the main gate and then turn left into the wooded area and follow the path through the trees to your right until it joins the *Molenbosstraat*.

This was the area where the front-line trenches ran south from the Caterpillar and Hill 60 on to Verbrandenmolen and the Bluff. Trenches 34, 35 and 36 here were often known as 'Bomb Corner'. A good description of this sector in 1915 is given by the 1/5th Battalion Leicestershire Regiment:

German trenches at Verbrandenmoelen.

The lines at this time were very close together, and at one point ... less than 50 yards separated our parapet from the Boche's ...

One's parapet in this area was one's trench, for digging was impossible, and we lived behind a sort of glorified sandbag grouse butt, six feet thick at the base and two to three feet at the top, sometimes, but not always, bullet-proof.

One or two amusing stories are told about the infantry opposite '35', who were Saxons, and inclined to be friendly with the English. On one occasion the following message, tied to a stone, was thrown into our trench: 'We are going to send a 40lb bomb. We have got to do it, but we don't want to. It will come this evening, and we will whistle first to warn you.' All of this happened![4]

This road effectively runs through where No Man's Land was and **now follow it until it meets the main road**. Turn **right then left** onto *Zwarteleenstraat*. Follow this to just before the railway bridge and then stop.

You are looking at the ground in front of a position known as the Caterpillar on British maps. For most of the war the British lines were just in front of the road, with the German trenches by the tree line. The main British line was Trench 37, and just before Second Ypres in April 1915 the machine-gun section of 9th Londons (Queen Victoria's Rifles) set up here and fired on the German positions on Hill 60 itself. For the Battle of Messines, the Caterpillar was selected as a target for one of the offensive mines. Started by the 3rd Canadian Tunnelling Company in 1916, after some six months it was taken over by the 1st Australian Tunnelling Company and eventually fired at 3.10am on 7th June 1917. A charge of 70,000lbs of Ammonal was used, forming a crater 275 feet wide and sixty feet deep, enabling the men of 23rd Division to capture the ground at minimal cost.

As part of the Great War Centenary this site has been redeveloped. There is a large panoramic photograph of the area during the war on an information panel by the bridge and a new path leads you across what was once No Man's Land into the woods. There is a German observation bunker visible to the right. Follow the path to the rim of the mine crater. This is arguably the most impressive of all the Messines mines as it shows the size and scale of what this mining offensive was all about. You can walk all round the crater and there are further paths off into the woods, where signs of shell holes can be seen.

Return to the road and then continue across the bridge.

HILL 60 was the centrepiece of much of the fighting around Ypres, in particular during the first half of 1915. An artificial hill, 60 metres above sea level (hence its name), it was created from the spoil when the railway cutting was dug in the nineteenth century. Known as 'Lover's Knoll' before the war, as it was a favourite haunt of courting couples, it later took on somewhat more ominous tones. The French occupied the hill in 1914, the British taking over in February 1915. Mine warfare had already begun at Hill 60 when the French miner Lieutenant Bruyeat began offensive operations against the German positions on the crest in December 1914. At this stage in the war no proper Tunnelling Companies existed in the British army and men of the Monmouthshire Regiment carried on from where Bruyeat had left off. It was not until the spring of 1915 that a group of Engineers from the newly formed 171st Tunnelling Company, under the inspiration of Major Norton Griffiths, blew a mine on 17th April to assist the 5th Division's attack on Hill 60. During these

Hill 60 railway cutting and bridge, 1916.

operations four Victoria Crosses were won on the hill, by Second Lieutenant Harold Woolley of the QVRs (the first Territorial officer to win the VC), and three men of the 1st Battalion East Surrey Regiment: Private E. Dwyer, Second Lieutenant B. Geary, and Lieutenant G. Roupel. Possession of the hill passed to the Germans on 5th May 1915 and it remained in their hands until the Battle of Messines in 1917. Mine warfare continued on both sides so that by 1916 No Man's Land directly below the hill was one long line of mine craters.

Meanwhile the German line was reinforced with concrete bunkers and it became clear that a full frontal attack on Hill 60 would be suicidal. As part of the Messines mining operations, Hill 60 became the northernmost target on the Messines Ridge. The 3rd Canadian Tunnelling Company prepared a mine that was handed over to the 1st Australian Tunnelling Company, as at the Caterpillar. A charge of 53,000lbs of Ammonal and gun cotton blew a chunk out of the right-hand sector of the hill, neutralising what was left of the German garrison and enabling men of the 11th Battalion West Yorkshire Regiment to take the position. A German account recorded:

Private Edwin Dwyer VC.

128

The Menin Gate Memorial, Ypres.

Remembering the missing on the Menin Gate.

Original war graves signs.

Reconstructed trench at Passchendaele Memorial Museum.

Mid-war British trench reconstructed at the Passchendaele Memorial Musuem.

Tree-lined avenue at Petite Douve near Messines.

The Flanders landscape near Messines.

nset at Messines.

reat War recycling: the neck of a rum jar being used as a fence insulator near Hooge.

Black Watch Memorial near
Polygon Wood.

Tunnellers Memorial
at Wytschaete.

The Menin Gate on Armistice Day surrounded by a Field of Remembrance.

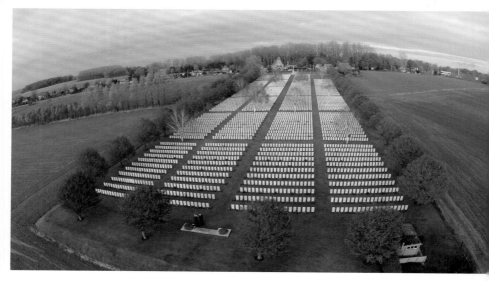

Above the battlefield: Hooge Crater Cemetery.

Battlefield archaeology at Messines: cleaning clips of .303 ammunition.

Battlefield archaeology at Messines: excavating a German trench.

Battlefield archaeology at Messines: inside an excavated German trench.

Lost battlefields: a German dugout at Zonnebeke in the 1980s, now collapsed.

Lost battlefields: Essex Farm before renovation of the site.

Lost battlefields: Hellfire Corner in the 1980s.

Lost battlefields: International Corner near Poperinghe, 1986, now demolished.

In Flanders Fields.

Mine crater at Kruistraat, Messines Ridge.

The Messines Ridge.

French Memorial, Kemmel.

Ypres: one family remembers.

British bunkers near Ypres.

Bunkers on Hill 60.

the ground trembled as in a natural earthquake, heavy concrete shelters rocked, a hurricane of hot air from the explosions swept back for many kilometres, dropping fragments of wood, iron and earth; and gigantic black clouds of smoke and dust spread over the country. The effect on the troops was overpowering and crushing.[5]

Modern aerial of Hill 60. (*John Giles archive*)

Following the capture of Hill 60, the front lines were further along the railway line at Battle Wood, near Hollebeke. Retaken by the Germans in April 1918, Hill 60 returned to British hands without a fight in September 1918.

Today Hill 60 is one of the few specifically British sectors of the Western Front left preserved in its 1918 state. It is a large site and was likewise redeveloped as part of the Great War Centenary. As you cross the bridge there is the memorial to the 14th (Light) Division, moved here from Railway Wood in 1978. It has no direct connection to this site but it shows clearly the outline Order of Battle of a British infantry division, which is useful to understand how the army operated. Nearby is the 1st Australian Tunnelling Company memorial which commemorates the Australian tunnellers who worked beneath Hill 60. It shows signs of Second World War battle damage. A new wooden walkway starts close by and takes you across the hill on foot, seeing first what seems like a natural gully; this is in fact the crater zone from all the mine explosions which took place here during 1915–16. On the crest you can see evidence of German concrete bunkers, the 1917 mine crater and a memorial to Harold Woolley's Queen Victoria's Rifles. The latter is a replacement of the original, which was destroyed during the fighting in May 1940. On the Battle Wood side is a rare example of a British bunker, this one

Zero Hour: the blowing of the Messines mines at Hill 60, June 1917.

Australian Tunnelling Memorial, 1920s.

The original Queen Victoria Rifles Memorial in the 1920s. It was destroyed in the Second World War.

The Hill 60 canteen: a haunt of battlefield visitors in the 1920s.

The former trench museum at Hill 60 in the 1930s.

constructed by Australian Engineers in 1918 and used as an observation post overlooking Hollebeke. The walkway takes you to a new car-park area close to a modern café and some houses. In the inter-war period there was a museum and 'trench experience' here, which was a system of trenches especially dug by British veterans who lived in the area. The museum closed at the time of the Second World War and no trace of it remains. The café serves as a good place for a drink or some lunch.

Return to the Hollebeke road by recrossing the railway bridge, and where this road meets the main road, turn left. After a short walk, take the first road on the right, signposted for Palingbeek, and tree-lined all the way to another café, car park and a wooded area by the canal.

When you reach the woodland you are on the area of the Bluff itself. Although now a nature reserve, signs of the war are never very far away among the trees. This is a popular local attraction for the people of Ypres, a setting now a world away from the horror which unfolded here during the war years. An officer in the 7th Battalion York & Lancasters recalls a typical episode in February 1916 after the Germans had blown a mine:

> I saw the Bluff . . . and it presented a haunting spectacle. Upon the slopes of the crater were the dead, frozen as they had been killed, for the weather was intensely cold . . . Silhouetted against the skyline, and plainly visible from the British line, was the figure of the only man who had looked upon the invisible enemy. Clad in his great coat, his shrapnel helmet was still on his head. His right knee was bent to the ground; his right hand grasped the barrel of his rifle, the butt of which also rested in the ground. He had been frozen stiff as he had died; turned into a terribly arresting sculpture by the frost.[6]

Captured in June 1917, the Bluff remained in British hands until April 1918, when German troops captured it during the Spring Offensive. At that time it was held by the 13th Battalion Royal Sussex Regiment (3rd South Downs), whose front-line companies, well under-strength following heavy casualties on the Somme in March, were quickly wiped out. The defence of the Bluff passed to the battalion headquarters, led by the commanding officer Lieutenant Colonel H.T.K. Robinson DSO, a veteran who had served in France since 1916. He roused his staff, cooks and stretcher-bearers and anyone else he could find for a final stand at his HQ dugout. They fought to the last man and were overwhelmed by sheer weight of numbers. Robinson and many of his scratch mob were killed; none has a grave and they are commemorated on the Tyne Cot Memorial.

The Great War period shell holes and mine craters can be accessed here by turning right just before the café area and following a path into the woods. The craters soon become visible on your left. This area has been redeveloped for the Great War centenary with information panels and a wooden walkway which takes you out above some of the craters. Trees have been cleared as well to allow better access to what remains of the Great War landscape. Nearby a path takes you down to the canal itself. Here **turn left** and follow the line of the canal to near the café and then cross over the canal by a small bridge. Further steps will take you up the other side and eventually out onto a metalled track just south of the Bluff. Follow this to where another joins it from the right. **Stop.**

Ahead of you in the trees was the wartime location of White Chateau. This was a large ornate house, in ruins by 1917, forming part of the German second line south of the Ypres–Comines canal between Oak Support and Oak Reserve trenches. For the Battle of Messines on 7th June 1917, the 140th Brigade of 47th (London) Division attacked here with the aid of four tanks. The 7th and 8th Battalions of the London Regiment captured the German front line, but were held up by a determined garrison holed up in the chateau grounds. This was cleared when a party led by Lieutenant J.F. Preston from the 7th Londons stormed the rubble and White Chateau was taken. In the fighting the 140th Brigade captured 282 prisoners, and lost forty officers and 956 men.

Take the minor road on the right, past the golf course, and continue until a military cemetery is reached on the left.

OAK DUMP CEMETERY
This small battlefield cemetery was started during the Messines offensive in June 1917 by units of the 47th (London) Division who captured this ground. Of the 109 British graves, fifty-nine are soldiers of the London Regiment. There are also two Australians, and of the total five are unknown. The bodies of seven men of 180th Siege Battery RGA, who were killed near White Chateau in March 1918, were found in 1927 and moved to this cemetery.

Return to the road and turn left, following it to the end where it joins another. Turn right, back towards the canal. Cross the bridge over the canal and there are two military cemeteries a short distance apart on the left of the road.

SPOILBANK CEMETERY
This cemetery takes its name from the nearby banks of spoil alongside the Ypres–Comines canal known to the British as Spoilbank. It was also known as Gordon Terrace Cemetery and was started in February 1915,

Spoilbank Cemetery, 1930s.

remaining in use until March 1918. Spoilbank Cemetery is particularly associated with the 2nd Battalion Suffolk Regiment, which was on the Bluff in early 1916, and a row of burials from the battalion can be found in Plot I Row B. After the war 116 graves were moved in from a wide area around Ypres. The total burials here are: 426 British, sixty-seven Australian and sixteen Canadian. Of these 125 are unknowns, and there are eleven Special Memorials.

Among the Special Memorials are an officer and six gunners of 298th Army Brigade Royal Field Artillery. Second Lieutenant H.C. Rowe (Sp Mem B-6) and his men had their guns alongside the canal at Lock 8, north of Convent Lane, when on 19th July 1917 they were killed by shell-fire while working on a new battery position.[7] Three officers from the headquarters of the 10th Battalion Royal Welsh Fusiliers are also buried here: Lieutenant Colonel S.S. Binney DSO (I-M-4), Major E. Freeman (I-M-5) and Captain & Adjutant W.T. Lyons (I-M-3). On 3rd March 1916 'a shell of large calibre made a direct hit on Battalion Headquarters in Gordon Post, killing the Commanding Officer, Second in Command and Adjutant'.[8] Binney was a regular army officer who had previously fought with the XIXth Hussars in the Boer War, winning the Distinguished Service Order. He latterly served on the Staff at Sandhurst and had retired when war broke out. In 1914 he was recalled and served as a Railway Transport Officer, becoming Deputy Director of Railway Transport in France. Promoted to Lieutenant Colonel, he went to command the 10th Royal Welsh in February 1916, a post he held for only a matter of weeks.

Two brothers are buried side by side here. Second Lieutenant G. Keating (I-H-3) and Lieutenant J. Keating (I-H-4), both of the 2nd Battalion Cheshire Regiment, died on 17th February 1915. On this day their battalion made a two-company attack from Chester Farm towards the Bluff, which was 'checked by hostile machine-guns which opened up at short range'.[9] Long-serving Regular soldiers with over twenty years' service each, they had been commissioned from the ranks in 1914. It is believed they were killed by the same burst of machine-gun fire.

Continue up the road to the next cemetery.

CHESTER FARM CEMETERY

Named after a farm which is almost opposite the cemetery, itself probably named by the 2nd Cheshires in 1915, the cemetery was started in March 1915 and was used by front-line units on the Bluff and Verbrandenmolen until November 1917. Many graves are grouped by regiment and battalion; for example in Plot I are buried ninety-two men of the 2nd Battalion Manchester Regiment who were killed between April and July 1915. In various parts of the cemetery are seventy-two officers and men from battalions of the London Regiment. In total there are 306 British graves, eighty-seven Canadian, twenty-one Australian, and four German prisoners.

The first two burials are soldiers from the 1st Battalion Norfolk Regiment. Privates W. Barnes (II-AA-1A) and O. Taylor (II-AA-1) were killed on 15th March 1915. Later graves include two young soldiers, both aged seventeen: Private H. Bagshaw (I-B-5) of the 1/6th Battalion Sherwood Foresters, who died on 21st September 1915, and Rifleman E.E.G. Miles (I-K-33) of the London Irish Rifles, killed on 12th June 1917. Lieutenant E.S. Carlos (I-K-36) was a talented artist who was killed here during the Battle of Messines on 14th June 1917 whilst serving with the 8th Buffs.

Return towards the canal, and just before it **turn right**, following a towpath. Continue until it brings you to the main Ypres–Messines road. Opposite is a Demarcation Stone. Cross the road carefully to see it.

This Demarcation Stone is one of a number on the Flanders battlefields. The stones were designed by French sculptor Paul Moreau-Vauthier and are often referred to as 'Vauthier stones', and all were erected on key sites along the Western Front in the early 1920s. There are three designs, each with a different helmet; this one has a British example. This stone marks the closest the Germans got to the southern side of Ypres in April 1918. The Bluff and other positions on the Messines Ridge, captured in 1917, were lost in a matter of days, but the line of the Ypres–Comines canal formed a natural barrier at this point and it was here that the Germans were slowed down and stopped, largely by the 7th Battalion Leicestershire Regiment. Bedford House and Lankhof Farm (see below) then became part of the front line.

Recross the road and follow the footpath in the direction of Ypres. Further along on the right some concrete bunkers by a farm, set back from the road, can be seen.

The buildings behind the bunkers were known as Lankhof Farm on British maps, and the bunkers took this name. Engineers of the 47th (London) Division made a headquarters here in 1916 but the concrete structures were built by a party from the 153rd Field Company Royal Engineers in 1917. However, they were not properly finished until early 1918, when Australian Engineers completed the work. A few months later, in April 1918, this area became part of the front line following the German attacks and the farm and bunkers fell into German hands. There was a series of raids on the position but it was not retaken until 1st September, when men from the 120th Infantry Regiment of the American Expeditionary Force captured the position. These were National Guardsmen from North Carolina taking part in their first major offensive of the war. The bunkers are on private land, and access is only gained by permission of the farmer.

From here continue along this road, which will shortly bring you back to Bedford House Cemetery and your vehicle.

Notes

1. Scott, F.G. *The Great War As I Saw It* (Goodchild 1922) p.126.
2. Bean, C.E.W. *The AIF In France 1917* (Angus & Robertson 1933) p.827.
3. Quoted in Brice, B. *The Battle Book of Ypres* (John Murray 1927) pp.61–2.
4. Hills, J.D. *The Fifth Leicestershire: A Record of the 1/5th Battalion the Leicestershire Regiment TF during the War 1914–1919* (Echo Press 1919) pp.45–7.
5. Edmonds, J.E. *Military Operations France and Belgium 1917 Volume II* (HMSO 1948) p.61.
6. Brice op cit. p.60.
7. 298th Army Brigade RFA *War Diary*, 19.7.17, TNA WO95/456.
8. 10th Battalion Royal Welsh Fusiliers *War Diary*, 3.3.16, TNA WO95/1436.
9. 2nd Battalion Cheshire Regiment *War Diary*, 17.2.15, TNA WO95/2276.

Chapter Seven

Langemarck Walk

STARTING POINT: Cement House Cemetery, Langemarck
GPS: 50°54.297′N, 2°54.418′E
DISTANCE: 10.2km/6.3 miles

WALK SUMMARY: *An easy walk looking at the ground around the key village of Langemarck (now Langemark), taking in one of the most important German cemeteries in the region, as well as where Harry Patch – the 'Last Fighting Tommy' – fought.*

Park your vehicle outside the cemetery; there is a large lay-by here.

CEMENT HOUSE CEMETERY
'Cement House' was the military name given to a fortified farm building on the Langemarck–Boesinghe (now Boezinge) road. The original Cement House Cemetery (now Plot I, an irregular group of 231 graves) was begun here at the end of August 1917 and used by the 4th and 17th (Northern) Division burial officers, by field ambulances and by units in the line until April 1918. In the years immediately following the Armistice most of Plots II–XV were added when Commonwealth graves were brought in from the surrounding battlefields and small burial

Cement House Cemetery, 1930s.

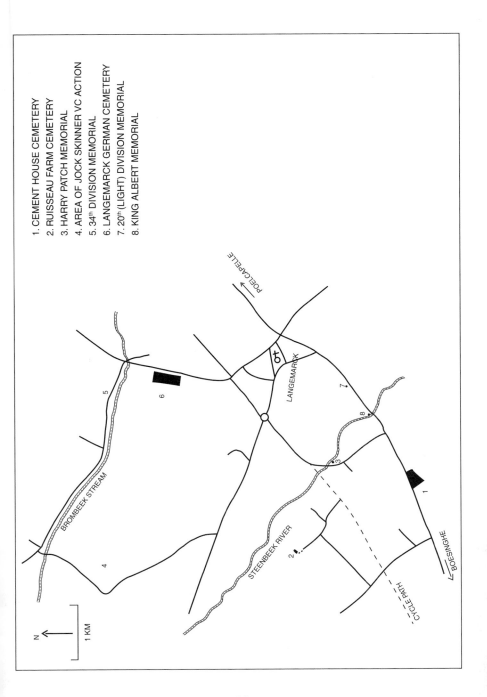

1. CEMENT HOUSE CEMETERY
2. RUISSEAU FARM CEMETERY
3. HARRY PATCH MEMORIAL
4. AREA OF JOCK SKINNER VC ACTION
5. 34th DIVISION MEMORIAL
6. LANGEMARCK GERMAN CEMETERY
7. 20th (LIGHT) DIVISION MEMORIAL
8. KING ALBERT MEMORIAL

POELCAPELLE

BROMBEEK STREAM

STEENBEEK RIVER

LANGEMARCK

CYCLE PATH

BOESINGHE

N

1 KM

grounds around Langemarck and Poelkapelle, mostly dating from the autumn of 1917. Almost 500 French graves in the original Plots XVI, XVII and XVIII made at this time were removed in 1922, and the space vacated was filled in the intervening years by graves brought in from communal cemeteries and churchyards in the wider area when their maintenance in these locations could no longer be assured. The cemetery was then used for the burial of remains that were discovered in the vicinity, and a number of plots were extended to accommodate these graves. There are now 3,566 Commonwealth servicemen of the First World War buried or commemorated in the cemetery, and 2,398 of the burials are unidentified. Of the twenty-two Second World War burials in the cemetery, five are unidentified. The cemetery was designed by Sir Reginald Blomfield.

Captain Jonathan Knowles.

Lieutenant Charles Garstin.

This is an important but often overlooked Ypres cemetery in that until the 1990s it was the only 'open' cemetery not just in Flanders but for the whole of Belgium. This meant that from the period of the end of the Second World War through to the 1990s the remains of any Great War soldiers found in Belgium were moved here for burial. This also included graves in civil cemeteries that were later closed or cleared. As such there are men who died in the Battle of Mons in August 1914 buried here. Captain Jonathan Edward Knowles (XVIII-D-1/16) died with the 4th Battalion Middlesex Regiment in the fighting at Obourg at Mons and was originally buried in a collective grave with other men at Maisieres Communal Cemetery, being moved to Cement House in 1957. Elsewhere is the grave of Lieutenant Charles William North Garstin (XVIII-A-19), who was killed with the 9th Lancers during a cavalry charge at Audregnies, on the flanks of Mons, on 24th August 1914, aged 20. His father was Sir William Garstin, a prominent Victorian civil engineer who had worked in Egypt. Lieutenant Garstin had originally been buried in Audregnies churchyard, close to the site of the action, but that was closed in 1953 and he was moved here.

The original graves in the cemetery in Plot I include a large number of men brought back wounded from the fighting around Langemarck and

Poelcapelle in September and October 1917, as there was an advanced dressing station located here. Later on the site had gun positions in the shell holes around it and the graves here also reflect that with men from the Royal Field Artillery buried here. The staggered nature of the graves here clearly indicates these early burials, which are in contrast to the neat rows of post-war concentrations.

In Plot II Rows AA to CC are the graves of men recovered by the local archaeology group, The Diggers, in the early 2000s at the Yorkshire Trench site near the Yser Canal (see the Yser Canal Walk). These were mainly men from units in the 4th Division who fell in an attack on 6th July 1915 but also include two Royal Welsh Fusiliers from 38th (Welsh) Division who died in a forward sap in early 1917. None of these men could be identified as nothing but regimental insignia was found intact with the bodies.

Leaving the cemetery by the gate **turn left** onto the main road and continue, then taking the **first road on the right**, *Groenstraat*. Walk down here until it joins the cycle path and **turn right** onto this. Where it meets the next road **turn left** and walk past the first farm on your left to the next farm, following CWGC signs to the cemetery.

RUISSEAU FARM CEMETERY

You have to walk through part of the farm, named Ruisseau Farm on British maps, to enter this burial ground.

Ruisseau Farm was a strongpoint in the German defences, some way behind their front line on the Pilkem Ridge. Although the cemetery register states the position was not captured until 8th October 1917, it actually fell to the 2nd Battalion Coldstream Guards on 31st July 1917. Their history records:

No 1 Company . . . succeeded in reaching Signal and Ruisseau Farms, where thirty of the enemy were captured, including a battalion commander and a number of officers . . . No 1 Company dashed on, and managed to cross the Steenbeek River, on the farther side of which it dug itself in.[1]

After that it formed part of the British front line around the Steenbeek river and while the fighting moved to Langemarck village and then beyond, the Guards Division returned to this area in early October in preparation for an attack towards a position called Wijdendrift to the north-east of the farm. During the attack on 8th October 1917 the cemetery was begun by the burial officer of the Guards Division and there are eighty-two graves at Ruisseau Farm, of which six are unidentified. It is one of only a small number of wartime battlefield cemeteries that still survive in the battlefields around Ypres, most having been concentrated into the large post-war cemeteries. The graves here are dominated by the Grenadier and Coldstream Guards who took this ground, and the Royal Field Artillery which had gun positions here when the fighting moved on beyond Langemarck.

Go back through the farmyard to the minor road and follow it back to the cycle path. **Turn left** onto the cycle path and follow it until a brick culvert is reached.

This cycle path is on the line of the old Roulers railway line; although it returned to use after the war, the line was dismantled in the 1960s and is now used as a main cycle route. Beneath this culvert is a section of the Steenbeek river, which had been an objective on the opening day of Third Ypres on 31st July, but was not properly cleared until October 1917. During the September 1917 fighting a soldier of the Duke of Cornwall's Light Infantry passed over this point, en-route to take part in the fighting beyond Langemarck. He was Harry Patch, the 'Last Fighting Tommy', who died in 2009 aged an incredible 111. Harry was a wartime conscript,

Memorial to Harry Patch: the 'Last Fighting Tommy'.

part of a Lewis machine-gun team, who was wounded by a shell fragment during the battle for Passchendaele on 22nd September 1917 and subsequently did not serve overseas again. In the years afterwards Harry wanted to forget the war, but in later life he returned to Flanders to pay his respects to fallen comrades and regularly attended the services of remembrance at the Menin Gate in Ypres on 11th November. Because of his status as the last British army veteran of the Western Front to pass away, in many respects Harry has come to symbolise an entire generation who fought here in Flanders Fields.

Continue on the cycle path to where it meets the road. **Turn right** towards what looks like a small lake, and take a track that runs alongside the Steenbeek, keeping the lake on your right.

On your left there is a small and modest memorial to Harry Patch, recording one of his visits and overlooking the battlefield where he moved up to take part in the Battle of Poelcapelle in September 1917.

Return to the road and follow it to the right, using the footpath, to the next roundabout. Here **turn left** and follow the road out of Langemarck village, then take the **second right** onto *Mangelaarstraat*. Follow this until the road bends sharply to the right. **Stop**.

In the fields to the right of this bend was the area where the 1st Battalion King's Own Scottish Borderers made an attack on 16th August 1917. Serving in the battalion was Company Sergeant Major John 'Jock' Skinner. A pre-war Regular soldier who had enlisted as a boy soldier and fought in the Boer War, Skinner had fought at Le Cateau in 1914, Gallipoli in 1915, on the Somme in 1916 and later at Arras. He had already been decorated for bravery but here he would take several German strongpoints, which would result in the award of the Victoria Cross:

For most conspicuous bravery and good leading. Whilst his company was attacking, machine gun fire opened on the left flank, delaying the advance. Although

Company Sergeant Major John 'Jock' Skinner VC.

C.S.M. Skinner was wounded in the head, he collected six men, and with great courage and determination worked round the left flank of three blockhouses from which the machine gun fire was coming, and succeeded in bombing and taking the first blockhouse single-handed; then, leading his six men towards the other two blockhouses, he skilfully cleared them, taking sixty prisoners, three machine guns, and two trench mortars. The dash and gallantry displayed by this warrant officer enabled the objective to be reached and consolidated.[2]

Jock Skinner VC DCM went on to fight at Cambrai but was killed in a quiet period at Ypres on 17th March 1918. He was buried at Vlamertinghe New Military Cemetery and it is said that six men who had been awarded the Victoria Cross carried his coffin to the grave.

Stay on this road until it meets another, *Beekstraat*, and here turn right. Walk a little way to the second bridge over the stream on your right. **Stop**.

This is the Brombeek (marked as the Broembeek on British maps). On 9th October 1917 the Guards Division made an attack over this position with French troops on their flanks working in co-operation with them. Many of the dead in Ruisseau Farm Cemetery were killed in this area. Opposite where you are standing was Ney Copse, which was roughly the dividing line between the British and French forces, and the Broembeek lay across the line of advance, presenting its own problems. Following heavy rainfall, the stream was swollen and many times its usual width. The ground was churned up by shell-fire and the mud was thick and glutinous. The assault waves from the Guards had mats and light bridges to assist and in the final attack fallen trees were used to get the men across as well. The Coldstream Guards recalled:

The German Division who held this part of the line appears to have been taken by surprise, for it made a very poor resistance, and in places where the crossing was difficult, the curious sight of Germans holding out their hands to help our men out of the mud could be seen. Its line was held by a series of posts, mostly converted shell-holes.[3]

This was typical of the fighting during Third Ypres; not trench warfare at all but advancing across a morass of mud to take a series of defended shell-holes. Further up in the field on the right is a small memorial to French soldiers who were killed here in the fighting in October 1917.

Continue along the road until you reach a British memorial in front of a bunker on the left.

This memorial commemorates the artillery units of the 34th Division. After the Broembeek was taken by the Guards, the 34th Division moved up and continued with the advance here. This dead ground close to the river proved suitable for gun positions but constructing gun pits among the mud and shell holes, let alone getting artillery pieces up there, was no easy challenge. The history of the 34th Division records:

> The Divisional artillery . . . had a very rough time in the muddy margins of the Broembeek, and they lost heavily, but they did right good service. The 152nd Brigade covered our front . . . and fired seven thousand eight hundred and fifty eight rounds in a day. An ordinary day's shooting was about two thousand three hundred rounds. They . . . [later] covered the fronts of the divisions that relieved us.[4]

Follow the *Beekstraat* until it reaches the main road and here **turn right** and continue until the German cemetery car park entrance is reached. Go in here.

LANGEMARCK GERMAN CEMETERY
Start your visit here in the visitors centre close to the car park. In 2014 the centre consisted of a long tunnel with images and film on display but there are plans to change it during the First World War Centenary period. Then follow the path into the cemetery.

Langemarck German Cemetery was started in 1915 with a number of field burials. In 1916 the cemetery was expanded and made into a permanent resting place for German dead largely from the 1914–15 period; at this time (and also into the post-war period) it was known as Langemarck-Nord (Langemarck North) Cemetery, as there were more

Langemarck German Cemetery as it looked from the 1920s to the 1950s.

Langemarck German Cemetery, 1930s.

than a dozen German cemeteries located close by, also in the Langemarck area. Despite the fact that fighting swept across this area in 1917/18, the cemetery survived the war and at the close of the conflict there were 10,143 graves.

In the post-war period the Volksbund Deutsche Kriegsgräberfürsorge (VDK) turned it into a permanent cemetery. Major renovation work began on the cemetery in 1930 and it was officially inaugurated on 10th July 1932. The design of the cemetery is often overlooked. The large moat at the 'top' of the cemetery symbolises the channel coast and the flooding of the Yser plain in 1914. The large concrete strongpoints symbolise German resistance and the small blocks in between, originally designed so that unit memorials could be placed on them, show the line of the Western Front in Flanders. These blocks were available for people to sponsor and commemorate particular regions or units. The plot of graves now between these blocks, the bunkers and the moat was originally empty of burials and was left to grow wild to symbolise No Man's Land. The graves there now were added after the Second World War. The cemetery was planted with oak trees, the German national tree and typical of the type of tree found on the graves of German warriors, along with a memorial designed by Munich sculptor Professor Emil Krieger showing four figures in mourning and chanting the German remembrance song *I Had A Comrade*. The memorial was inspired by a photograph Krieger had seen in the German press in 1918 showing men of a local regiment performing such a ceremony on the battlefield.

At the entrance to the cemetery a memorial room was created with oak panels to remember 10,000 student soldiers who had died in what is now accepted as a myth – the 'Death of the Innocents' (or *Kindermode* as the Germans called it). Following an attack near Langemarck on 11th November 1914, during the First Battle of Ypres, the German press reported that groups of young German soldiers recruited from schools, colleges and universities in Germany were massacred while walking into battle, arm in arm, singing *Deutschland über alles*. This was not then the national anthem but a very popular patriotic song. Later Hitler and the Nazis leapt on this episode to show how the German nation had been betrayed by a corrupt state that had sent the cream of Germany to die in a pointless battle. But modern historians know that the losses were exaggerated, covered a much wider period than one day, and the date chosen by Hitler to become Langemarck Day – a national day of remembrance in the Nazi calendar – was a rebuke to the commemoration of the fallen of the Great War in the west: Armistice Day. Today the students' memorial room remains but needs to be seen in its wider context.

Following renovations here as part of the Great War Centenary, visitors enter via the original entrance and now see the cemetery in the way it was initially envisaged. A path extends to the right into the main burial area, while ahead the area of the mass grave can be seen. Here the visitor is immediately faced with a row of plaques showing regions of Belgium, with a wreath in the middle bearing an inscription in German that states 'I have called you by your name and you are mine'. These plaques read at first sight like a list of battle honours, and in some respects they are, but they are also places across Belgium where there were once German war cemeteries from the First World War, all of which were closed in the 1950s and moved to Langemarck. Beyond the plaques is a raised planted area surrounded by blocks listing names, and at the head of the grave are the figures designed by Emil Krieger. This area forms the mass grave, or comrades' grave as the Germans call it. It was not a feature of the original cemetery but was created in the 1950s when the VDK, now funded only by West Germany following the post-Second World War division of the country, simply could not afford to maintain all the existing cemeteries, and so closed them and moved the bodies to several sites, including Langemarck, where they were placed in this mass grave. No list of names of those buried here was added until the early 1980s, and it has given the impression somehow that Germany does not care for her dead from the Great War. Many modern visitors look at this mass grave, which contains the bodies of 24,916 men, and look at the oak trees, now more than eighty years old, and they see a dark and foreboding place in great contrast to the British and Commonwealth cemeteries. Aside from the mass burials, a further 9,500 identified soldiers were moved into the cemetery and buried in individual graves. All this work brought the total of burials by the late 1950s to 44,294. It is not the largest German cemetery in Flanders – the cemetery at Menin eclipses it with 47,864 burials – but it is certainly among the most visited.

The graves in the cemetery and the names on the memorial for the mass grave cover a broad spectrum of the German experience in Flanders. By the end of the Great War Germany had lost more than two million men in the conflict. Nearly half of these were men aged between nineteen and twenty-four, and many of those with the rank of *Kriegsfreiwillige* (wartime volunteer) found in this cemetery are among those young soldiers, a considerable number of them here at Langemarck student soldiers who died in the early battles of Flanders. Some twenty per cent of all officers who served in the war died, but in cemeteries like this one it is rare to find anyone with the rank of Major or above as the Germans had a policy of repatriating them home to be buried in a military cemetery in Germany or in the family grave. One of Germany's greatest aviators is commemorated on the mass grave panels. Werner Voss transferred from the cavalry into a fighter squadron and was credited with forty-eight victories by the time he was shot down over Frezenberg on 23rd September 1917, aged only twenty. James McCudden VC, one of Britain's greatest air aces, described him as 'the bravest German airman'.

On the name panels for the mass grave is a noticeable bronze plaque commemorating two British soldiers, Albert Carlill of the 1/4th Battalion Loyal North Lancashire Regiment and Private Leonard Harry Lockley. Carlill was a nineteen-year-old from Brough in Yorkshire, who died as a prisoner of war on 4th November 1918. He was originally buried at Louvain Communal Cemetery but his grave was later lost; a Special Memorial to him was erected at Cement House Cemetery in 1957. Lockley was from Portsmouth and died as prisoner of war on 30th October 1918 while serving with the 4th Battalion Seaforth Highlanders. Originally he was commemorated with a Special Memorial in Jemappes Communal Cemetery, as the location of his grave in Belgium had been lost. What appears to have happened is that in fact both men were buried in German cemeteries and their remains were subsequently moved to Langemarck in the 1950s without the knowledge of the Commonwealth War Graves Commission. As it proved impossible to remove them from the mass grave, their memorial is now here.

Leaving the cemetery by the entrance, **turn right** and follow the

The battlefield between Langemarck and Poelcapelle in 1917.

footpath into Langemarck. In the main square walk to the other side of the church and take a side road, *Korte Ieperstraat*, down to the main road. Here **turn right**.

Further up on the right-hand side is the memorial to the 20th (Light) Division. This was a formation which had been raised in 1914 and was made up of Light Infantry regiments, including the Duke of Cornwall's Light Infantry, with which Harry Patch served here in 1917. Harry visited this memorial on one of his return visits.

Continue along the road to the bridge over the Steenbeek river. **Stop**.

On the bridge is a Belgian memorial to King Albert of the Belgians and his troops. It carries the date 28th September 1918, which was when Belgian troops under the command of their King finally liberated this region of Belgium. With the memorial in front of you, turn round and look across the road bridge to some modern houses on the other side of the road. This is the site of Au Bon Gite, a large German concrete bunker. This two-tiered bunker was attacked by the 11th Battalion King's Royal Rifle Corps, part of the 20th (Light) Division, on 16th August 1917. Sergeant Edward Cooper of the 11th KRRC was later awarded the Victoria Cross for his bravery here at that time:

149

Langemarck church in 1915.

Langemarck church in 1919.

Au Bon Gite bunker, 1917.

For most conspicuous bravery and initiative in attack. Enemy machine guns from a concrete blockhouse, 250 yards away, were holding up the advance of the battalion on his left, and were also causing heavy casualties to his own battalion. Sjt Cooper, with four men, immediately rushed towards the blockhouse, though heavily fired on. About 100 yards distant he ordered his men to lie down and fire at the blockhouse. Finding this did not silence the machine guns, he immediately rushed forward straight at them and fired his revolver into an opening in the blockhouse. The machine guns ceased firing and the garrison surrendered. Seven machine guns and forty-five prisoners were captured in this blockhouse. By this magnificent act of courage he undoubtedly saved what might have been a serious check to the whole advance, at the same time saving a great number of lives.[5]

Continue on the road. At the next junction **bear left** and follow the main road back to Cement House Cemetery and your vehicle.

Notes

1. Ponsonby, Sir F. *The Grenadier Guards in the Great War 1914–1918* (Macmillan 1920) p.231.
2. *London Gazette*, 14th September 1917, TNA ZJ1.
3. Ponsonby op cit p.252.
4. Shakespear, Lt-Col J. *The Thirty Fourth Division* (Witherby 1921) p.164.
5. *London Gazette*, 14th September 1917, TNA ZJ1.

Steenbeek River battlefield, 1917.

151

Chapter Eight

Passchendaele Walk

STARTING POINT: Memorial Museum Passchendaele, Zonnebeke
GPS: 50°52'14.6"N, 2°59'14.8"E
DISTANCE: 13km/8.1 miles

WALK SUMMARY: *A walk covering the ground fought over in some of the final phases of the Battle of Passchendaele, starting at the excellent local museum and visiting bunkers, memorials and cemeteries in the area connected with the 1917 battle.*

Park your vehicle in the car park of the Memorial Museum Passchendaele. The local library is also located here and there is plenty of space. From the car park head to the main entrance of the museum.

The Memorial Museum Passchendaele (www.passchendaele.be) is located in the old Zonnebeke Chateau and tells the story of the Zonnebeke–Passchendaele area during and after the Great War. There are good displays of artefacts, weapons and uniforms, and some interesting recreations. The museum also has an outside feature with a network of reconstructed trenches that help explain the evolution of trenches on the Flanders battlefield. A visit here will easily last two hours and helps to put the rest of the walk into context.

'I Died in Hell: They Called it Passchendaele' – the battlefield in 1917.

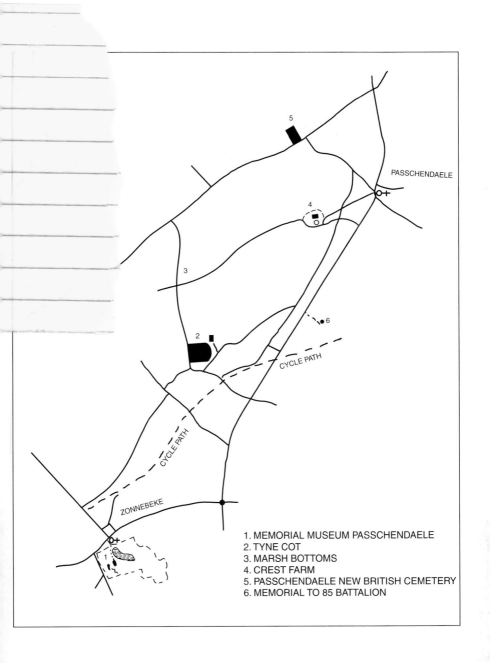

PASSCHENDAELE

CYCLE PATH

CYCLE PATH

ZONNEBEKE

1. MEMORIAL MUSEUM PASSCHENDAELE
2. TYNE COT
3. MARSH BOTTOMS
4. CREST FARM
5. PASSCHENDAELE NEW BRITISH CEMETERY
6. MEMORIAL TO 85 BATTALION

From the front steps of the museum go **left** and walk past the lake and then go right through the trees towards the church. The Germans constructed a massive dugout system beneath the church, part of which was exposed in the 1980s, and an information panel explains it, showing the extent of the work the Germans carried out. From the church cross the road and walk down Langemarkstraat, then take the **first right** into Astridstraat. Follow this through the houses and built-up area until it reaches a walking and cycling track. This is the site of the old railway; now take this route and follow it towards the Passchendaele Ridge. Further up it meets a road from the left; **stop**.

The 3rd (Australian) Division made an assault on the Broodseinde Ridge line ahead from here on 4th October 1917. Commanded by John Monash, who would become the Australian Corps commander in 1918, the men attacked at 6am and found the Germans attempting to attack at the same time. Up against a much stronger force, the German assault troops faltered and were pushed back, although there was much heavy fighting for the bunkers in this area which the Germans used as the lynch-pins of their in-depth and flexible defence which formed part of the so-called *Flanderen Line*. C.E.W. Bean later wrote: 'The day's success was a very great one – indeed the most complete yet won by the British Army in France in that war.'[1]

Even so, it cost the Australians more than 6,500 casualties on this day and the subsequent days in this area. There is an Australian Memorial here and some German bunkers can be seen across the fields to the right.

Continue up the walking/cycle track. Further along there is a modern farm on the right, and just to the side of the track is an example of the common type of bunker the Germans constructed in the *Flanderen Line*. Many of these bunkers were makeshift but they allowed machine-gun teams to anchor the defence for rifle teams who were often just in shell-holes around them. The battlefield by October 1917 was a vast quagmire, a moonscape of shell craters, and the construction of new trench systems was not only easy to spot, but often physically impossible to achieve. An information panel here explains more about the site.

Again continue on the track until it meets a road. Go **straight over** and stay on the track. At the next road, **go left** and follow Tynecotstraat to the next junction; take the **left-hand fork** and follow past the houses around the original entrance to Tyne Cot Cemetery. The site has changed since the cemetery first opened, and the main entrance is now to the rear but on foot you can enter from here. Go into the cemetery.

TYNE COT CEMETERY AND MEMORIAL

Tyne Cot is the largest British military cemetery in the world, from either

Author Henry Williamson at Tyne Cot Cemetery in the 1920s. (*Henry Williamson family*)

world war, with 11,908 graves. It is also the most visited; visitors are found here on every day of the year and in the summer months lines of cars and coaches almost block out the entrance. It is often used by school parties to give their students an impression of the scale of losses suffered by all sides in the Great War, and although many find it impressive, some feel the sheer numbers make a visit here impersonal – there are simply too many graves to take in.

Tyne Cot, or Cottages, was the name given to a small collection of Flemish buildings on the Broodseinde Ridge. The origins of this name have long been in dispute; one account claims that British troops from north-east England could see farm cottages here that reminded them of cottages back home in Tyneside. A more likely explanation is that trench maps in this area named a number of key features after the names of major rivers; close by was Thames House and here Tyne Cottages, shortened to Tyne Cot on the maps. By 1917 the cottages, such as they were, had gone, blasted by shell-fire. The area had been reinforced, as elsewhere on the Passchendaele battlefield, with a complex of German concrete bunkers – machine-gun positions with inter-locking fields of fire. Five of them were at Tyne Cot, with a command bunker; three are now preserved within the confines of the cemetery. As you stand here today, the advantage afforded by this position is obvious. Even on a misty day the spires of Ypres are visible; the ground attacked over and captured by the Australians in October 1917 was clearly dominated by this low ridge: the Broodseinde Ridge. The original graves, found behind the Cross of Sacrifice, date from November 1917 to February 1918, when the command bunker (now under the Cross) was used as a regimental aid post. Those who died of wounds were buried in shell holes nearby, including several German prisoners, and this explains the random nature of these burials.

As early as 1919 the Imperial War Graves Commission selected this site to construct a main Ypres battlefield cemetery, concentrating graves from all over the Salient. The movement of over 11,000 bodies, a mammoth task, was not completed until 1922, when King George V came to see what was then a hillside of wooden crosses. As part of his tour some steps had been placed against the command bunker; from the top were some excellent views across the ground here. He suggested that this feature should be incorporated into the final cemetery and today there are steps up the side of the Cross allowing access to the top, although they are very steep and care should be taken, as well as giving the Cross the respect it deserves. Work to make the cemetery permanent began after the King's visit, and Herbert Baker designed the layout and design of both the main cemetery and the eventual memorial to the missing. A friend and colleague of Edwin Lutyens, Baker also worked on the memorials at Neuve Chapelle, Loos and Delville Wood. Tyne Cot was completed within five years and it was officially opened on 19th June 1927.

The burials at Tyne Cot Cemetery are arranged in sixty-seven plots and total:

British	8,953
Australian	1,368
Canadian	966
New Zealand	520
South African	90
Newfoundland	14
Channel Islands	6
German	4
West Indies	2
French	1

Of this number 8,366 are unknowns: seventy per cent of the total. Those buried here represent a myriad of units, of actions, of battles and engagements large, small, forgotten or much lauded. Casualties from all four battles of Ypres can be found, and there are three Victoria Cross winners.

Captain Clarence Smith Jeffries VC (XL-E-1), of the 34th Battalion AIF, was killed on 12th October 1917. His citation in the *London Gazette* of 18th December 1917 reads:

Captain Clarence Jeffries VC.

For most conspicuous bravery in attack, when his company was held up by enemy machine-gun fire from concrete emplacements. Organising a party, he rushed one emplacement, capturing four machine guns and thirty-five prisoners. He then led his company forward under extremely heavy enemy artillery barrage and enfilade machine-gun fire to the objective. Later, he again organised a successful attack on a machine-gun emplacement, capturing two machine guns and thirty more prisoners. This gallant officer was killed during the attack, but it was entirely due to his bravery and initiative that the centre of the attack was not held up for a lengthy period. His example had a most inspiring influence.

Sergeant Lewis McGee VC (XX-D-1), of the 40th Battalion AIF, was killed on 13th October 1917. His citation from the *London Gazette* of 23rd November 1917 reads:

For most conspicuous bravery when, in the advance to the final objective, Serjt. McGee led his platoon with great dash and bravery, though strongly opposed, and under heavy shell-fire. His platoon was suffering severely and the advance of the Company was stopped by machine gun fire from a 'Pill-box' post. Single-handed, Serjt. McGee rushed the post armed only with a revolver. He shot some of the crew and captured the rest, and thus enabled the advance to proceed.

Sergeant Lewis McGee VC.

He reorganised the remnants of his platoon and was foremost in the remainder of the advance, and during consolidation of the position he did splendid work. This Non-commissioned Officer's coolness and bravery were conspicuous and contributed largely to the success of the Company's operations. Serjt. McGee was subsequently killed in action.

Private James Peter Robertson VC (LVIII-D-26), of the 27th Battalion Canadian Infantry, was killed on 6th November 1917. His citation from the *London Gazette* of 8th January 1918 reads:

For most conspicuous bravery and outstanding devotion to duty in attack. When his platoon was held up by uncut wire and a machine gun causing many casualties, Pte Robertson dashed to an opening on the flank, rushed the machine gun and, after a desperate struggle with the crew, killed four and then turned the gun on the remainder, who, overcome by the fierceness of his onslaught, were running towards their own lines. His gallant work enabled the platoon to advance. He inflicted many more casualties among the enemy, and then, carrying the captured machine gun, he led his platoon to the final objective. He there selected an excellent position and got the gun into action, firing on the retreating enemy who by this time were quite demoralised by the fire brought to bear on them. During the consolidation Pte Robertson's most determined use of the machine gun kept down the fire of the enemy snipers; his courage and his coolness cheered his comrades and inspired them to the finest efforts. Later, when two of our snipers were badly wounded in front of our trench, he went out and carried one of them in under very severe fire. He was killed just as he returned with the second man.

Among the others are many interesting characters who are often overlooked by visitors. H. Barries (Sp Mem 60) was a Piper in the 1st Battalion Cameron Highlanders, killed while piping his comrades forward on 5th November 1914. RSM C.F. Jagger (XVI-A-5) of the 1/4th Battalion East Yorkshire Regiment died on 13th December 1917. He was among that rare breed of soldier, a Warrant Officer who was awarded the Military Cross. Royal Flying Corps graves are numerous, particularly in Plot I, Row AA, where two eighteen-year-old pilots are buried. Elsewhere is Captain V.N.H. Wadham (LXII-C-5), a veteran RFC officer. Killed on 17th January 1916, the register records he was 'one of the 34 pilots who flew from Salisbury Plain to France on 12th August 1914'. The two most senior officers at Tyne Cot are Brigadier General J.F. Riddell (XXXIV-H-14), a Northumberland Fusiliers officer who was killed in action commanding 1/1st Northumberland Brigade near St Julien on 26th April 1915, aged fifty-two, and Lieutenant Colonel S.H. Dix MC (XLVI-B-1), the commanding officer of the 12th/13th Northumberland Fusiliers, who fell at Passchendaele on 4th October 1917, aged thirty-nine.

Brigadier General J.F. Riddell.

Reading the inscriptions on the headstones at Tyne Cot gives a good impression of how the families of these men viewed the sacrifice of their loved ones in the post-war world. There are countless references to Country, Empire and God. Today most modern pilgrims are inclined to write 'Why?' in the cemetery visitors' book, but the grave of Second Lieutenant A.C. Young (IV-G-21) bears one of the very few anti-war inscriptions to be found anywhere on the Western Front battlefields. Commissioned into the 7/8th Royal Irish Fusiliers, Young was a veteran of the Somme. He was killed near the Steenbeek on 16th August 1917, aged twenty-six. His father, a diplomat who had served in Japan for most of his career, was moved to write 'Sacrificed to the fallacy that war can end war'.

The **TYNE COT MEMORIAL** forms the large arched wall to the rear of the cemetery. This takes over from where the Menin Gate leaves off, and commemorates those killed at Ypres from 16th August 1917 to the end of the war. The majority of names are men who died during Third Ypres and the German spring offensive in April 1918. The memorial records 34,927 soldiers; aside from British names, 1,176 are from New Zealand, and one from Newfoundland. Australian, Canadian and South African 'missing' are on the Menin Gate. Arranged regimentally, the names are engraved on low stone walls. Among the casualties are three Victoria Cross winners from Third Ypres:

Lieutenant Colonel Philip Eric Bent VC DSO (Panel 50), 9th Battalion Leicestershire Regiment, killed on 1st October 1917. His citation from the *London Gazette* of 11th January 1918 reads:

For most conspicuous bravery, when during a heavy hostile attack, the right of his own command and the Battalion on his right were forced back. The situation was critical owing to the confusion caused by the attack and the intense artillery fire. Lieutenant Colonel Bent personally collected a platoon that was in reserve, and together with men from other companies and various regimental details, he organised and led forward to the counter attack, after issuing orders to other officers as to the further defence of the line. The counter attack was successful and the enemy were checked. The coolness and magnificent example shown to all ranks by Lieutenant Colonel Bent resulted in the securing of a portion of the line which was of essential importance for subsequent operations. This very gallant officer was killed whilst leading a charge which he inspired with the call of 'Come on the Tigers'.

Corporal William Clamp VC (Panel 52), 6th Battalion Yorkshire Regiment, killed on 9th October 1917. His citation from the *London Gazette* of 19th December 1917 reads:

For most conspicuous bravery near Poelcapelle on the 6th October 1917, when an advance was being checked by intense machine-gun fire from concrete blockhouses and by snipers in ruined buildings, Corporal Clamp dashed forward with two men and attempted to rush the largest blockhouse. His first attempt failed owing to the two men with him being knocked out, but he at once collected some bombs and, calling upon two men to follow him, again dashed forward. He was first to reach the blockhouse and hurled in the bombs, killing many of the occupants. He then entered and brought out a machine gun and about twenty prisoners, whom he brought back under heavy fire from neighbouring snipers. This non-commissioned officer then again went forward, encouraging and cheering the men and succeeded in rushing several snipers' posts. He continued to show the greatest heroism until he was killed by a sniper. His magnificent courage and self-sacrifice were of the greatest value and relieved what was undoubtedly a very critical situation.

Corporal Ernest Seaman VC (Panel 70), 2nd Battalion Royal Inniskilling Fusiliers, killed on 29th September 1917. His citation from the *London Gazette* of 12th November 1918 reads:

On 29th September 1918 at Terhand, Belgium, when the right flank of his company was held up by enemy machine-guns, Lance-Corporal Seaman went forward under heavy fire with his Lewis gun and engaged the position single-handed, capturing two machine-guns and 12 prisoners, and killing one officer and two men. Later in the day he again rushed another enemy machine-gun post, capturing the gun under very heavy fire. He was killed

160

immediately afterwards, but it was due to his gallant conduct that his company was able to push forward to its objective.

Others of interest on the Tyne Cot Memorial include:

A LIFE WITH HORSES: Charles Eddy was born in Bath, Somerset, and joined the Regular army in the last few years of the nineteenth century. He was posted to the Hussars, with whom he served in the Boer War; discovering a particular skill with horses, he rose to the rank of Farrier. He married a Rhodesian woman in 1909, and after discharge from the army worked with horses there until he returned to Bath just before the outbreak of war, where he resumed his trade as a farrier. In August 1914 he joined the Army Service Corps as a Farrier Staff Sergeant and served at Gallipoli with a veterinary unit in 1915. He came to France in a similar position with a RAMC Field Ambulance of 11th (Northern) Division, and for a reason that remains unknown applied for a commission in 1917. A vacancy was found in the Middlesex Regiment, and he was sent to join the 16th Battalion at Ypres. Perhaps considered an unlikely platoon commander, he was appointed the unit's transport officer, continuing his lifelong army connection with horses. It was while performing these duties, bringing up the rations for the battalion located in positions north-east of Poelcapelle, that he was killed by a shell.

Second Lieutenant Charles Eddy.

FATHER AND SON: The commemoration of brothers is an all too familiar occurrence in the cemeteries and on the memorials of the Western Front battlefields. A woman losing both her husband and son is somewhat rarer, and marks a tragedy impossible to imagine. Lieutenant Colonel Harry Moorhouse DSO commanded the 1/4th Battalion King's Own Yorkshire Light Infantry; his son, Ronald Wilkinson Moorhouse MC, was a Captain and company commander in the same unit. On 9th October 1917 the battalion was attacking near the Ravebeek, and Ronald was killed leading his men forward on Belle Vue. His father died only half an hour later, from a stray bullet which struck him as he was leaving his headquarters.[2] The

Lieutenant Colonel Harry Moorhouse DSO.

Captain Ronald Moorhouse.

161

dreadful nature of the ground and the terrific shelling meant that after the war their bodies could not be found. One wonders how this double tragedy was compounded for Mrs Moorhouse, having no graves to visit.

The cemetery can be exited via a gate at the rear of the Memorial to the Missing. There are public toilets here next to the car park. Take a path to the **left** and follow this to the Tyne Cot Visitors Centre. The centre was opened by Queen Elizabeth II in 2007 and helps explain the fighting here in 1917. Artefacts from the Memorial Museum Passchendaele are on display, along with the stories of some of the casualties in the cemetery and on the memorial; there is a rolling slide show of images of Passchendaele casualties.

Exit the Visitors Centre and follow the new path along the cemetery wall back down to the road which runs past the main entrance to Tyne Cot. On reaching the road, **turn right**, and follow this downhill to a crossroads. **Stop.**

This is the area known as Waterfields and Marsh Bottoms on trench maps. In late October 1917 the Canadians took over the front line on Broodseinde Ridge, opposite the village of Passchendaele, from the Australians. Private Donald Fraser, then serving with the Canadian Machine Gun Corps, left a vivid description of the battlefield at this time:

> The countryside [was] bare and open and looked as if it had been fought over recently. Shell holes were everywhere and most contained slimy, muddy water. The terrain was a wilderness of mud . . . We watched the shells send up fountains of mud and water as they exploded. For quite some distance you could see eruptions taking place at various points resembling geysers or mud volcanoes.[3]

The valley is cut by the Ravebeek, a small stream, the banks of which had been smashed by the continuous shell-fire from both sides. This flooded the ground and front-line conditions for the infantry were almost beyond imagination. In this part of the battlefield British trench maps show no trenches, as such, just a system of inter-connected shell holes forming an outpost line. This meant that all relief had to be done above ground at night, further adding to the problems and misery of battalions going in and out of action here.

Take the right-hand road and follow it until another meets it from the left. **Stop.**

About half way up this road on the right were two positions known as Duck Lodge and Snipe Hall. It was here on 30th October 1917, the opening day of the Canadian attack on Passchendaele, that the Princess

British dead in a trench at Passchendaele.

Patricia's Canadian Light Infantry (PPCLI) moved forward from the assembly positions. As the companies crossed No Man's Land a shell burst and killed one of their officers, Major Talbot Papineau MC. An original PPCLI officer, he was arguably the most important Canadian to die in the Great War; for further details of his life see the entry for the Menin Gate in the Ypres Town Walk. Today he has no known grave, but in 1917 his comrades found his shattered body in a shell hole near Duck Lodge and he was buried on the spot, the grave marked by a rough cross bearing his name. Later, shell-fire destroyed it, although the Canadian War Graves Office and Papineau's mother speculated in post-war correspondence that his body may

Major Talbot Papineau MC.

have been found in the 1919 battlefield clearance which took place; perhaps he is in Tyne Cot or Passchendaele New British Cemetery under an unknown soldier's headstone?[4] In the fighting of 30th October

Papineau was one of twenty officer casualties in the PPCLI, along with 343 other ranks, of whom 150 were killed. The battalion had numbered twenty-five officers and 600 men that morning, so these losses were heavy. Two members of the unit were awarded Victoria Crosses for their bravery: Lieutenant H. McKenzie was a PPCLI officer attached to the Canadian Machine Gun Corps. He received a posthumous VC for capturing a pillbox, during the final attack on which he was killed. Like Talbot Papineau, McKenzie's name is on the Menin Gate. Private George Henry Mullin was the other; an American by birth, he was one of the battalion snipers:

> On 30th October 1917 near Passchendaele in Belgium, a company of the PPCLI was attempting to eliminate a German 'pillbox' fortification that was blocking its advance and causing heavy casualties. While one group of Patricias led by Lieutenant Hugh McKenzie made a frontal attack on the pillbox and drew its fire, Sergeant Mullin approached from the flank and crawled onto the top of the concrete structure, disposing of an enemy sniper's position on the way. From this vantage point, Mullin shot two German machine gunners with his revolver before compelling the other ten occupants of the pillbox to surrender.[5]

Continue as the road climbs to higher ground. Follow it right, then left, until the steps of the Canadian Memorial are reached.

This is Crest Farm. A high point on the battlefield, it was a small farm complex overlooking the valley where the Canadians attacked in October 1917. The ground here was reached by the 72nd Battalion Canadian Infantry (Seaforth Highlanders of Canada) on 30th October, when the unit closely followed the creeping barrage and was able to get into the German positions with minimal losses: 280 all ranks. Canon Scott, a Canadian chaplain, recalled an episode on the battlefield at this time:

> The bodies of dead men lay here and there where they had fallen in the advance. I came across one poor boy who had been killed that morning. His body was covered with a shiny coating of yellow mud, and looked like a statue made of bronze. He had a beautiful face, with a finely shaped head covered with close curling hair, and looked more like some work of art than a human being.
>
> The huge shell holes were half full of water, often reddened with blood and many of the wounded had rolled down into the pools and been drowned.[6]

After the war Crest Farm was selected as a suitable site for the Canadian Battlefield Memorial commemorating the CEF's involvement in the Battle of Passchendaele. It takes the usual form of a granite block with text in English and Flemish. There is a visitors' book in a bronze locker, which you are invited to sign and leave your comments.

Leave by the steps and turn left, and follow the road around the memorial site. Follow the road past the first turning on the right and continue up to a crossroads where you turn left. This leads to another crossroads. Here turn left and follow the road up to the high ground north of the village. It eventually meets another road; turn left and the cemetery is immediately on the right.

PASSCHENDAELE NEW BRITISH CEMETERY

This cemetery lies on a ridge overlooking Passchendaele village, in an area attacked by the 49th Battalion Canadian Infantry on 30th October 1917. However, there was no burial site here during the battle, this being a post-war concentration cemetery. Burials total 1,019 British, 646 Canadian, 292 Australian, 126 New Zealand, four Royal Guernsey Light Infantry, three South African and one Newfoundlander. Of these 1,602 are unknowns, some seventy-five per cent.

Outside of Tyne Cot and Lijssenthoek, this is the third largest grouping of Canadian casualties on the Ypres battlefield. The men buried here, although largely unknown, give a good cross-section of the Canadian Expeditionary Force (CEF) at this time. There are immigrant workers from Latvia and Denmark. A Canadian Indian, Private Alexander Decoteau (XI-I-28), was one of many Indians employed as a sniper. He

Passchendaele New British Cemetery.

died on 30th October 1917. There are several Americans, often men who had crossed the border in the early part of the war, ashamed that their own country was not participating. There are long-serving officers like Captain Rider Lancelot Haggard (VII-A-19) of the PPCLI, a 1914 man who had risen from the ranks and commanded a company at Courcelette and Vimy Ridge. He fell not far from Talbot Papineau. Haggard had a literary connection; his uncle was Sir Henry Rider Haggard, author of *King Solomon's Mines*.

A Special Memorial at the rear of the cemetery commemorates the Chaplain of the 1/28th Battalion London Regiment (Artists' Rifles), the Revd Harry Dickinson. He fell on 30th October 1917 when his battalion was attacking alongside the Canadians near a position about a mile from this cemetery, known as Varlet Farm. The Artists' Rifles was an unusual formation, before the war being similar to a gentleman's club, and by late 1914 acting as an officer training unit. It was re-formed in 1917 and became part of the 63rd (Royal Naval) Division, and Passchendaele was its first major action as a front-line battalion. The following account of its part in this battle gives a good impression of the problems facing units at this time:

> Immediately the attack started the forward troops came under intense MG fire from an almost unseen enemy, who were cunningly posted in carefully chosen tactical positions, having taken refuge in the pill-boxes during our intense bombardment . . . The ground to be traversed was nothing but a deep sea of mud and undoubtedly many men were drowned in the mud-filled shell holes, particularly those who were already wounded. Further, the mud clogged up rifles and Lewis guns in the first few minutes of the attack, and rendered them entirely useless. Consequently it was not long before the attack was brought to a complete standstill.[7]

The Artists' Rifles had gone into this attack 470 men strong, and suffered 350 casualties, of whom 170 were killed. Few of these have graves; lost in the mud, their names appear on the Tyne Cot Memorial.

Return via the same route back towards the centre of Passchendaele, but at the crossroads go straight on into the main square opposite the church.

Passchendaele, now Passendale, which makes the hissing 's' sound of the name seem even more sinister, is known more to the locals in this smart Belgian village for its cheese, rather than any connection with the Great War. Many visitors come to Passchendaele and are disappointed;

All that remained of Passchendaele, 1919.

they think of the vast crater zone which covered the battlefield, of the mud and the snow which engulfed the Canadian attacks, and they are not a little saddened to find normality. The only reminder of the fighting in the village itself is a memorial window in the church to the 66th (West Lancs) Division, which fought in the approaches for Passchendaele, and a Western Front Association plaque from the 1980s. I once knew a veteran of the battle who in later life showed his son a 1917 aerial photograph of the Passchendaele front, asking him where he thought it was. His son replied, 'the moon'. The frightful nature of the ground in this corner of Flanders cannot be overstated. Now we have houses, shops and bars. It is time for the pilgrim to move on.

From the church take the road opposite, Canadalaan, and follow it back towards the Canadian memorial. At the crossroads **turn left** onto Rozestraat and follow this out of the village, running parallel to the main N37 road across to your left. After some time turn left onto the continuation of Rozestraat and at the main road go across to the right and follow a grass path to a memorial.

This small memorial commemorates the men of the 85th Battalion Canadian Infantry (Nova Scotia Highlanders) who fell in the fighting for Passchendaele. During these operations the battalion suffered heavy casualties, particularly amongst the officers,

Memorial to the 85th Battalion Canadian Infantry, 1919.

167

Broodseinde Ridge, 1918.

and the names of the 148 dead are listed here on a bronze plaque. It was erected in the spring of 1919, and a photograph of it appears in the Michelin guide to Ypres published the same year. It is one of only a handful of Canadian battalion memorials on the Western Front and was renovated some years ago.

Return to the main road, and cross back onto Rozestraat. At the end turn left onto another road and where it forks, **take the left-hand fork**. Follow this and a road appears on the left. **Stop**.

The ground to the right is where Captain C.S. Jeffries VC of the 34th Australian Infantry was killed and it was close to here that his remains were found prior to reburial at Tyne Cot. When this area was well behind the German lines in 1915 a large cemetery was opened further along this road to the right. This cemetery was completely destroyed by shell-fire in 1917 and it seems no graves were recovered from it after the war. It is one of several 'lost' German cemeteries on the Western Front.

Take the road to the left and go downhill to the main road. Here **turn right** and then take the **next right** onto the walking/cycle track. This is the continuation of the walking route used earlier. Follow this back towards Zonnebeke; information panels and part of the old railway line are seen further ahead. Where it meets the road go straight across and

168

stay on the track all the way back to the outskirts of Zonnebeke. In the village retrace your steps back to the grounds of the Memorial Museum Passchendaele and your vehicle.

Notes

1. Bean, C.E.W. *Anzac to Amiens* (Canberra 1948) p.371.
2. 1/4th Battalion KOYLI *War Diary*, 9.10.17, TNA WO95/2806.
3. Roy, R.H. *The Journal of Private Fraser* (Sono Nis Press 1985) p.313.
4. This is evident from papers in his personnel file in the Canadian National Archives, which itself runs to over 200 pages; I am grateful to Ron Jack, of MARRS, for his assistance in acquiring a copy of it.
5. Canadian Military website, last accessed October 2012, http://www.cmp-cpm.forces.gc. ca/dhh-dhp/gal/vcg-gcv/bio/mullin-gh-eng.asp.
6. Scott, F.G. *The Great War As I Saw It* (Goodchild 1922) p.228.
7. From papers in the archives of Tony and Joan Poucher.

An abandoned trench system near Zonnebeke, 1919.

Chapter Nine

Behind the Lines Walk:
Brandhoek–Vlamertinghe

STARTING POINT: Brandhoek New Military Cemetery No 3
GPS: 50°50′07.4″N, 2°54′11.1″E
DISTANCE: 12.2km/7.5 miles

WALK SUMMARY: *A pleasant walk in the Flemish countryside between Poperinghe and Ypres, which was a hive of activity during the Great War. The sites of former camps and casualty clearing stations are also visited, along with associated cemeteries.*

Park your vehicle outside Brandhoek New Military Cemetery No 3 and take time to visit the cemetery before moving off.

BRANDHOEK NEW MILITARY CEMETERY No 3
There were many medical units in and around this area during the fighting for Ypres. One of three cemeteries in the small village of Brandhoek, New Cemetery No 3 was opened in August 1917 and became the main burial ground for soldiers who died of wounds in the casualty clearing stations (CCS) located at Brandhoek. It was used until 1918, and a quarter

Brandhoek Military Cemetery No 3.

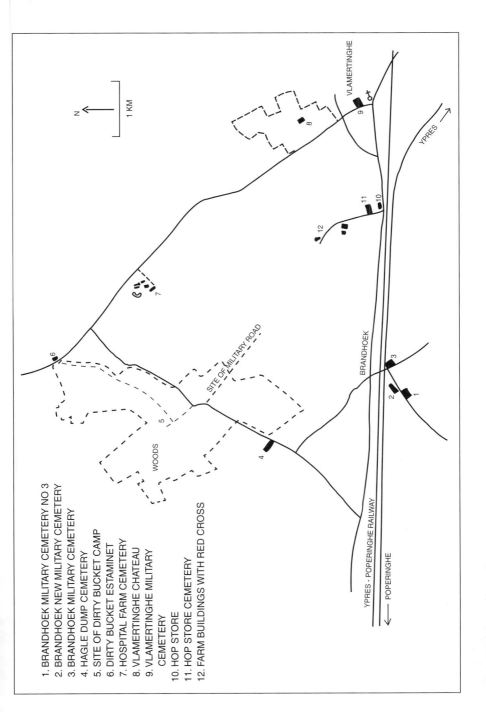

1. BRANDHOEK MILITARY CEMETERY NO 3
2. BRANDHOEK NEW MILITARY CEMETERY
3. BRANDHOEK MILITARY CEMETERY
4. HAGLE DUMP CEMETERY
5. SITE OF DIRTY BUCKET CAMP
6. DIRTY BUCKET ESTAMINET
7. HOSPITAL FARM CEMETERY
8. VLAMERTINGHE CHATEAU
9. VLAMERTINGHE MILITARY
   CEMETERY
10. HOP STORE
11. HOP STORE CEMETERY
12. FARM BUILDINGS WITH RED CROSS

of the graves are men from artillery units who also had their gun sites in the nearby fields. The bronze cemetery gates were given by the family of Lieutenant Anthony Herbert Strutt (IV-A-5) of the 16th Battalion Sherwood Foresters, who died of wounds received near Rifle Wood on 27th April 1918. From Belper in Derbyshire, Strutt was educated at Harrow and Cambridge and was a keen sportsman, who was commissioned from the Inns of Court Officer Training Corps. He fought on the Somme in 1916 but was sent home with trench fever, returning to Flanders in 1917. There are 849 British, forty-six Australian, forty-six Canadian, eighteen New Zealand, five South African, one British West Indies Regiment and one Chinese Labour Corps burials.

Two senior officers were buried here. Lieutenant Colonel T.C. Irving DSO (I-N-26) was a staff officer with 4th (Canadian) Division Engineers and died on 29th October 1917, aged thirty-eight. Lieutenant Colonel S.J. Somerville (II-F-17) was one part of a family tragedy. He died of wounds received near the Steenbeek on 16th August 1917 whilst commanding the 9th Battalion Royal Irish Fusiliers. He was aged forty-six and was a long-serving officer, whose son had been killed on the Somme in 1916 and buried in Authuille Military Cemetery (see *Walking The Somme*). The register records a further tragic occurrence for an RAMC man. Corporal William Bathgate (II-B-10), of 113th Field Ambulance, died of wounds on 15th August 1917 and 'was laid to rest by his brother Robert (Sergeant 112th Field Amb)'.

Leaving the cemetery, turn right, and after only a few yards a CWGC sign on the left indicates a grass path to the next cemetery.

BRANDHOEK NEW MILITARY CEMETERY

This cemetery took over from Brandhoek Military Cemetery in July 1917 when the 3rd (Australian), 32nd and 44th Casualty Clearing Stations (CCS) arrived at Brandhoek in preparation for Third Ypres. It was used in the opening phase of the operations and then closed in August 1917 when the cemetery you have just come from was started. There are 513 British, twenty-eight German, eleven Australian and six Canadian graves in the cemetery.

The most visited grave here is undoubtedly that of Captain Noel Godfrey Chavasse VC and bar MC (III-B-15), Royal Army Medical Corps. Chavasse was the medical officer of the 1/10th Battalion King's Liverpool Regiment (Liverpool Scottish), and served with that unit from the outbreak of war. He was awarded the Military Cross for bravery at Hooge in 1915 and his first Victoria Cross at Guillemont on the Somme in August 1916. He returned to the Salient with his battalion in time for Third Ypres and was in action near Wieltje from 31st July 1917 until he was mortally wounded, dying in a CCS at Brandhoek on 4th August. For his further bravery in this attack he was awarded a bar to his VC: one of only three men in the history of the medal to achieve this.

But there are other soldiers at Brandhoek, often overlooked by the casual visitor. In addition to Chavasse, a further thirteen RAMC men have graves in the cemetery. Two of them were medical officers like Chavasse: Captain F.R. Armitage DSO (I-E-8), who died of wounds on 30th July 1917, attached to the 232nd Brigade Royal Field Artillery; and Captain H.D. Willis (VI-F-12), attached to the 3rd Battalion Worcestershire Regiment, killed on 12th August 1917. Of the others, three in Plot IV Row D died while serving with the 47th Sanitary Section on 5th August 1917, a unit rarely encountered but which performed an important job in areas behind the lines where vast numbers of men were camped out and clean toilet facilities were needed to stop the spread of disease.

The other burials are dominated by Irish regiments. Among them is a battalion commander, Lieutenant Colonel T.H. Boardman DSO (III-F-1), who died of wounds on 5th August 1917 with 8th Battalion Royal Inniskilling Fusiliers. CSM E. Power (III-E-5) was a Regular soldier with the 2nd Battalion Royal Irish Regiment, who had served at Mons and was the holder of the Military Cross, rare among Warrant Officers. He died of wounds on 8th August 1917, aged thirty-eight.

Leaving the cemetery, return to the road and turn left. Continue to a T-junction and cross another road to the next cemetery, visible opposite.

BRANDHOEK MILITARY CEMETERY

Because of its location and distance from the front, Brandhoek was for much of the war not within range of German field artillery and was therefore considered 'safe'. As such, RAMC Field Ambulances operated in the village from 1915 onwards, and as a consequence the cemetery was started by them in May, in a field next to the then advanced dressing station (ADS). The cemetery was closed in July 1917, just prior to Third Ypres. By this time CCSs had replaced the ADS, and they eventually used the two cemeteries you have just come from. Graves here number 600 British, sixty-three Canadian, four Australian, two Bermuda Rifle Volunteer Corps and two German. Of this number only four are unknown.

The graves are roughly in date order, the earliest ones being close to the entrance. Artillery units had their gun positions at Brandhoek, and so there are many Royal Artillery graves to be found here. Second Lieutenant Rowland T. Cobbald (I-F-19) was serving in the 6th Battery RFA when he was killed in action on 25th September 1915, aged twenty-three. The register records he had returned to England from Argentina in

Brandhoek Military Cemetery.

order to enlist. Likewise, Second Lieutenant J.S. Leeds (I-D-2), who died on 19th September 1915, aged twenty-eight, while serving with the 1st Honourable Artillery Company, had also returned from Argentina in September 1914. There are several 1st HAC men buried elsewhere in the cemetery, casualties from the almost constant fighting around Hooge. Also among them was a journalist, a writer for the *Daily Chronicle*: Private George Mascord (I-E-5), who died of wounds on 20th September 1915, aged twenty-six.

There are four senior officers in the cemetery, who between them had many years of service. Brigadier General F.J. Heyworth CB DSO (II-C-2) of the Scots Guards died on 9th May 1916 while commanding 3rd Guards Brigade; he was shot by a sniper while touring the front line. Lieutenant Colonel C. Conyers (I-C-21) was 'killed while leading a charge of the 2nd Leinsters' at St Eloi on 12th May 1915, aged forty-six. A Boer War veteran, his original unit was the 2nd Battalion Royal Irish Fusiliers. Lieutenant Colonel J. Clarke CB (I-B-19) is buried behind him, and died a few days earlier on 10th May 1915, aged fifty-six. He was serving with the 1/9th Battalion Argyll & Sutherland Highlanders when he was mortally wounded during Second Ypres. Also buried close by is Lieutenant Colonel A.F. Sargeaunt (I-D-20) of the Royal Engineers, who died on 31st July 1915, aged forty-four.

Two Royal Flying Corps Balloon officers are buried next to each other; Lieutenant T.F. Lucas (I-L-1) and Captain E.A. Wickson (I-L-2) were killed when their observation balloon of 20th Balloon Company RFC fell to earth on 16th July 1917. Both men were in their thirties; Wickson had previously served in the 51st Battalion Canadian Infantry, and Lucas had a titled father.

A concentration of graves from one unit is found in Plot II Row G: a row of men from the 1st Welsh Guards who died of wounds received while holding the Canal Bank sector near Boesinghe between 1st March and 24th July 1916. Similarly, in Plot II Row H are twelve graves of men from the 42nd Battalion Canadian Infantry (Black Watch of Canada) who died on 3rd August 1916. This unit was out of the trenches at the Ypres Ramparts on the evening of 3rd August when a large calibre shell struck their billets and caused nearly sixty casualties, of which these were the fatalities.

Leaving the cemetery by the gate, turn right and walk to the new Poperinghe–Ypres road and cross it via the pedestrian crossing. This is a very busy road and care should be taken. Once across, follow the footpath to the railway and go over that down a minor road.

The railway ran here during the war and by Third Ypres there were several sidings at Brandhoek so the wounded could be brought straight to the CCSs. Casualties requiring further treatment could be taken on other trains along the same line to the main CCS at Remi Siding, south-west of Poperinghe (now Lijssenthoek Cemetery – see Poperinghe Walk),

Behind the lines in Flanders.

British camps behind the lines.

or further back to a base hospital on the French coast. On 31st July 1917 and subsequent days, given the number of burials in the Brandhoek cemeteries alone, this must have been a very busy area.

The minor road brings you out into the centre of Brandhoek and onto the old Poperinghe–Ypres road. The church, now rebuilt, is to your right. There is a modern memorial to Noel Chavasse VC and Bar in the grounds of it; visit this first and return to the crossroads. Then **turn right** to join Kleine Branderstraat. Continue down what soon becomes a quiet country lane past older houses on the left that were here during the war.

Further along, past a bend to the right, and just before a white farm cottage, was the site of B Camp. This was one of dozens of military camps between Poperinghe and Ypres which were used during the war years by troops going to and from the line. Many, such as this one, were simply known by a single letter; others had more unusual names like Chippewaw and MicMac. Conditions in these camps varied greatly; some had tents, others wooden huts or even the newly designed Nissen Huts. An officer of the 12th Battalion Rifle Brigade recalled a typical camp like B Camp at the time of Third Ypres in 1917:

> There are about twenty bivouacs per company and every officers' mess has a big tarpaulin as head-cover. With numerous 4.5 ammunition boxes and sundry pieces of timber . . . which we found in close proximity to our camp, the place was soon made quite comfortable.[1]

Continue along this route, past several old Flemish houses, until it meets another road. Turn right at this junction and a little further up on the left is Hagle Dump Cemetery.

HAGLE DUMP CEMETERY

Hagle Dump was the name given to a large ammunition and supply depot 2 miles south-west of Elverdinghe and close to the site of this cemetery. Nearby was another camp, used extensively during the fighting of 1917–18, but the cemetery itself was not started until April 1918 during the Battle of Lys. It remained in use until October, and after the war 207 graves were moved in from various points in the Ypres Salient to what are now Plots III and IV. Twenty-six Americans and two French soldiers were moved to other cemeteries. Today there are 397 British, twenty-six Australian, fourteen Canadian and two German burials. Of this number 142 are unknown.

Many of the original graves in Plot I represent behind the lines units that operated in this area: siege battery gunners, light railway units and army tramway companies. However, in Plot I Rows C and D there is a large concentration of men from the 10th Battalion Royal West Kents, all of whom died on 27th April 1918. They bear testimony to the folly of placing a rest camp so close to an ammunition dump. Their *War Diary* records what happened that day:

> A serious explosion occurred behind the Detail Camp about 12.30pm caused by a H.V. [High Velocity] enemy shell striking an ammunition and gun cotton dump. The camp was wrecked and

Soldiers of the Chinese Labour Corps at an ammunition depot.

numerous huts set on fire by the explosion. Rescue parties at once set to work to assist in recovering the numerous casualties from the debris, and extinguishing the fires, in face of great danger from recurring explosions.[2]

Lieutenant D.F. Anderson (I-D-7) was among the dead, along with seventeen other ranks. A further twenty-eight men were wounded and one man missing. The blow to the battalion was heavy; most of the dead and wounded were Warrant Officers and Sergeants, arguably the men who keep a unit together in the field; indeed, there are two CQMS and four Sergeants buried in this plot.

Elsewhere in the cemetery there are some interesting inscriptions on headstones. On that of Private F.C. Healy (III-E-11), 1/4th Suffolks, who died on 25th September 1917, it simply states, 'A Gamekeeper'. Second Lieutenant A.C. Ransdale (II-G-6) 'came from the Argentine at his nation's call for help'. He was killed with the 15th Battalion Loyal North Lancs on 1st September 1918. A soldier with an unusual name was Private William Henry Jubilee Kitchen (III-F-15), 1st Battalion Gloucestershire Regiment, who died on 1st November 1914, aged twenty-seven. Presumably he was born on or close to one of Queen Victoria's jubilees? To the rear of the cemetery are graves moved in after the war, which include that of CSM James William Dames DCM MSM (III-H-12), who died on the Bellewaarde Ridge with the Princess Patricia's Light Infantry on 8th May 1915. For many years his grave was marked as an unknown soldier but recent research showed that the original burial report noted the sequence of awards found on the uniform of the soldier. These were unique to Dames and included not just his decorations but also many ribbons for service in several of Queen Victoria's 'small wars'. Nearly ninety years after he had died, Dames's true resting place was recognised.

Leaving the cemetery turn left and continue along the road (Sint Pieterstraat). There is a useful shop close to the cemetery, which sells drinks, food and other supplies and is usually open. Soon the road approaches a large wooded area and enters it from the south side. On a sharp bend, with a house set in the wood to your left, there is a notice board just to the left of the road recording the fact that these woods once contained Dirty Bucket Camp.

Dirty Bucket Camp was one of the largest camps in the Salient during the Great War, and comprised a series of hutted and tented areas covering several square miles. Some were in the wood itself, others bordered on it. It took its name from a local estaminet known to the troops as the Dirty Bucket, and the modern notice board on this bend gives further

Royal Marine gunners at Dirty Bucket Camp, 1917.

German prisoners at Dirty Bucket Camp in 1919.

information in English and Flemish about the camp. An officer of the 11th Battalion Royal Fusiliers felt that Dirty Bucket Camp was 'a very aptly named place'.[3] Edwin Campion Vaughan was serving as an officer in the Royal Warwickshire Regiment and came to the area in August 1917:

> . . . we turned off to the left towards Dirty Bucket Corner and shortly halted outside a wood wherein our camp lay. It was a nondescript camp consisting of bivouacs, tents, huts and tarpaulin shelters into which we stowed the troops as best we could. For our combined mess and bedroom we had a small hut with a table and a couple of forms. It was a baleful place for the shell holes and shattered trees bore testimony to the attentions of the German gunners. Amongst the trees was a great concentration of tanks – and the name of the camp was Slaughter Wood![4]

From this bend a plank road took troops from the camp along what was known as Military Road all the way to Vlamertinghe, and from there up to the front line around Ypres. Although the planks have long gone, a track can be seen going through the trees and can be followed as the woods are now open to the public; there is little to see but it is worth a diversion before returning to the main road. Edmund Blunden recalled this planked route just prior to Third Ypres when he was here with the 11th Battalion Royal Sussex Regiment (1st South Downs):

> Wooden tracks led this way and that in puzzling number through the crowded airless shadows, and new roads threw open . . . a district only suited for the movements of a small and careful party. At the corner where one swaggering highway left the wood eastward, an enormous model of the German systems . . . was open for inspection, whether from the ground or from stepped ladders raised beside, and this was popular, though whether from its charm as a model or value as a military aid is uncertain.[5]

Tens of thousands of British soldiers spent their time out of the trenches at this camp. It was often shelled. Prior to Third Ypres, long-range German guns fired at Dirty Bucket, and German Gotha bombers were also active in the area from 1917. In one incident men of C Battalion Tank Corps came under fire on 4th July 1917 when the battalion orderly room was hit, wounding two officers and two men, killing four Gunners and a Corporal. A tank also received a direct hit, damaging a sponson, breaking some rollers and cutting the track.[6]

British troops doing gas mask practice behind the lines.

From the road take the **left-hand** path into the woods. Further up take the **first path on the right** and follow this through what was the heart of Dirty Bucket Camp. The track comes out near a small restaurant; here **turn right** and follow the road to the next junction. This is Dirty Bucket Corner. From here continue until you are parallel with a farm – Hospital Farm – in the fields to your right. A little further on a green CWGC sign can be seen. Go through the turnstile gate, and follow a line of trees to the cemetery entrance.

HOSPITAL FARM CEMETERY
This rarely visited cemetery is in an unspoilt, quiet and secluded spot, typical of the area between Poperinghe and Ypres. Hospital Farm was the name given to several farm buildings, which you have passed on the way into the cemetery. These were used by the RAMC as an ADS, cases being evacuated back here from Elverdinghe and Vlamertinghe station. During the war a light tramway ran close to the farm. The ADS was expanded by the West Riding Field Ambulances of the 49th (West Riding) Division when they held the Canal Bank sector at Boesinghe in mid- to late 1915. Graves total 116; all but one are British, the other is a French civilian killed nearby in August 1916.

Aside from the ADS, there were many gun sites in the Hospital Farm area, and the graves here reflect this. Three officers from the 2/1st (1st Lancs) Heavy Battery Royal Garrison Artillery are buried side by side: Captain A.D. MacNeil (B-5), Captain R.W.C.M. Rodgers (B-6) and

Lieutenant A.E. Voysey (B-4). All died on 27th July 1917, in the lead-up to Third Ypres when the number of artillery units operating on this part of the front expanded greatly; by this time there were 752 heavy howitzers and 1,422 field guns participating in the preliminary bombardment.

Lieutenant Lambert Playfair (B-9) was an early officer of the Royal Flying Corps. Born in India, where his parents lived in Upper Assam, he was educated at Sandhurst (where he won a prize cadetship), and was commissioned into the 1st Battalion Royal Scots in January 1913, later joining the RFC as an observer. On 6th July 1915, while serving with No 1 Squadron, his Avro 504 was on artillery observation duties over St Julien. At 11.04am his pilot came into combat with two German Aviatiks, and a burst of machine-gun fire hit the Avro's engine; Playfair was found to be dead when the aircraft made a forced landing near Hospital Farm.

The cemetery register indicates further evidence of German bombing raids on the camps around Hospital Farm and Dirty Bucket Corner. RSM W. Walker (E-24), of the 1/4th Battalion Gordon Highlanders, is recorded as having been 'killed by a bomb from a German aeroplane' on 15th September 1917. Another soldier of the same unit, killed on the same day, is buried next to him.

Return to the road via the same route you accessed the cemetery, and turn right after the turnstile. From here it is about thirty minutes' walk into Vlamertinghe; take care on this road as cars can speed along it, as well as heavy farm machinery.

Just as you approach the outskirts of the village, a small park borders the road on the left, and soon some large white gates are visible. They mark a private drive; respecting this, go in and look at Vlamertinghe chateau, an impressive building. Poet Edmund Blunden was here with the 11th Battalion Royal Sussex Regiment in July 1917 and a plaque now records his connection with the place. He recalled the visit here in a poem:

Vlamertinghe: Passing the Chateau July 1917
'And all her silken flanks with garlands dressed' –
But we are coming to the sacrifice.
Must those have flowers who are not yet gone West?
May those have flowers who live with death and lice?
This must be the floweriest place
That earth allows; the queenly face
Of the proud mansion borrows grave for grace
Spite of those brute guns lowing at the skies.
Bold great daisies' golden lights,
Bubbling roses' pinks and whites –

Such a gay carpet! Poppies by the million;
Such damask! Such vermilion!
But if you ask me, mate, the choice of colour
Is scarcely right; this red should have been duller.[7]

Continue into Vlamertinghe via Hospitaalstraat and the military
cemetery is on the left.

VLAMERTINGHE MILITARY CEMETERY

This cemetery was started by French troops in 1914, and the six British
burials made here at that time are now in the north-west corner. Field
Ambulances operating in Vlamertinghe subsequently used the cemetery,
as did fighting units returning from the line to bury their dead. It was
closed in June 1917, as there was no further space available, the ground
surrounding the cemetery then being used by railway units. Burials
thereafter moved to Vlamertinghe New Military Cemetery south of the
village. In total there are 1,114 graves of British soldiers, fifty-two
Canadians, four Australians, two South Africans, two Newfoundlanders,
one Indian and one German. The wrought-iron gates were given by Lord
Redesdale in memory of his son, Major the Hon. C.B.O. Mitford DSO
(I-E-8), who was killed on Frezenberg Ridge with the 10th Hussars on
13th May 1915, aged thirty-eight, and is buried here.

Of the total number of graves, nearly 250 are soldiers from Lancashire
Territorial units, largely men from the 55th (West Lancs) Division, which
in early 1917 used this cemetery for both soldiers who died of wounds
and those killed in the front line; these are now in Plots IV, V and VI.
There are also a large number of officers and men from Cavalry units
who fell in the fighting on Frezenberg Ridge in May 1915, such as Major
Mitford noted above. Among them are other officers from equally well
known families, such as Captain Guy Bonham-Carter (I-G-3), 19th
Hussars, killed on 15th May 1915, and Captain Francis Octavius Grenfell
VC (II-B-14), 9th Lancers, who died on 24th May 1915. Twin brother of
Riversdale, and cousin of poet Julian, Francis had been awarded the
Victoria Cross for saving the guns at Audregnies on 24th August 1914.
The Grenfells lost heavily in the war; brother Riversdale fell on the Aisne,
and the fighting at Frezenberg eventually consumed both Julian and
Francis. Elsewhere are two other important Frezenberg casualties:
Lieutenant Colonel E.R.A. Shearman (I-D-7) and Captain & Adjutant
G.C. Stewart (I-D-6), both of whom died on 13th May 1915 serving with
the 10th Hussars.

Other interesting graves include Corporal C.E. Brookes (VII-B-9) of
the 8th Battalion Royal West Kents, killed in action on 27th May 1917,

French troops pass British soldiers near Vlamertinghe, 1915.

who, the register records, 'after serving over 18 months on the battlefields he was killed on the eve of obtaining his commission'. Private N. Finucane (V-C-11) was 'one of the crew of the *Lusitania*'; he survived the sinking and served at Gallipoli, but was killed with the 1/10th Battalion King's Liverpool Regiment near Ypres on 4th January 1917.

Second Lieutenant Harold Parry (VI-L-12) is shown in the register as 'one of England's soldier poets'. Born in 1896, he was educated at Queen Mary's Grammar School and won a scholarship to Oxford in 1915. After only a short period as a student he decided to enlist and was commissioned in 1916. He later joined the 17th Battalion King's Royal Rifle Corps and served on the Somme. From his experiences there he wrote the following poem, humorously entitled *'River that runs into everyone's dugout'*:

> I come from trenches deep in slime,
> Soft slime so sweet and yellow,

184

And rumble down the steps in time
To souse 'some shivering fellow'.

I trickle in and trickle out
Of every nook and corner,
And, rushing like some waterspout,
Make many a rat a mourner.

I gather in from near and far
A thousand brooklets swelling,
And laugh aloud a great 'Ha ha!'
To flood poor Tommy's dwelling.[8]

Parry came to Ypres with his battalion in November 1916, and was killed somewhere on the Yser canal sector by shell-fire on 6th May 1917. His poems were published posthumously in 1918, in a memoir prepared by his family.

Leave by the cemetery gate and turn left, going into the centre of Vlamertinghe. Continue to the church.

Vlamertinghe was a main route up to Ypres and the front-line trenches, and during the major offensives – particularly Third Ypres – the roads here were crowded with traffic, guns and limbers, ambulances, lorries and buses. Virtually every division going up to the fighting north-east of Ypres came through this village. The chateau was used as a headquarters, while buildings in the village became store dumps and depots, billets for the troops and quarters for the many artillery units in operation here. RAMC Field Ambulances established several ADS, the most famous of which was in Vlamertinghe Mill, of which, sadly, there is no trace today. There are several bars and shops in the village, and a visit to the church is worthwhile if you have the time.

Vlamertinghe Mill, 1916.

From the church go west on the road to Poperinghe. Follow this for some distance, passing on the left the site of Vlamertinghe windmill. Henry Williamson described the scene here during the Battle of the Menin Road Ridge in September 1917:

> There was a Casualty Clearing Station in the boarded mill beside the road . . . Inside the lower rooms white sheets hung on the walls, and across the ceilings. Two RAMC surgeons, in white aprons, smoked unconcernedly outside. They had been at work on case after case all day. A convoy of motor ambulances was arriving. Lightly wounded men, more or less content, having had their wounds dressed, were sitting in the shade of elms lining the road, smoking and talking as they awaited transport to the train. Their faces were almost carved in earth by dried sweat-runs through grime.[9]

Continue until the outskirts of the village are reached. Almost the last building on the right is the large brick-built Hop Store, which was also used as an ADS during the Great War. It bears the date 1868 and is virtually in its original condition. Just past the Hop Store is a CWGC sign indicating a minor road which takes you to the cemetery of the same name.

HOP STORE CEMETERY
Medical units established an ADS in the Hop Store in early 1915, and burials began in May of that year. The cemetery expanded, and many more graves were added in 1917 during Third Ypres. One Canadian and 247 British soldiers are buried in the cemetery. Fifty-eight of them are men from artillery units, reflecting the many gun sites in this area, and there are also a number of RAMC personnel.

An unusual headstone is that of Major Harold Payne Philby DSO (I-A-16). Philby was a Regular army officer, having been commissioned into the York & Lancaster Regiment in September 1908. His service before the Great War included an attachment to the West African Frontier Force, and he returned to England in August 1914 to join the 2nd York & Lancs, then on its way to France. He fought on the Aisne and at First Ypres, and was awarded the Distinguished Service Order for bravery at Hooge on 9th August 1915. By the end of that year he was acting adjutant, and moved to the Canal Bank sector, where he was appointed to command the battalion in early 1916, although he did not live long enough to be promoted to the rank of Lieutenant Colonel. Philby met his death opposite Morteldje estaminet, north-east of Ypres, on the night of

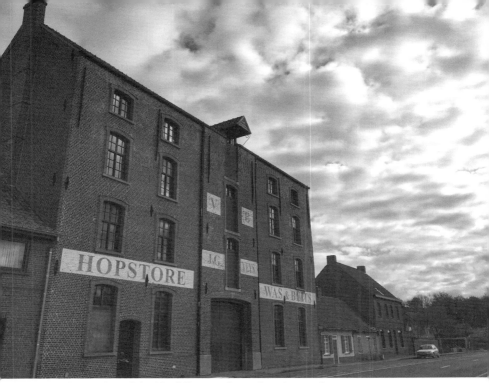

Hop Store: the original building used as a dressing station.

17th/18th May 1916. A much loved officer, his body was brought back to Vlamertinghe by his men. One wonders what such a long-serving and brave officer would have made of his nephew, the spy Kim Philby?

The graves are roughly in date order and the lettering on many of them is of a different style from that encountered in other cemeteries. This was one of the earliest cemeteries constructed at Ypres by the Imperial War Graves Commission, which was then still experimenting with style and design. In Plot I Rows D and E are the graves of men from a variety of famous cavalry regiments, all of whom died during Second Ypres in 1915. Among them are two officers of the 1st Dragoons who died of wounds received at Frezenberg Ridge in May: Captain W.H.J. St Leger Atkinson (I-D-18), aged thirty-three, and Captain H. McLaren Lambert (I-D-17), aged thirty-six.

Leaving the cemetery, **turn right** and continue up the minor road past some farm buildings. A little further up are some more farm buildings and a painted Red Cross can be clearly seen on the outside: one of the few places left where this is visible. The ground here was used by medical units throughout the war.

Indian troops prepare food near Vlamertinghe, 1915.

Return to the Poperinghe road, and stop.

Many troops marched down this road during the Great War and its then cobbled surface would have echoed to the sound of thousands of British army boots. In this direction, knowing that a billet in one of the many camps lay ahead of them, such men might have been singing: a good commanding officer allowed the men to talk in the ranks if the route ahead was not too long. Files of soldiers coming in the opposite direction, heading for Ypres and the front line, would have looked on with envy. These silent columns passed their happy comrades with unmoving faces, particularly if they knew what lay ahead.

Cross the main road into a minor road opposite and follow it to the end. Take a footpath crossing the railway line to the next main road beyond. Cross this very busy road by the pedestrian crossing and **turn left** and then **first right** into Casselsestraat. Follow this road round until it begins to run parallel to the busy main road, now across on your right.

This part of the walk takes you through countryside once covered with hutted camps, among them Montreal Camp and Thistle Camp. There were railway sidings to your right, known as Hospital Spur and used to evacuate casualties from the CCSs further back, and by 1918 gun sites here protected the front lines which were then very close to Ypres.

Continue on this road until it meets a crossroads. Here **turn right** and walk back to Brandhoek. Before the main road **go left**, following the CWGC signs back to the Brandhoek cemeteries and your vehicle.

Notes

1. Seymour, W.W. *The History of the Rifle Brigade in the War of 1914–1918* Vol II (Rifle Brigade Club Ltd 1936) p.120.
2. 10th Battalion Royal West Kent Regiment *War Diary*, 27.4.18, TNA WO95/2638.
3. O'Neill, H.C. *The Royal Fusiliers in the Great War* (Heinemann 1922) p.199.
4. Vaughan, E.C. *Some Desperate Glory* (Frederick Warne Ltd 1981) p.190.
5. Blunden, E. *Undertones of War* (Cobdean Sanderson 1928) pp.192–3.
6. C Battalion Tank Corps *War Diary*, 4.7.17, TNA WO95/106. The fatalities were once buried in Oosthoek Wood, part of Dirty Bucket Camp, but their graves were moved to Gwalia Cemetery, near Poperinghe, after the war.
7. Blunden op cit. p.256.
8. Parry, H. *In Memoriam* (WH Smith 1918).
9. Williamson, H. *Love And The Loveless* (Panther Books 1963) p.253.

Chapter Ten

Poperinghe Town Walk

STARTING POINT: Railway Station, Poperinghe
GPS: 50°51′16.7″N, 2°44′09.8″E
DISTANCE: 2.5km/1.6 miles

WALK SUMMARY: *This short walk visits the main sites in central Poperinghe (now Poperinge), including the famous 'Talbot House' where Toc-H began in 1915. It also recommends two follow-up visits to nearby military cemeteries.*

You can either leave your vehicle in the parking area outside the railway station (remember to buy a parking ticket!), or you could leave it in Ypres itself and sample Belgian railways by taking the train to Poperinghe; times are available from the tourist office or at the railway station in Ypres. Return fares are inexpensive, and there are reasonably frequent trains. It is also a very pleasant journey, along a line used in the Great War.

British troops in Poperinghe, 1915.

Uitgever: Sansen-Vanneste, Poper

OORLOG 1914-1915

RUINEN TE POPERINGHE — RUINES DE POPERINGHE — RUINS OE POPERINGHE
Zvvynslagery Muyllaert, Groote Markt — Charcuterie Muyllaert, Grand'Place

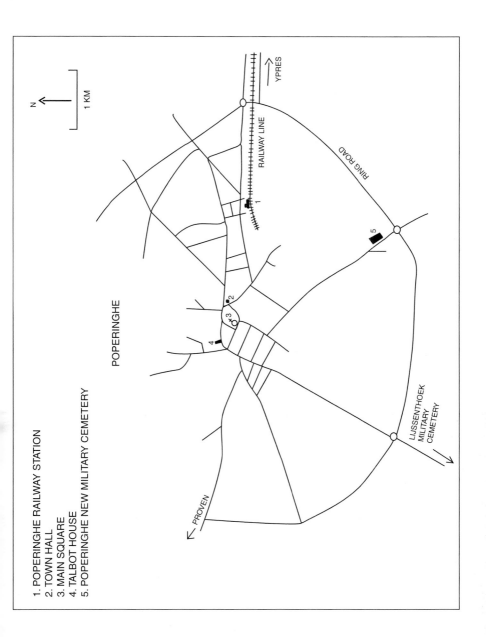

1. POPERINGHE RAILWAY STATION
2. TOWN HALL
3. MAIN SQUARE
4. TALBOT HOUSE
5. POPERINGHE NEW MILITARY CEMETERY

POPERINGHE

N

1 KM

YPRES

RAILWAY LINE

RING ROAD

LIJSSENTHOEK
MILITARY
CEMETERY

PROVEN

British soldiers photographed at Poperinghe in 1916.

Poperinghe, alternatively known as Pop or Pops to the British Tommy, was an important bastion in the lines of communication behind the Ypres Salient during the Great War. A town of 12,000 inhabitants in 1914, it was never completely evacuated and as such was often seen as something of an oasis by British troops out of the trenches. Many houses, factories and other buildings were commandeered for use as headquarters, administrative offices, billets, baths and even semi-legalised brothels. In the fields and hamlets around the town vast hutted camps were constructed and large medical establishments erected, around which grew military cemeteries. Military detention camps run by the Military Provost Staff Corps were also located at Poperinghe (including in the town hall, see below), where deserters and defaulters were kept awaiting trial, or as part of their punishment. Some suffered the ultimate fate and were 'shot at dawn', executed for a number of different military crimes.

Troops were always in Poperinghe, and the local inhabitants came to know men from every corner of the British Empire. Because the civilians remained in the town, soldiers were able to visit and enjoy the famous 'estaminets', where food and drink could be obtained, and one of the few places where men could actually relax and forget the war. Local photographers did a roaring trade in portrait photographs, and shops sold picture postcards, silks and other souvenirs to send home to family and friends. Officers had their own restaurants and cafés, but all mixed together in Talbot House, just off the main square, where there were films and shows to entertain them. Although it suffered from shell-fire and bombing, particularly in 1918, Poperinghe was never damaged to the extent that Ypres was and retains many of its original buildings today. It is an attractive and quiet Flemish town, with many good restaurants and hotels, and offers a suitable alternative to Ypres as a base for touring the area.

Poperinghe station was an important railway junction for the British forces in the Salient. It was linked to the railhead of Hazebrouck in France, so that troop and supply trains could move up here from any of the channel ports and the major camps behind the lines at Étaples or

French soldiers on Poperinghe station, 1915.

Rouen. Men of the Royal Engineers Railway Operating Division (ROD) took over the organisation of Poperinghe station almost as soon as the BEF arrived here in 1915, and continued to control it for the rest of the war. Some distance from the battlefield, Poperinghe was hit by the occasional long-range shell although it was rarely threatened by concentrated shell-fire, but by 1917 the Germans were operating Gotha bombing raids over the town and the railway became a prime target. A main route to and from the Salient, officers and men went on, and returned from, leave at this station, and tens of thousands of troops arrived here in cattle trucks marked 'Hommes 40, Chevaux 8' – 40 men, 8 horses – although a lot more than that were usually packed in. When you stand on the platform today it is easy to wonder how many of those who passed through here were on a one-way journey to a shallow grave in Flanders? Henry Williamson remembered a visit in 1917. By this time trains could not stop at the main platforms as they had been so badly damaged. A new siding was therefore made further up the track.

> The troop trains arriving at 'Pop' by day used to behave peculiarly as they approached the station through acres of hospital hutments and military cemeteries. Card parties squatting on the floors of the wooden trucks were liable to be thrown forwards, jerked upright, and flung backwards. Cling! – clang! – plonk! – plink! – crank! ran from buffer to buffer along the grey length of the train. Then another jerk, the frantic puffing of an engine whose wheels were racing on the rails, and the train went on, faster and faster, rattling through the station, and stopping half a mile past it.[1]

Harry Kendall, serving with King Edward's Horse in the Poperinghe area about this time, recalled that many of the troops noticed how regularly the shells arrived just as a train was approaching, and many suspected the civilian stationmaster; Kendall claimed he was later shot as a traitor.

Leaving the station by the main entrance, cross the square in front onto Ieperstraat, the main road that runs from left to right.

This was known as Rue d'Ypres in 1914 and there were cafés and restaurants here during the war, and many local photographers offering cheap portraits and group photographs. A few shops existed, but low pay in the British army meant that the average Tommy could rarely afford any luxuries. Some of these houses in this street were used as billets in the early part of the war, and the occupants were not always accommodating to their allies. Lieutenant Colonel John Humphrey, the Town Major of Poperinghe, recorded in July 1915, that 'Monsieur Emile, Rue d'Ypres, complains of damage done to his property by British

The main square, Poperinghe, 1914.

soldiers billeted there – statue broken 75F, crockery 25F; forwarded a claim to APM V Corps.'[2] He also recorded that prostitutes were active at No 51 in the same street, one being forcibly evacuated on 20th July 1915 because of venereal disease. In September a house at No 94 was broken into and 170 bottles of alcohol stolen; the culprits, whether civilian or military, were never discovered!

In Ieperstraat **turn left** towards the centre of Poperinghe, but take the **first road on the right**, Prootstraat. This is only a short road. At the end **turn left** onto Bruggestraat and follow it for some distance past a small square set back from the road, on the left. After this the street becomes Guido Gezellestraat. A little way further on the town hall building is on the left. Follow the signposted entrance into the main courtyard.

The Town Hall is at the heart of Poperinghe and it was here that a number of soldiers sentenced to death, following a Field General Court Martial (FGCM), were executed. The courtyard was arranged with a sandbagged wall at one end and a wooden execution post placed in front. A firing party then carried out the sentence, usually at dawn, with an officer on hand to implement the 'coup de grace' with a service revolver if death was not instantaneous. Standing to one side was a chaplain with a burial party, and a medical officer to pronounce that life was extinct and issue a death certificate. Considering this courtyard is only a short distance from the main square, troops in, and coming to and from, Poperinghe would have certainly heard what was going on. But perhaps this was all part of the 'for the sake of example' process these executions were meant to perform? Wilfred Saint-Mande, in his fictionalised memoirs *War, Wine and Women*, recalled a typical FGCM and execution near here in 1916:

> One night a private lost his nerve as we were going up to the trenches with ammunition, rations and stores. The shelling was too much for him, and he disappeared into the darkness . . . nothing was heard of him for fourteen days; he was then arrested at le Havre wearing civilian clothes. The military policemen who caught him said he was hanging about at the docks, trying to sneak on a ship bound for England.
>
> The scene in court was impressive, and I had a foreboding that he was doomed . . . He had enlisted in the first days of the war at the age of eighteen and had been in many fierce engagements. However, according to military law the crime was clear and so was the penalty . . . The prisoner was sentenced to death and the sentence was carried out at dawn a few days later. We formed up in a large square and the prisoner had to be dragged to a post in the middle of the ground. He was gagged and bound before being blindfolded. The firing party looked stern and grim. . . . After the wretch had been tied to the post his hands kept twitching and his limbs trembled . . . An officer dropped a handkerchief and the volley rang out.[3]

The first British execution took place at Poperinghe in 1916, and the last in 1919 when a soldier of the Chinese Labour Corps was shot for murder. For many years an original execution post was on display in this courtyard, encased in plastic but with bullet holes and bloodstains grimly visible.[4] However, this was replaced with a new memorial to those executed on this spot, which stands in a different location from where the executions actually took place.

Go back to the courtyard entrance. On the left is the door to the so-called 'death cells'. These were ancient cells attached to the town hall and used by the local police. The British army took them over during the Great War, and they became holding pens for soldiers arrested in Poperinghe before being either moved on for trial, returned to their battalion or sent on to a proper military prison. It is also believed that several men executed in the courtyard were detained here at some point prior to their trial, but it is unlikely any were kept here immediately prior to execution, although information panels here claim otherwise. The cells are now restored and on the walls is a great deal of original graffiti from men held prisoner here, now protected behind plastic. In the right-hand cell there is some very crude American 'artwork' from when the 27th and 30th (US) Divisions were here in 1918 but this cell is closed and part of a 'sound and light' show.

Leave the cells and return to Guido Gezellestraat. Turn left and follow the wall of the town hall into the main square. To your left, in the basement of the town hall itself, is the local tourist office (Tel: 057 34 66 76). As at Ypres, all the staff speak very good English and are happy to provide information about the town or answer any queries. You can also pick up good tourist information on the local area and Poperinghe's role in the Great War.

French cavalry passing through Poperinghe in 1915.

Go back into the square and cross to the other side. There are several bars and restaurants, if needed. One to the left was known as 'A La Poupée', a famous officers' only bar during the war where it was said that more champagne corks were popping than shells falling on Poperinghe! Outside is a new memorial to 'Ginger', the daughter of the owner. Ginger was actually Mademoiselle Eliane Cassey. Edward Campion Vaughan recalled her in 1917:

> The two rooms were full of diners but we found a table in the glass-roofed garden. A sweet little sixteen-year-old girl came to serve us. I fell a victim at once to her long red hair and flashing smile. When I asked her name, she replied 'Gingair' in such a glib way that we both gave a burst of laughter. We had a splendid dinner with several bottles of bubbly, and Ginger hovered delightfully about us.[5]

197

Poperinghe, 1914.

Elie Cassey kept La Poupée open after the war and it became a favourite location for inter-war battlefield visitors. She even ran trips out to the battlefield sites from Poperinghe. She died aged only 42 in London, having emigrated to Britain just before the Second World War. This new memorial now recalls one of the town's most celebrated young ladies!

From the square take the road to the left of a large café called De La Paix and go into Gasthuisstraat. Follow it for several hundred yards to a building **on the right**, signposted Talbot House.

Perhaps the most famous building in Flanders, Talbot House was a Belgian town house acquired in 1915 by two 6th Division chaplains, the Revd Neville Talbot and the Revd P.B. 'Tubby' Clayton. They set to work with men from the 16th Battalion London Regiment (Queen's Westminster Rifles), creating an oasis out of the front line for men billeted in or passing through Poperinghe. It was named after Clayton's friend and Neville's brother – Lieutenant Gilbert Talbot of the Rifle Brigade, who fell at Hooge in 1915 – and opened soon after his death. An early sign placed by the entrance warned visitors to 'abandon rank all ye who enter' and both officers and men mixed freely inside. There was a library, a cinema in the cellar showing Charlie Chaplin films, a concert hall, quiet rooms for relaxation and letter writing, and even rooms available for those given leave but having nowhere to go or not wanting to return to England. Notice boards where soldiers could leave details of their name and unit helped friends and brothers stay in touch. In the hop loft was a chapel, the altar made from an old carpenter's bench, where over 20,000 soldiers attended services between 1915 and 1918. The genesis of the Toc-H organisation started here, and throughout the war Tubby Clayton stayed with his beloved house. However, in 1919 the owner returned and it went back to being a residential dwelling. Toc-H recovered the building again ten years later when Lord Wakefield bought it for what became the Talbot House Association. It has remained open ever since, and during the Second World War many of its treasures were hidden by the local population.

Today Talbot House (www.talbothouse.be) has museum status and entrance is gained not via the front door but by a new entrance on Pottestraat, down the **first road** on the right past the house. Here you enter a Behind The Lines museum which tells the story of life out of the trenches and the history of Talbot House. The museum is located in what was the concert hall at Talbot House, where it is said comedians Flanagan and Allen first performed together in 1917. You can then visit the garden and finally go into the main house where you can see the reconstruction of 'Tubby's Room' and take the long climb to the hop loft chapel ('The Upper Room'), preserved as it was during the war. The original carpenter's bench is still there, and a roll of honour records men confirmed in the chapel who later fell in action. The original cross from Gilbert Talbot's grave is on the wall, and another cross from an unknown soldier's grave hangs above the altar. The atmosphere in this place of tranquillity is like no other, and we must all be grateful to Toc-H for allowing continued access to it. The museum area has a shop and it is

The 'Upper Room' in Talbot House.

also worth remembering that rooms are still available at Talbot House for those visiting the battlefields. These are only available on a self-catering basis but are extremely popular. Volunteer wardens look after the house and are always on hand to make a cup of tea and have a chat, and they really help make a visit to this very special corner of Flanders Fields.

Leaving the house, return to Gasthuis-straat and turn right. Further up, on the right, is a building made from light brown brick, with white framed windows. It used to have a 'Hotel Skindles' sign above the main door, but this has now been removed.

Hotel Skindles was a famous restaurant and club frequented by officers during the Great War. This is not the original, which was located in Rue du Nord (now Casselstraat), but one that opened in the 1920s and was used by pilgrims to the battlefields between the wars. It closed many years ago and is now a local business, and should be respected as such. Skindles was originally the Hotel de la Bourse du Houblon. It got its wartime name

Wartime concert party.

from an officer of the Rifle Brigade who, in June 1916, remarked to a friend over a plate of egg and chips, accompanied by a bottle of wine, that it was as good as a pub called Skindles in Maidenhead. The name stuck and the three rooms on the ground floor were always full.

Continue along this street and follow as it bends left, then take the first road on the left, Priesterstraat. Follow it to the end and continue on the road that circles the church on your left. Just before the town hall is a road to the right, Ieperstraat, signposted for Ieper. Take this and follow it back to the railway station. This walk takes about twenty minutes.

FOLLOW UP VISITS
There are a number of interesting military cemeteries in and around Poperinghe, but two are particularly important and should be visited as a follow-up to this walk.

POPERINGHE NEW MILITARY CEMETERY
This cemetery is in Poperinghe itself, located just off the main ring road in Deken De Bolaan opposite the road to Reninghelst. It is well

signposted. There is parking in a lay-by outside the cemetery, or by a shop opposite.

While Poperinghe grew as a British military base, soldiers who died in the medical establishments or whose bodies were brought back from the line were buried in the communal cemetery on the Reninghelst road. This became known as the Old Cemetery and was started during First Ypres in 1914. Graves were added until May 1915, when a New Military Cemetery was opened on this site in June and remained in use until the end of the war. There were no post-war concentrations of graves into the cemetery, and the total burials number: 596 British, fifty-five Canadian, twenty Australian, three New Zealand, two British West Indies, one Chinese Labour Corps and three unknowns. A separate plot for French and Belgian soldiers is adjacent to the cemetery.

Today Poperinghe New Military Cemetery is frequently visited because of its connections with the executions that took place in and around the town during the Great War. Buried here are seventeen soldiers executed for various military crimes which fell under the main categories of cowardice and desertion. Their stories are well related in *Shot At Dawn*, and readers are directed to that publication for further information.

Visitors should remember that there are others buried in the cemetery, who are also worthy of consideration. Senior officers are numerous. Lieutenant Colonel G.H. Baker (II-G-1) died of wounds on 2nd June 1916, aged thirty-eight. Commanding the 5th Canadian Mounted Rifles,

Indian troops in Poperinghe.

OORLOG 1914-1915 — Indianen te Poperinghe.
Indiens à Poperinghe.
Indians in Poperinghe.

Visé, Paris N.° 43   UITGEVER-Sansen Vannesten, Poperinghe

he was mortally wounded during the German attacks on Hill 62. The son of a member of the Senate of Canada, he himself was a member of the Canadian House of Commons. Lieutenant Colonel R.V. Doherty-Howell DSO (II-B-12) was a senior Sapper; Assistant Director of Army Signals of VIII Corps, he was killed near Ypres on 9th January 1917. A titled senior officer was Lieutenant Colonel Sir R.B.N. Gunter (II-H-21) of the Yorkshire Regiment, a Regular army soldier who died of wounds on 16th August 1917, aged forty-six. Lieutenant Colonel H.S. Smith DSO (I-E-23) was another Regular, aged forty-seven, who was killed commanding the 1st Battalion Leicestershire Regiment on 22nd October 1915. In addition there are eleven officers with the rank of Major in this cemetery. Captain H.H. Maclean MC (II-G-35), a Highland Light Infantry officer serving as Brigade Major to 153rd Brigade, was 'killed in action by shell-fire with his own GOC' on 29th July 1917. His GOC was Brigadier General A.F. Gordon CMG DSO, who is buried in Lijssenthoek cemetery; see below.

Family tragedies are also evident. Private G. Ryan (II-C-8) died of wounds received in a gas attack on the 2nd Hampshires at Potijze on 9th August 1916. The register records that 'his brother, Pte H. Ryan, was also killed on the same day'. Among the many RE tunnellers in the cemetery is Lieutenant E.J. Maxwell-Stuart (I-B-29). From Arundel in Sussex, he was killed with the 175th Tunnelling Company on 26th April 1916, being 'one of four brothers killed in the war'.

LIJSSENTHOEK MILITARY CEMETERY

To reach this cemetery take the Poperinghe ring road and make a left-hand turn south-west of the town following signs for Abeele, or Abele. This road eventually crosses the border into France. Follow it before that for a few kilometres, and take a minor road to the left following a green CWGC signpost for the cemetery. At a crossroads, with a café on your left, turn right and continue along this road to the parking area in the Visitors Centre on the right just before the cemetery.

The main road you used to get here was at one time a railway line which ran from Hazebrouck in France to Poperinghe. During the war it was a main arterial route for British soldiers coming to and from the Salient, and branch lines were tapped off to camps and depots. One ran to a small farm complex, still visible to the rear of the cemetery, which the British called Remi Farm or Remi Sidings. RAMC casualty clearing stations were established at Remi in June 1915, and remained in use until the spring of 1918, when long-range shell-fire forced them further back. Field Ambulances then took over, from both the British and French forces operating in Flanders at that time. Twenty-four soldiers, now in Plot

Lijssenthoek Military Cemetery, 1919.

Airmen's graves at Lijssenthoek.

Chinese Labour Corps graves at Lijssenthoek.

Poperinghe 1920 - Cimetière '' Remy '' Kerkhof.

Le coin des travailleurs Chinois.
Het hoekje der Chineesche werkers.
The corner of the Chinese workers.

American graves at Lijssenthoek. These were removed in the 1920s.

The entrance to the Remi Siding CCS.

XXXI, were brought in from isolated locations near Poperinghe after the war. These were the only concentrations. Burials total:

British	7,350
Australian	1,131
Canadian	1,053
French	658
New Zealand	291
German	223
Chinese Labour Corps	32

Next to Tyne Cot, this is the largest British military cemetery in Flanders, and it gives the visual impression of being much bigger. It is arguably a much more important cemetery than Tyne Cot, as all but twenty-two of the men buried here are known; at Tyne Cot most are unknowns. Lijssenthoek therefore represents a good cross-section of not only the type of men who served in the Ypres Salient, but also the types of units and men that made up the army as a whole.

Given the variation and scope of the units in this cemetery, it is quite possible that every rank in the army up to major general is represented on a headstone. Indeed, senior officers are particularly noticeable, with one Major General, three Brigadier Generals and sixteen Lieutenant Colonels. Major General M.S. Mercer CB (VI-A-38) was the most senior Canadian officer to die at Ypres; he was mortally wounded commanding 3rd (Canadian) Division at Hill 62 on 3rd June 1916. Brigadier General A.F. Gordon CMG DSO (XIV-A-13) was a Gordon Highlander officer of many years' service who had been wounded at Festubert in May 1915. On 29th July 1917 he was inspecting the assembly trenches of his brigade, the 153rd of 51st (Highland) Division, which had been dug for the forthcoming Third Ypres offensive. A shell fell close by, killing his Brigade Major, Captain MacLean (see Poperinghe New Military Cemetery; above), and mortally wounding Gordon, who died in the 10th CCS on 31st July 1917, just as his men were going over the top. Of the Lieutenant Colonels, one was said to be the last British officer to die in the Salient. Lieutenant Colonel G.E. Beatty-Pownall DSO (XXX-B-14) died of wounds on 10th October 1918 while commanding the 1st Battalion King's Own Scottish Borderers.

A Victoria Cross winner is also buried here. Major F.H. Tubb VC (XIX-C-5) was one of the first Australians to win the VC. While serving as a Lieutenant in the 7th Battalion Australian Infantry at Lone Pine, Gallipoli, in August 1915, he repulsed a Turkish counter-attack, despite being seriously wounded in the head and arm. After recovery he returned to the 7th Battalion, serving on the Somme and at Ypres, and was mortally wounded in the fighting around Polygon Wood on 20th September 1917.

There are many other interesting characters in the cemetery. Private J. Gaspe (VIII-B-17A) died on 25th June 1916 while serving with the 20th Battalion Canadian Infantry. His father was chief of the Iroquois tribe of Canadian Indians. Captain Atherton Harold Chisenhale-Marsh (XXV-H-27) was an old Etonian who joined the 9th Lancers in 1914 and served with them in the famous charge at Audregnies where Lieutenant Grenfell was awarded the VC (see Vlamertinghe Cemetery in the Behind The Lines Walk). He came to the Salient in 1915 and fought on the Frezenberg Ridge. By 1918 he was a staff officer in the 34th Division and died of wounds received near Wytschaete on 28th September 1918. Captain W.A.M. Temple (XXXI-D-19) was the son of Colonel W. Temple VC RAMC, who had been awarded the coveted medal in the New Zealand Wars of 1863. Temple junior, a forty-two year old Captain in the 1st Battalion Gloucestershire Regiment, died of wounds on 21st October 1914.

Captain A.H. Chisenhale-Marsh.

Staff Nurse Nellie Spindler (XVI-A-3), of Queen Alexandra's Imperial Nursing Service, is the only woman buried at Lijssenthoek. She was killed on 21st August 1917 while attached to 44th Casualty Clearing Station at Brandhoek – probably the only woman killed that close to the front at Ypres. The CCS *War Diary* records what happened:

> Yesterday morning the enemy began to shell the railway alongside the camp and with the third or fourth shell killed S/Nurse N. Spindler. She was hit in the chest and died in about five minutes.[6]

Staff Nurse Nellie Spindler.

Four other nurses were concussed by the same shell burst, and as a consequence of these events 44th CCS evacuated all its nurses the next day to St Omer. It also moved back to Remi Sidings, where the officers and men from the unit held a burial service for Nurse Spindler. The diary records that during the chaos of the bombardment the nursing sisters 'behaved splendidly' and one of them, Sister M. Wood, was subsequently awarded a Military Medal for her bravery that day. She is one of only a handful of women to win the MM during the Great War.

The buildings of Remi Farm are at the rear of the cemetery. They are on private land and can only be visited with the permission of the owner. British and French graffiti is evident on the farm walls in several places.

A Visitors Centre opened at Lijssenthoek in 2012 and tells the story of the cemetery and follows the stories of several hundred men and women buried here, from all nations and all backgrounds. There are toilets here and parking, and the cemetery is accessed from the Centre on foot, following a marked path.

Notes

1. Williamson, H. *The Wet Flanders Plain* (Faber & Faber 1929) p.36.
2. Town Major Poperinghe *War Diary*, 2.7.15, TNA WO95/4042.
3. Saint-Mande, W. *War, Wine and Women* (Cassell 1931) pp.271–3.
4. For further information on executions see Putkowski, J. and Sykes, J. *Shot At Dawn* (Pen & Sword 1989, new edition 1998).
5. 'The Story of Gorgeous Ginger' website, last accessed 18th December 2015, www.users. telenet.be/aandeschreve/ginger.htm.
6. 44th Casualty Clearing Station RAMC *War Diary*, 21.8.17, TNA WO95/345.

The Flanders battlefield in 1917.

Chapter Eleven

Locre – Kemmel Walk

STARTING POINT: Outside Locre Church
GPS: 50°46′56.2″N, 2°46′18.6″E
DISTANCE: 10.5km/6.5 miles

WALK SUMMARY: *Suitable for the more experienced walker, this walk follows a pleasant route across the Flanders countryside in an area that was behind the lines for most of the war, and climbs Kemmel Hill – one of the highest points on the Ypres battlefield and affording spectacular views of the Salient.*

Leave your vehicle in one of the parking bays outside Locre (now Loker) church. There are several shops and cafés in the village. War graves in the churchyard are visible to the left of the main entrance.

Locre village was located several miles behind the front line after the stalemate of trench warfare set in following First Ypres in 1914. It was a main route up to the trenches in the Messines Ridge sector, and was used for billeting battalions going to and from these positions. RAMC Field

The village of Locre in 1914.

LOCRE — La Douane Belge

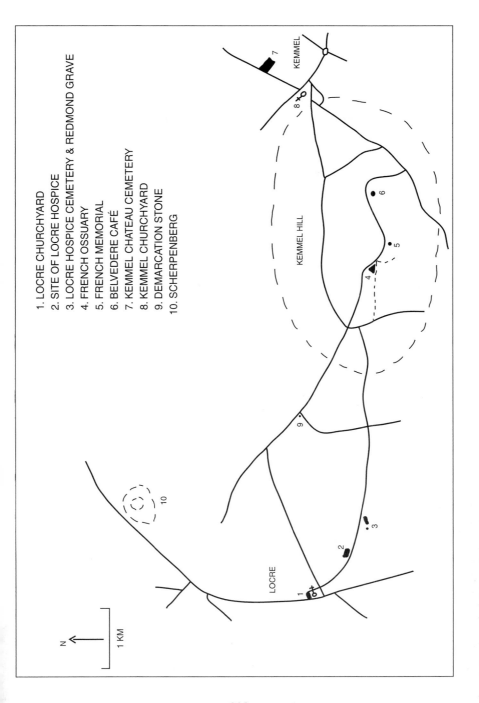

1. LOCRE CHURCHYARD
2. SITE OF LOCRE HOSPICE
3. LOCRE HOSPICE CEMETERY & REDMOND GRAVE
4. FRENCH OSSUARY
5. FRENCH MEMORIAL
6. BELVEDERE CAFÉ
7. KEMMEL CHATEAU CEMETERY
8. KEMMEL CHURCHYARD
9. DEMARCATION STONE
10. SCHERPENBERG

KEMMEL

KEMMEL HILL

LOCRE

N

1 KM

Locre church, 1915.

Ambulances also set up an advanced dressing station here and artillery units had gun sites in the fields and valleys nearby. What had started as a pretty Flemish village was soon turned to rubble by the cruel hand of war. Private Donald Fraser of the 31st Battalion Canadian Infantry came to Locre in October 1915 and found it weary after a year of war, but not untypical of many locations behind the lines:

The village is dirty and the buildings seem old and unsanitary. The inside of the houses are bare and untidy. What pictures or ornaments there are, are usually emblematic of Catholicism. The people themselves are unkempt. Most of them have a smattering of English picked up from the soldiers and often use swear words not knowing what they mean. The troops air their French which usually amounts to madam, café, compres [sic], oui and a few other words. A conversation between a soldier and a Belgian is very amusing. Every third word is punctuated with 'compres' [sic] and 'oui' with gesticulations.[1]

As the war continued, the number of men requiring billets far outstripped the number of suitable buildings in Locre, and around the village vast military camps were constructed, on similar lines to those between Poperinghe and Ypres. Some took the form of huge tented areas, others were more permanent, with wooden buildings or Nissen huts. Each one was named, and marked on trench maps; several here were called after famous battles of the Crimean war. Fighting finally came to Locre in April 1918 when the Germans launched their spring offensive in Flanders, recapturing Messines Ridge and taking Kemmel Hill. French troops were brought up to support the British, and the line was finally held just outside the village.

LOCRE CHURCHYARD
Burials in the churchyard are split into two plots; one here, and another on the opposite side of the church. It was used by Field Ambulances and fighting units from December 1914 until the Battle of Messines in June 1917. Between the two plots are 184 British and thirty-one Canadian graves; two of them are unknowns. The use of this area by artillery units means that they are well represented; in one row alone are six men of the same artillery battery all killed on the same day in May 1917.

The grave of Second Lieutenant C. Hawdon (I-D-6) records a family tragedy; the inscription reads 'His two brothers also fell. In death they are not divided.' Hawdon died on 27th June 1916, aged twenty-two, while serving with the Yorkshire Regiment. His brothers both died in November 1918; one was an army chaplain. In the next row is Bugler J.H. Weatherall (I-E-1), who was killed with 6th Battalion Durham Light Infantry on 13th July 1915. The Canadian graves are largely from early 1916, among them two majors buried side by side: Major W.H. Belyea (I-E-12), 26th Battalion Canadian Infantry, was killed on 20th March 1916, aged thirty-nine. Three days later, on 23rd March, Major W. Bates (I-E-13) of 25th Battalion was also killed, and buried here.

211

An 'Old Bill Bus' bringing troops to the front near Kemmel in 1915.

Leave this part of the churchyard by the gate and go onto the road in front of the church, turning left and going round to the other side. More war graves are seen at the back.

These are earlier graves from the 1914–15 period and they include many Territorial battalions which were amongst the first of the 'Saturday Night Soldiers' to come to Flanders. Among them are burials from, for example, the Honourable Artillery Company and the 10th Battalion Liverpool Regiment (Liverpool Scottish), whose medical officer at this time was Captain Noel Chavasse; he later won the VC and bar. A young soldier is Private Frank Eke of the Devonshire Regiment, who was killed on 28th March 1915, aged sixteen. Young Frank had only been at the front for a few weeks when he was killed.

Return to the road in front of the church and **go left**. On the left is the village war memorial. Close by is a French memorial to the 2nd Brigade of Light Cavalry, which fought here alongside the British in April 1918. Continue past it and **turn left** at the Kemmel sign. Then take the **first right** down Godtschalckstraat. There are good views towards

All that remained of Locre in 1918.

Kemmel Hill as you come out of the built-up area. Continue and go past a large building resembling a hospital; this is the new Locre Hospice; there is an information panel by the road in front of it. The site of the original is further along this road, on a bend with a military cemetery in the fields to your right. There is an old brick gatepost on the left, now an entrance to a field.

This was the site of the original Locre Hospice, which comprised a large group of brick buildings. One wing was taken over by the RAMC, which established an ADS here that remained in use until 1918. The nuns who lived in the hospice provided meals for British officers during the war, and the complex housed many refugees from Ypres, who made lace while the fighting was going on less than two miles away. Several soldiers were at one time buried in the grounds, but their graves were removed after the war. The Hospice was destroyed by shell-fire in April 1918, when it became part of the front line after the Germans captured Kemmel Hill.

Stay on the road; a path to the cemetery soon appears on your right, just past a house. Follow this path to the cemetery.

LOCRE HOSPICE CEMETERY

Started by Field Ambulances which used Locre Hospice during the Battle of Messines in June 1917, the cemetery remained open until April 1918, when this area became part of the front line. Four graves from the hospice itself were moved here after the war and now there are 255 British burials along with two Australian, one Canadian, one New Zealander and two Germans. Two senior officers lie in the cemetery: Brigadier General R.C. MacLachlain DSO (II-C-9) of the Rifle Brigade, who was killed commanding the 112th Brigade on 11th August 1917, aged forty-five; and Lieutenant Colonel R.C. Chester-Master DSO and bar, a battalion commander who was killed by a sniper while serving with the 13th Battalion King's Royal Rifle Corps on 30th August 1917, aged

Lieutenant Colonel R.C. Chester-Master DSO.

forty-seven. Known in the regiment as 'The Squire', Chester-Master was from an old Gloucestershire family. He had commanded the 13th Battalion since March 1915, and had served on the Somme, at Arras and at Ypres.

A path to the right side of the cemetery leads to the isolated grave of Major William Redmond MP. He was an Irish Nationalist Member of

Major Willie Redmond MP.

Contemporary
illustration of Willie
Redmond marching with
his men to the front.

A very faded but rare image of Willie Redmond's grave and one of the nuns
who tended it. (*Mike Stockbridge*)

Willie Redmond's grave today.

Parliament who was really too old for military service, but through his contacts had secured a commission in the 6th Battalion Royal Irish Regiment. He died of wounds received in the attack on Wytschaete on 7th June 1917, his first major action. Originally his grave was in the garden of Locre Hospice, and it is still flanked by two stones from the old hospice buildings. The grave was moved to this spot after the war and it remains one of only a few in Flanders where the original grave marker still remains.

Return to the road via the grass path and turn right in the direction of Kemmel Hill. At the first crossroads continue straight on, and at the second turn right. Then, opposite a building on the right, take a winding track uphill on the left. This brings you to the lower slopes of Kemmel Hill.

Almost at the end of this track, on the left, is an illustrative orientation panel that supplements the commanding view you have from here. Even before reaching the summit, you can already, particularly on a clear day, see as far as Poperinghe, and to the south the Lorette spur near Arras and close to Vimy Ridge in Northern France. The importance of high ground in the flatlands of Flanders is very apparent here. Just up the track where it meets the road is the FRENCH OSSUARY. French troops were fighting at Kemmel in April 1918 and this mass grave

The view to Kemmel Hill in 1919.

An old dugout on
Kemmel Hill, 1919.

The ruins of the Belvedere
Café in 1919.

commemorates 5,294 'Poilus' who died in the 'violent combat around Ypres', as the memorial proclaims. Of this number only fifty-seven are identified. Take time to sign the visitors' book as this cemetery receives few visitors compared to British ones.

From the ossuary gates go straight up the cobbled road ahead of you, which will lead to the crest of Kemmel Hill. On the way is another French memorial to the fighting of April 1918. Follow the road for a few hundred yards to a café-restaurant on the right, noticing signs of trenches and shell holes amongst the trees as you progress.

This is the Belvedere Café, which makes a good stop for liquid refreshment, although meals tend to be a little on the heavy side for most walkers. The huge tower to the rear of the building replaced one that was here before 1914 and was used as an observation post by British officers during the war. On the edge of the car park, in an area clear of trees, is another illustrative orientation panel which overlooks the area from Ypres to Messines.

It was up these slopes that the battle for Kemmel Hill took place in April 1918. During Ludendorff's spring offensive in Flanders, the dominating position of Kemmel Hill was one of the key objectives for

Some of the defenders of Kemmel Hill in April 1918: officers and NCOs of the 19th Lancashire Fusiliers.

the Germans. A determined attack on the hill was made on 17th April and repulsed, with a similar story two days later. By this time the German advance appeared to be faltering, and most of the line was handed over to a French Corps which occupied positions from Kemmel to Messines. The 9th (Scottish) Division, however, remained in the sector. On 25th April a further German attack came which swamped the French positions, and at one point the 12th Battalion Royal Scots suddenly found German troops 2,000 yards behind their right flank. With the French pushed back, the hill was finally captured by the Germans. Next day the weary 25th Division made a counter-attack which reached Kemmel village, but the French had failed on their flank and they withdrew. The line settled down between Locre and Kemmel, until American troops from the 27th and 30th (US) Divisions took over the positions here in September 1918. Fighting at that time finally returned the hill to Allied hands.

From the car park go downhill for a short distance and then turn left onto a track. This leads to a junction of the tracks which run across the hill; take the right-hand track, again going downhill. This track eventually meets a minor road; here turn right and then continue to the main road where you turn left and follow it into Kemmel village, and the main square with its bandstand. There are several shops and cafés here; in particular 'Het Labyrint' combines food and drink with a fascinating array of antiques, old toys and archaeological artefacts. It is well worth visiting if you have the time. Also in the main square is the local tourist office.

Kemmel, like Locre, was a village that remained behind the British lines for most of the war. Nearer the trenches, battalions were billeted in the farms and buildings here, and there were headquarters in the main houses and also in a large chateau, set in an elaborate park. Medical units also established an advanced dressing station near the chateau and several cemeteries grew up as a consequence. Thousands of soldiers passed through Kemmel during the Great War, and many have left their impressions of it. In the winter of 1914/15 Captain G.A. Burgoyne spent several months here with the 2nd Battalion Royal Irish Rifles. He described a typical billet:

> The reserve are in a fine farm, the buildings run three sides of a square, in the centre of which is the usual stinking midden and pond. The roof has been blown in over the living rooms, but we occupy the kitchen . . . We've now installed the Flemish stove taken from the ruined sitting room, and it keeps the room a little warm . . . The men are in a huge loft, and in the barn on the west side of the square where there is plenty of hay and flax to lie on.[2]

Kemmel village in 1914.

He also recalled the village itself at that time:

> Took a walk around Kemmel town this morning. I don't think that
> out of a town of some 4,800 inhabitants there is one house quite
> intact and undamaged by shrapnel, and half the place is in ruins,
> blown down completely. We passed one building, the front of
> which is completely wrecked. The wretched occupier has partly
> blocked up the frameless windows with bricks, above which one
> can see a shattered interior. However, outside the door hung a pig;
> inside we saw portions of the other half, a plate of apples and a
> few other things on sale. There are some dozen shops of sorts
> where bread, butter, candles, chocolates and sweets . . . can be
> bought, and milk and eggs can be easily obtained . . . The interior
> of the church is smothered in masonry dust. A shell has pierced
> the chancel behind the High Altar and shattered it, and littered the
> chancel with debris . . . A lot of the stained glass windows are
> shattered with shrapnel. It is remarkable that the Christ on the
> outside wall of the church is quite untouched, though a shell burst
> at the foot of the cross and the wall all round is pitted with
> shrapnel.[3]

Stories of spying also dominated life in these villages in the early part
of the war and Burgoyne noted that in January 1915 two locals were
found manipulating the hands of the church clock – seemingly signalling
to the Germans – and were discovered by men of the Northumberland

219

5 KEMMEL. — Le Château. — Château de M. Bruncel de Montveliier, bourgmestre de Kemmel.
Ancien Château féodal, a été récemment artistiquement restauré   Edition Grignet

Kemmel Chateau in 1914.

Fusiliers who shot them. He also recorded that an officer of the Honourable Artillery Company occupied a billet in Kemmel, which the French had used as a dressing station earlier in the war. One room contained a macabre collection of amputated arms and legs, thrown there in a pile by the orderlies following operations on badly wounded French soldiers.

Despite being behind the lines, Kemmel was often shelled by long-range guns, and on 4th June 1915 two lieutenant colonels became casualties. They were using the old doctor's house as a billet when:

> Colonel Jessop, of the 4th Lincolnshires, was talking to Colonel Jones [5th Leicesters] in the road outside the house, while an orderly held two horses close by. The first shell fell almost on the party, killing Colonel Jessop, the two orderlies . . . and both horses. Colonel Jones was wounded in the hand, neck and thigh.[4]

Jessop and the orderlies were taken back to Dranoutre for burial, and their graves can be found in the cemetery there.

By the end of 1915 there were fewer civilians in the village, and even more damage had been done to it. The Canadians had by this time taken over the sector east of Kemmel and among them was Private Donald Fraser of the 31st Battalion Canadian Infantry, who left this description:

Kemmel, in peace time one of the loveliest and most frequented spots in Belgium, was, when we entered it, in a badly battered condition. Still there was quite a number of civilians and several stores were in operation. The town pump, situated in the centre of the square, was intact and from it we replenished our water supply. A fairly elaborate hostel, called the Maison Communale, was doing business as usual; a rather prepossessing young girl of about fifteen dispensing drinks to both soldiers and civilians. Lower down was the Ypres Hotel of doubtful repute. The Brewery, or Brasserie as it is locally called, seemed to be the outstanding industrial establishment though at this time it had ceased activities.[5]

From the main square go south on Polenlaan to a junction opposite a Spar shop. Here **turn left** and continue to the steps in front of the church; now take the road opposite on the right, Nieuwstraat. This was known as Sackville Street during the war and leads to a military cemetery further up on the right.

KEMMEL CHATEAU CEMETERY
The original chateau was located in the park to the rear of this cemetery. It was owned by the son-in-law of the famous Hennessy brandy family, and Private Donald Fraser found it in November 1915 a 'magnificent and imposing turreted building surrounded by a moat, crossed by a little suspension bridge'. During the war it at various stages housed brigade and divisional headquarters, and the RAMC set up an advanced dressing station in the chateau grounds. The cemetery was started in December

Kemmel Chateau Cemetery in 1919, showing the original wooden crosses.

1914, and used by front-line units burying their dead. The RAMC added to it when soldiers died of wounds, as did units in the trenches opposite Wytschaete when they suffered casualties. The cemetery remained in use until March 1918 – the area being taken by the Germans in April – and was partially damaged by shell-fire in later fighting. In total there are 1,030 British graves, with eighty Canadian, twenty-four Australian, and one New Zealander.

The cemetery has a distinct 'regimental' feel with, for example, sixty-six graves out of ninety-five in Row E belonging to men of the Sherwood Foresters, largely the 1/8th Battalion from April/May 1915. Fifty-eight of the eighty-three soldiers in Row N are from Irish regiments, who are well represented in the whole cemetery. Canadian burials abound in Row K, and the 2nd Battalion Royal Scots have a large plot in Row E; eight of them died on 21st April 1915, one of them a seventeen year old soldier, Private A. Darrock (E-17).

There is a very high proportion of officers in this cemetery, with company commanders, adjutants, medical officers and battalion commanders among them. Of the latter, Lieutenant Colonel G.L.B. Du Maurier DSO (L-4) has a well-known name, being an uncle of writer Daphne Du Maurier. He died commanding the 3rd Battalion Royal Fusiliers on 9th March 1915, and his death was noted by Captain Burgoyne in his diaries:

> Just heard over the telephone from Brigade Head Quarters that Colonel Du Maurier . . . was killed this morning by a shell which blew up Alston House, the old farm which is always used as Battalion Head Quarters when the Battalion is in the trenches . . . He was the author of 'An Englishman's Home', the brother of Gerald Du Maurier and the son of the artist . . . I hear . . . he had just ordered everyone out and into dugouts outside and was waiting in the house for his Sergeant-Major to report that everyone was in safety before he took cover himself.[6]

Du Maurier was a long-service officer and was forty-nine years old when he died. He had fought in both the Burmese and South African Wars.

Kemmel was often the home of Tunnelling Company units operating beneath the Messines Ridge and in 1916 Major Cropper's 250th Tunnelling Company was here. Under the battlefield near Petit Bois one of their tunnels was collapsed by an enemy charge and only one man escaped, Sapper William Henry Bedson. Those who did not survive are buried in Row D. Their bodies were recovered when the rescue party got to the collapsed section and found only one man alive:

Kemmel in 1919.

This man, Sapper Bedson, told how the entombed men had collected at the broken end of the gallery, where a little air was coming through the air pipe which they had disconnected. They then began by turns to dig their way out. This effort they soon abandoned and spaced themselves along the gallery. Gradually, however, they were overcome by the foul air, and in three days all but one were dead. Bedson, however, was an experienced miner. He avoided the broken end, where heavy air accumulated, and lay by the face, which was a little higher. He comforted himself by the reflection that a party of coal miners were entombed for thirteen days and then rescued alive.

He kept his head marvellously. His only food consisted of two army biscuits and a bottle of water. He dare not eat the biscuits nor drink the water. From time to time he rinsed out his mouth with water and returned it to the bottle. To keep himself warm he improvised a suit from sandbags. Every night he slept on a crude bed made by placing sandbags on a bogie truck, winding up his watch before retiring! And when after six and a half days he was rescued – hauled through a small hole in the broken ground – his first words were: 'For God's sake give me a drink! It's been a damned long shift!' He was taken to the shaft on a mine stretcher placed on a bogie wagon in charge of the M.O. At the shaft he was rested for two hours. During this time his mind was quite clear and he could answer quite sensibly.

Even then Bedson's perils were not all over. As he was being

223

carried down the communication trench he and his stretcher party had the narrowest of escapes from shell-fire![7]

Bedson was a former Yorkshire miner in his late thirties who was married with a large family. He had previously served at Gallipoli before joining the Tunnellers and not only survived this scrape with the war underground, but went home to his family near Rotherham in 1918.

Leaving the cemetery, return towards Kemmel via the same road you used to get here. At the end, opposite the church, cross over and climb the steps into the churchyard. The first plots of war graves are to the right of the entrance.

This is KEMMEL CHURCHYARD. You are in the main plot, with graves scattered elsewhere around the church. Most date from 1914/15, with a few of the 1st Gordons from the attack near Wytschaete on 14th December 1914. Among the officers here is Major G.G.P. Humphreys, of the 127th attached 129th Baluchis, Indian Army. He died of wounds received near Hollebeke on 30th October 1914, aged forty-one. Born in Ireland, he had been commissioned in the Welsh Regiment in 1892. Some years later he transferred to the Indian Army and fought in the Uganda Campaign in 1897, with the China Field Force in 1901 and was present at the Delhi Durbar in 1911. His grandfather had served under Nelson at Copenhagen.

Major G.G.P. Humphreys.

From these graves return towards the main gate, but go past it and follow the path round past the civilian graves and the church. On the other side of the church is the local tourist office, which is worth a visit. Turn left at the Kerkplein sign towards the main square in Kemmel, but as you come out of the churchyard **turn sharp right** following a Camping sign on the right into Lokerstraat. Follow the road uphill, past the entrance to the campsite, and Pingelarestraat, until a wooded area is reached. Here follow signs on the right through the trees and then go down some wooden steps to the left.

These are the Lettenberg Bunkers. Unearthed by local archaeologists, they are structures built of concrete and set into the slopes of the hill. At various stages they were used as headquarters, possibly as a brigade headquarters, and there were medical facilities as well, as an original painted Red Cross on one bunker indicates. The site has been restored and there are information panels that give a good impression of how the whole area was once covered with dugouts, headquarters and medical posts like these.

The battlefield near Kemmel in 1919.

Return via the path to the road and **turn right**. Continue for some distance until you reach a crossroads just past a farm on the right. Here **turn right**, following a road signposted for Loker, and continue.

Further along on the left, where a minor road meets this one, is a DEMARCATION STONE. This is one of several placed in the Salient by the Belgian Touring Club in the early 1920s to 'mark the limit of the German invader', as it proclaims. Here the stone denotes where the front lines settled down after the German spring offensive of April 1918. Although you are in the flatlands below Kemmel Hill, there are good views from here in a north-eastern direction towards Ypres; indeed on a clear day the spires of the Cloth Hall and St Martin's Cathedral can be seen.

Continue along the Loker road to another cross-roads. Stop.

Ahead of you in the distance the ground rises to another hill known as the Scherpenberg. As with much of the ground covered by this walk, the Scherpenberg lay behind British lines until April 1918 and there were many hutted camps close by. Indeed, by these crossroads stood the large Sebastopol Camp and the even larger Leeds Camp. On 25th April 1918 the Germans swept down the slopes of Kemmel Hill in an attempt to capture the Scherpenberg, pushing back the French troops who were then holding this sector. However, the French 39th Division stopped the Germans and the hill was held, the valley between it and Kemmel becoming No Man's Land until September 1918.

At the cross-roads turn left and follow a long straight road back to

A large unexploded German shell near Kemmel in 1919.

Locre. This last part of the journey I find very evocative; this road is so typical of the routes to and from the back areas of Flanders. How many battalions marched up this road to the line, and how many men marched back again afterwards? With these thoughts in mind, Locre is soon reached. The road comes into the village at the rear of the churchyard; follow it round to the front of the church and your vehicle.

Notes

1. Roy, R.H. *The Journal of Private Fraser* (Sono Nis Press 1985) pp.37–8.
2. Burgoyne, G.A. *The Burgoyne Diaries* (Thomas Harmsworth 1985) p.47.
3. ibid. pp.114–15.
4. Hills, J.D. *The Fifth Leicestershire: A Record of the 1/5th Battalion the Leicestershire Regiment TF during the War 1914–1919* (Echo Press 1919) p.34.
5. Roy op cit. p.49.
6. Burgoyne op cit. pp.135–9.
7. Grant Grieve, W. and Newman, B. *Tunnellers* (Herbert Jenkins 1936).

Chapter Twelve

'Whitesheet' Walk

STARTING POINT: Main Square, Wytschaete
GPS: 50°47'08.7"N, 2°52'57.3"E
DISTANCE: 11.6km/7.2 miles

WALK SUMMARY: *An easy walk covering the positions on the Messines Ridge around the village of Wytschaete, known as 'Whitesheet' to British troops. It links well with the Messines Ridge Walk and an experienced walker might even consider doing them together as one long walk. The walk includes a visit to the trenches at Bayernwald: tickets for this need to be purchased in advance at the Kemmel Tourist Office (www.heuvelland.be).*

Wytschaete, or Wijtschate as it is known today, is just off the main Ypres–Armentières road. There is plentiful parking in the main square, or in the road close to the church. There are a few shops here and some cafés.

From the main square go towards the church; just in front of it is a memorial. This commemorates the men of the Tunnelling Companies of the Royal Engineers who worked beneath Flanders Fields in the Messines

Wytschaete Military Cemetery, 1930s.

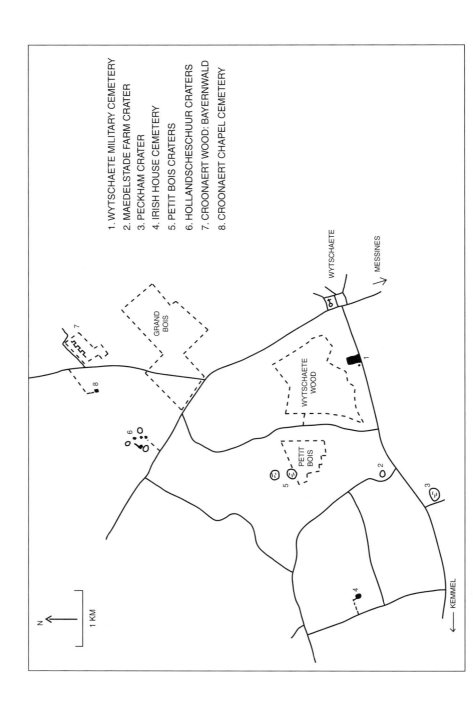

1. WYTSCHAETE MILITARY CEMETERY
2. MAEDELSTADE FARM CRATER
3. PECKHAM CRATER
4. IRISH HOUSE CEMETERY
5. PETIT BOIS CRATERS
6. HOLLANDSCHESCHUUR CRATERS
7. CROONAERT WOOD: BAYERNWALD
8. CROONAERT CHAPEL CEMETERY

GRAND BOIS

WYTSCHAETE WOOD

PETIT BOIS

WYTSCHAETE

MESSINES

KEMMEL

N

1 KM

Ridge sector and were the units responsible for the blowing of nineteen mines along the ridge during the Battle of Messines in June 1917. The memorial is a recent one; as several tunnelling experts have pointed out, the Sapper is holding a standard entrenching tool, a type that was rarely used in the war underground.

Return towards the main square and then **go across to the right** onto Wijtschatestraat. Follow this out of the village until you reach the military cemetery on your right.

WYTSCHAETE MILITARY CEMETERY

No cemetery existed on this site during the war, and all these graves were brought in from burial sites in a wide area about the Messines Ridge, and indeed from other parts of the Salient. Today it contains 486 British graves, along with thirty-one Australian, nineteen Canadian, eleven South African, seven New Zealand and one German. Of these 423 are unknown: the vast majority of the burials here. Twenty-five Special Memorials commemorate men whose graves were lost.

There are 1914 casualties here from the fighting around Messines. Captain Alastair Grant Gwyer (VI-C-11) was a thirty-one year old Scotsman from Pitlochry who had been in the army since 1902. After only six weeks at the front with the 6th Dragoon Guards he was killed on 22nd October 1914. Privates C.A. Wallace (III-B-44) and E.G. Chapman (III-B-45), who both died with the London Scottish at Messines on 1st November 1914, are among the few from that unit who died in the fighting there who have a known grave. The parents of Lance Corporal W. Waygood (Sp Mem A4) added the inscription 'Fought and Died Like An Englishman' to his gravestone; he died with the 9th Lancashire Fusiliers near Hollebeke on 12th June 1917. The mother of Private Harry Barnes (II-C-4) echoed many when she added the inscription 'I Miss My Boy'. Barnes was a nineteen year old Londoner and Regular soldier who had joined the army as a Boy Soldier before the war; he died in January 1915 on a quiet day in the trenches. Among the Special Memorials is a row of Royal Engineers, once buried at a cemetery called RE Beaver Farm. In fact this was 'RE Farm' close to a point called Beaver Corner, north of Kemmel village. The 56th and 57th Field Companies buried three of their men here after they were killed on 12th March 1915. Two of them were decorated Sappers: C.J. Amphlett and A.W. Kay had both been awarded the Distinguished Conduct Medal for bravery in the battles of 1914.

Close by the cemetery is the memorial to the 16th (Irish) Division. Raised in 1914 from New Army battalions of southern Irish regiments, it had fought with distinction at Guillemont and Ginchy in 1916. During

Memorial to the 16th (Irish) Division.

the Battle of Messines in June 1917 it fought alongside the 36th (Ulster) Division in the capture of Wytschaete; it was the first time these two Irish units had fought side by side. Another memorial to this division, of the same design, exists at Guillemont on the Somme.

Leave the cemetery by the main gate and turn right, following the Kemmel road westwards. It is advisable to keep on the right-hand side of the road in the cycle lane, although beware of cyclists who can approach from either direction! As you come out of the village, past some modern houses, the trees surrounding Spanbroekmolen mine crater can be seen to the left (see Messines Ridge Walk). Further along **turn right** at the Oosthoeve signboard down Oosthoevestraat to the area known as Maedelstade Farm on British maps.

Maedelstade Farm was a farm complex which formed part of the German lines here on this sector of the Messines Ridge. No Man's Land was over 300 yards wide here, and a network of trenches had grown up around the farm since the lines stabilised in the winter of 1914. On high ground, Maedelstade Farm afforded good views across to the British trenches and beyond to the rear areas towards Kemmel. All the German lines in this sector had names beginning with N, and Nap Trench protected the ruins of the farm buildings. Infantry assaults earlier in the war had proved this a formidable defensive work and by 1916, when plans for an attack on the Messines Ridge were being formulated, it was decided that this would be a suitable area for one of the mines which would open the attack.

The 250th Tunnelling Company Royal Engineers was brought in to this sector to prepare this and the other mines for Messines, from Hollandscheschuur Farm to Peckham – the largest area covered by a

The ruins of Wytschaete in 1919.

single Tunnelling Company. This unit was commanded by Major Cecil Howe Cropper, an Australian-born officer and former civilian miner who had transferred into the Royal Engineers from the infantry. Under his command, the 250th Tunnelling Company made one of the greatest contributions to the mining offensive that would become the Battle of Messines in 1917. The tunnel towards Maedelstade Farm was started by his men in 1916, but the final charges, amounting to 94,000lbs of explosive (a mixture of Ammonal and gun cotton), were still being laid as late as 2nd June 1917, only five days before the battle was due to start. The gallery leading to the main charge was over 1,600 feet long, and 100 feet below ground at its greatest depth, and the mine was designed to explode behind the farm buildings under a spot where a network of trenches was located. A second gallery, branching off from the main one, had been directed towards Wytschaete Wood, but lack of time prior to the battle meant this ambitious plan had to be abandoned.

On 7th June 1917 the 16th (Irish) Division occupied this part of the line, alongside their comrades in the 36th (Ulster) Division on the right; it was the first time these two formations had fought side by side. At 3.10am the mines on this front were blown using detonators or were ignited by electricity, and at Maedelstade Farm a smoking crater 205 feet across was created. The total area of destruction was more than another 100 feet around this. Units from Brigadier General Pereira's 47th Brigade then attacked the farm; the shock of the mine explosions here and at Petit Bois and Peckham broke the back of the German defences and the position was easily captured. From here the Irishmen pushed on into Wytschaete Wood and the village itself.

Today Maedelstade Farm crater is still impressive, but it lies in private land and is used for fishing competitions, and is often closed off from public access during the winter months. Opposite is a café with an information panel in Flemish and English about the area, and refreshments can be bought here, although opening times seem to vary.

From the café **continue** along the road as it moves north from the craters and past a farm on the right. Just beyond the farm is your first view to the right towards Petit Bois. Continue through a partially sunken area and **take the first minor road on the left**, Maedelstadestraat, then on the rise turn round to view Petit Bois. **Stop**.

Going north along the Messines Ridge, Petit Bois, a small wood (hence its name) incorporated into the German front line, was the next key objective in this sector for the fighting on 7th June 1917. Opposite the British trenches on Vandamme Hill, Nancy Trench constituted the German forward positions and mining activity had already begun as early as 1915; several small craters littered No Man's Land. In early 1916 Major

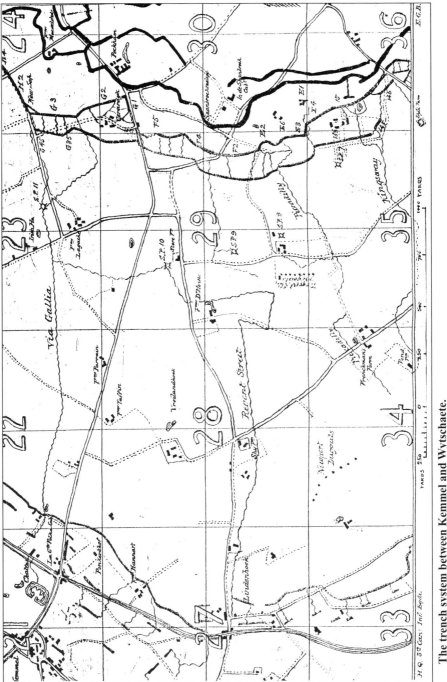

The trench system between Kemmel and Wytschaete.

German front-line trench near Petit Bois.

Cropper's 250th Tunnelling Company began work here and constructed a gallery with two branches, each of which would eventually contain charges of 30,000lbs of explosive. Uniquely for the tunnellers who worked on the Messines Ridge, Major Cropper had brought up a mechanical mining machine similar to those used in constructing underground railway tunnels in England. It was an impressive piece of equipment:

> The machine consisted of a chassis on wheels carrying a pair of rotating cutters at the front. These cutters were powered by a two-

cylinder compressed air engine which was in turn driven by a miniature generating station installed on the surface. As the compressed air blasted into the cutters they screwed themselves forward, tearing out the face ahead and feeding the spoil back. While cutting went on the machine was stabilised by top and bottom jacks.[1]

The cutter was broken down into its component parts and taken piece by piece down a narrow shaft, and assembled in the mining gallery. The heavy sections were brought up at night by trench railway, but it soon became impossible to disguise that work was going on and the German artillery began to concentrate its fire on the positions near the shaft entrance. Wild rumours – beloved of all soldiers in any war – began to circulate and there was much speculation that this was a secret, war-winning weapon which had been brought up to clear the Germans off the Messines Ridge in one go. After final assembly it was first used on 4th March 1916, and the initial results were good. However, after it was turned off for maintenance it failed to restart and Cropper discovered the machine had entangled itself in the clay and had to be dug free. This continued to happen each time it was operated and a catalogue of mechanical problems eventually led to the 'secret weapon' being abandoned after it had cut only 200 feet of tunnel. This gallery was then sealed up and abandoned, and the machine lies there to this day, 80 or more feet below the surface.

The Petit Bois craters are visible from here with a good pair of binoculars; they appear as indents in the ground from this angle, and are surrounded by several small trees. The craters are on private land and cannot be visited, but will be seen more clearly later on in the walk.

Turning round again, continue along Maedelstadestraat to where it joins another road and here **turn right**. Continue past the farm to a gate opening on to a grass path across the field to a military cemetery.

IRISH HOUSE CEMETERY
Irish House was the name given by British troops to the original of the farm building you have just passed. The cemetery was started after the Messines offensive in June 1917 when units of the 16th (Irish) Division buried their dead here. It remained in use until September 1918, falling into German hands in April that year. There are 103 British burials, and fourteen Australian. Several artillery graves reflect the nature of this position and the use of the natural valley in which the cemetery is located – it was an ideal gun site out of view of German positions on and beyond the Messines Ridge.

After the Battle of Messines, the 11th Battalion Royal Irish Rifles cleared this part of the battlefield and discovered the remains of a large group of Gordon Highlanders who had been lying in No Man's Land since their deaths in December 1914. The thirty-three officers and men recovered and buried in a mass grave at Irish House (A-30/32) were from the 1st Gordons, part of 3rd Division, who had been killed in an ill-thought-out attack near Wytschaete on 14th December 1914. The battalion *War Diary* gives the following account of what happened:

> At 7am our artillery bombardment commences. Many of our shells fell short of the German position, some even in rear of our reserve.
>
> At 7.45am . . . [we] advanced from the fire trenches and pushed on in extended order in spite of very heavy rifle fire which was immediately opened on us. The sodden nature of the ground and the fact that the men had been standing for several hours in trenches deep in mud rendered a rapid advance impossible.
>
> The heavy rifle and machine-gun fire which was opened from the German trenches showed at once that the artillery bombardment had failed in its purpose and that the German trenches were still strongly held. Many casualties occurred as our men left the trenches but the advance was not checked. The attacking companies soon disappeared from view and in default of any means of communication with them it was impossible to tell how they were progressing.[2]

The 1st Gordons had managed at one point to enter the German positions, but were in isolated groups up and down the line. Slowly these groups were pushed back, overwhelmed or taken prisoner, and by the close of the fighting that day the battalion had lost seventeen officers and 253 men: over fifty per cent casualties. As trench warfare settled down to stalemate, the bodies of the Gordons could not be recovered and were left on the battlefield. Units in and out of the line could see them but could do nothing. Many speculated as to their fate, and as time progressed, stories abounded as to what had happened here. Captain G.A. Burgoyne of the 2nd Battalion Royal Irish Rifles reported in January 1915:

> . . . one of our MG section was telling me of the charge of the Gordons made on December 14th . . . An officer drew his claymore, yelled 'Advance' and they were up and out over the poor parapets, and went real well. One young NCO he noticed, galloping ahead, his rifle in the air, yelling 'Come on boys' . . . he

pointed out to me what he thought was the poor boy's body, not 50 yards from the German lines . . . Our guns were pouring heavy shrapnel fire into the German lines and many poor Highlanders were knocked over by our own shrapnel . . . The whole affair was apparently very badly organised; never thought out at all. But then the whole time I have been out I never once saw any of our Brigade or Divisional staff come up to the trenches.[3]

Nearly a year after the action, in November 1915, the bodies were still lying there and were noticed by Private Donald Fraser of the 31st Battalion Canadian Infantry; he took a special interest as he himself was a Scot by birth and instantly recognised these kilted troops as fellow countrymen. While exploring No Man's Land at night, Fraser and his comrades discovered:

. . . a fairly even line of dead three or four hundred yards long . . . Most of the bodies were skeletons or partly mummified and fell to pieces when moved. Some were half buried. One Highlander was fairly intact. On two of them we found paybooks, a watch and some money. Their names were Robb and Anderson, and they belonged to Aberdeen, Scotland. Robb was married and had several letters in his possession. There was one written by himself to his wife. Of course it was never posted. It was dated . . . December 1914. He was very optimistic regarding the war, went even as far as to say it would be finished in a week or two, and expected to be home for Xmas. His paybook had only one entry, a payment made in October. He was clothed in winter garb and had his equipment over a light coloured goatskin. He was lying facing the German line and his rifle, with bayonet fixed, was lying about a foot to his right.[4]

One can only imagine the state the bodies were in when they were eventually laid to rest by the 11th Royal Irish Rifles in June 1917. Indeed it is a miracle that any bodies had survived to bury. Only three of the thirty-three are known; the unknowns are all marked by one unique headstone. Those whose identity could be ascertained were Lieutenant W.R.F. Dobie (A-30), Lieutenant J.J.G. MacWilliam (A-30) and CQMS A. McKinley (A-31). MacWilliam was a nineteen year old subaltern from Edinburgh who had joined the battalion in September 1914, and had already been wounded at La Bassée in October. One of his men wrote to MacWilliam's parents after the action describing what had happened to their son:

237

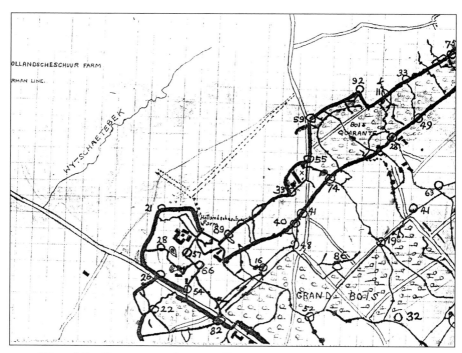

Map of the German trenches near Hollandscheschuur Farm to Croonaert Wood (Bayernwald).

When the order came to advance, he was the first out of the trenches. Smiling and waving his stick, he encouraged his men on. When he had got to within fifty yards of the German trenches we had to lie down for a minute to get our breath before making the final assault. It was when he raised his head to give the order to advance that he was killed.[5]

Leave the cemetery by the same path and return to the road. **Turn right** and continue. At the end of this road **turn right**. Further on, as the road climbs uphill, it forks; **take the left-hand fork** towards a farm on Mandesstraat. Go past the farm (Vandamme Farm on British maps), and then further on, by a new house on the right where the road bends, **stop**.

From here you have a good view towards the trees of Petit Bois. The edges of the craters are just visible, and small stumpy trees can be seen growing round the lips of them. From left to right the view here takes in Hollandscheschuur Farm, Croonaert Wood, Grand Bois, Unnamed Wood and Petit Bois, with Wytschaete Wood and the spire of Wytschaete church beyond. Work on the Petit Bois mines had started in December 1915. Six

238

months later, in June 1916, as the work progressed, German tunnellers blew two counter-mines which caved in 250 yards of the workings. Twelve Sappers were entombed at the German end, cut off from their comrades by the fall-in. A rescue party laboured for ten days to get them out and,

> . . . when at last they got through they discovered the bodies of the imprisoned men, who had collected near the block to listen for the sounds of the rescue work, and had all been suffocated, as this point, happening to be the lowest, was a pit of foul air. But one man, a miner by trade, had stayed in a higher part of the gallery, and he was found alive. He owed his life to finding half a pint of water in a bottle, which he kept taking into his mouth and returning to the flask.[6]

The tunneller who survived was Sapper William Henry Bedson; his comrades are buried in Kemmel Chateau Cemetery (see Locre-Kemmel walk).

Despite this setback, the two mines designated for this sector were completed by August 1916, each containing a charge of 30,000lbs. Brigadier General P. Leveson-Gower's 49th Brigade of the 16th (Irish) Division successfully attacked and captured Petit Bois on the morning of 7th June 1917. The Official History reports that these mines were fired twelve seconds late, causing casualties in the leading battalions and blowing many men off their feet, as at Spanbroekmolen nearby (see Messines Ridge Walk).

Continue along this road until it meets the main Vierstraat–Wytschaete road. At this junction stop and look up the sloping ground towards Hollandscheschuur Farm.

Hollandscheschuur Farm stands on a high point overlooking this part of the battlefield and was fortified by the Germans as part of their defences in this sector of the Messines Ridge. Three mines were started in December 1915 and completed between June and August 1916. Number 1 Mine was a charge of 34,200lbs, and the others were 14,900lbs and 18,500lbs respectively. On 7th June 1917 the 56th Brigade of 19th (Western) Division attacked across this ground, greatly assisted by the explosions which neutralised the German garrison. The divisional *War Diary* records, 'there was little resistance from the Germans, who either ran forward to surrender, or, if they could do so, ran away; very few of them put up a fight'.[7]

Follow the main road uphill in the direction of Wytschaete. The main entrance to Hollandscheschuur Farm is passed on the left, but this

A German illustration of Hollandscheschuur Farm in 1915.

is private and access to the mine craters cannot be gained without permission of the owners, although you can walk part way up the main drive to get a view of the nearest crater and a sense of the advantage the Germans gained from this position. Just before Grand Bois there is a minor road to the left, Hollandseschuurstraat. **Stop here** before taking this route and look back; there is a good view from the German perspective towards the British positions you have just walked across. Follow Hollandseschuurstraat to the end and turn left on the outskirts of Grand Bois towards another wood which is soon reached on the right.

Croonaert Wood, or Bois Quarante (from when the French held this sector), formed part of the German line from October 1914 until it was captured in the Battle of Messines. It was part of the Flanders battlefield that Adolf Hitler knew well, having been awarded an Iron Cross 2nd Class near here in 1914. On 7th June 1917 this was part of the attack area of Major General Shute's 19th (Western) Division, and men of the 9th Battalion Cheshire Regiment were present in the attack on the wood itself. For many years Croonaert Wood was home to a trench museum similar to that in Sanctuary Wood, and run by the enterprising Andre Becquart. It was interesting as it showed the contrast between the German trenches here and the British at Sanctuary Wood. A larger section of the front line could be explored, with mine craters, shell holes, concrete bunkers and a mine shaft, in which at one time visitors could be winched up and down in a bucket seat. On display was a wide variety of battlefield relics,

A German illustration of trenches in Bayernwald in 1915.

including human skulls which adorned Andre's front-room window, still wearing Picklehaubes! A great storyteller, Andre claimed that Hitler had been wounded here in 1916 and placed in a concrete bunker to await evacuation. Later that night there was a British trench raid, and a British officer entered the trench, saw the bunker, pulled back the gas blanket and made his way inside. There he found the pathetic figure of the wounded Hitler, lying on a stretcher. Levelling his revolver, the officer paused for a moment and on reflection said, 'I won't shoot you, you'll do no harm.' It is one of those stories the truth of which is lost to history itself, although Andre certainly did have photographs of Hitler returning to Croonaert Wood in May 1940.

The wood was abandoned after Andre's death in the mid-1980s, and later taken over by the local tourist authorities. It transpired that Andre's trench system was fake and bore no relation to what had been there during the war; perhaps that's not surprising when you consider the Hitler stories he told! After much research a team of battlefield archaeologists excavated the site and created a new trench system based on what had been there during the war. Using original construction methods and the same sorts of materials used in the same way, a very impressive trench system was created which gives a good insight into early war German trench systems in Flanders. The site is now accessible by walking up Voormezelestraat and reaching the main gate, where a code is required to enter the wood. Inside you can wander around the trenches and bunkers, and see where the mineshafts were, and there is a visitors area with photographs and maps, and an excellent 3D bronze map of the Messines Ridge. The site can only be accessed via a ticket, which has to be obtained in advance from Kemmel Tourist Office (www.heuvelland. be).

From here, return to the road and turn right, then go downhill slightly until a grass path is found on the left. **Stop.**

The small, now heavily weathered, French memorial by the access path is to Lieutenant Paul Marie Lasnier and his comrades of the 1st Battalion Light Infantry (Chasseurs à Pied) who died in this sector in 1914. The thirty-one year old Lasnier was from Brignolles in the Var; he had been at the front since the start of the war, and had taken part in several engagements. His unit was holding the wooded area on the ridge and on 2nd November 1914 came under almost continuous shell-fire from weapons of all calibres. Lasnier was killed by one of these shell blasts and was originally buried here, although his grave was moved to the French National Cemetery at Notre Dame de Lorette, in France, after the war.

From the memorial follow the path to the cemetery.

CROONAERT CHAPEL CEMETERY

A small battlefield cemetery of seventy-four British graves, plus one man of the Chinese Labour Corps, it was begun in June 1917 by burial officers

Memorial to Lieutenant Paul Lasnier near Croonaert Chapel.

of the 19th (Western) Division. Soldiers from several units of that division are found here, all of whom died in the early stages of the Battle of Messines, among them Second Lieutenant Frank Bannatyne Gadsdon (A-14) of the 9th Battalion Cheshire Regiment, who died in the fighting for Croonaert Wood. The cemetery stayed in use until November 1917, with two graves being added in April 1918. Most of the later graves are from artillery units that had their gun positions on this part of the ridge defending the ground taken in June 1917.

Return via the grass path to the road. Turn right and go back past Croonaert Wood and stay on this road, passing through the wooded area, until it takes you back to the Vierstraat road. Here **turn right**, then immediately left on another minor road, Kroonardstraat. This road follows the contours of the Messines Ridge and passes a modern house on the left. Just past this, **stop**. There is an information panel here and there are good views down towards the Petit Bois craters. From here, perhaps more than anywhere else on this walk, it is quite apparent how important a feature the Messines Ridge was; the field of vision even on a dull day is considerable.

Continue as the road passes between Wytschaete Wood and Petit Bois. Here a signposted track on the left goes towards Wytschaete Wood. Follow this into the trees. Just inside on the left is a concrete structure. **Stop**.

243

This is one of the German entrances to their mining system on the Messines Ridge known as the Dietrich Shaft. Just as the British were tunnelling, so were the Germans but not on the same scale. A lot of their work was seeking out the British tunnellers and destroying them with charges blown alongside the workings. This system of mine shafts was inspected by Major Cropper's 250th Tunnelling Company after the Battle of Messines and Major H.W. Laws later reported:

There is a concrete power house at O.19.a.0 which contained an electrical generating set. At N24.b.9.0 and N19.a.0.7 there are two circular shafts of concrete segments 5 feet diameter. They had electrical winding gear, lighting and blowers with 6″ air pipe and flexible canvas joints and pump lines of 2″ iron piping. The shafts were nearly full of water and depth unknown. The equipment indicates extensive work or preparation for it. It is highly improbable that offensive operations would be commenced from this point and it would therefore seem that the rumour of our mining under Wytschaete carried some weight with the enemy and that this was an attempt to intercept it.[8]

The site is now protected and there is an information panel with photographs and maps.

Return via the path to the road and **go left**. Follow it to the end, where it meets the Kemmel road. Here **turn left** and stay on the cycle path back to the centre of Wytschaete and your vehicle.

Notes

1. Barrie, A. *War Underground* (House Journals 1964) p.183.
2. 1st Battalion Gordon Highlanders *War Diary*, 14.12.14, TNA WO95/1421.
3. Burgoyne, G.A. *The Burgoyne Diaries* (Thomas Harmsworth 1985) pp.50–1.
4. Roy, R.H. *The Journal of Private Fraser* (Sono Nis Press 1985) p.55.
5. Quoted in Clutterbuck, L.A. (Ed.) *The Bond of Sacrifice* Volume I (Anglo-African Publishing 1915) p.248.
6. Brice, B. *The Battle Book of Ypres* (John Murray 1927) pp.169–70.
7. Quoted in Edmonds, J.E. (Ed.) *Military Operations France and Belgium 1917* Volume II (HMSO 1948) p.59.
8. 250th Tunnelling Company RE *War Diary*, June 1917, TNA WO95/551.

Chapter Thirteen

Messines Ridge Walk

STARTING POINT: St Quentin Cabaret Military Cemetery
GPS: 50°45.429′N, 2°51.373′E
DISTANCE: 14.1km/8.8 miles

WALK SUMMARY: *This is one of the longest walks in the book, and is best spread over the course of a day. However, it is also one of the most rewarding as most of the route is off road and along tracks. The views of Messines and the ridge itself are also quite impressive at times.*

St Quentin Cabaret Military Cemetery is on a minor road going south from the centre of Wulverghem, and is clearly signposted. There is ample parking outside the cemetery, with plenty of room to leave your vehicle.

ST QUENTIN CABARET MILITARY CEMETERY

St Quentin Cabaret was the name given to an old Flemish inn 500 yards east of Kandahar Farm on the south side of Wulverghem, the cellars of which were used as a battalion headquarters and aid post during the Great War. The inn building is opposite the cemetery, and is now a private house. Units in the line opposite Messines in the River Douve sector knew it well and the nearby military cemetery was started by battalions of the 46th (North Midland) Division which came to this area in February 1915; Plot I Rows E and F contain these early graves. The cemetery remained in use until 1918, although only two graves were added after

British supply lorries and Belgians behind the front opposite Messines in 1915.

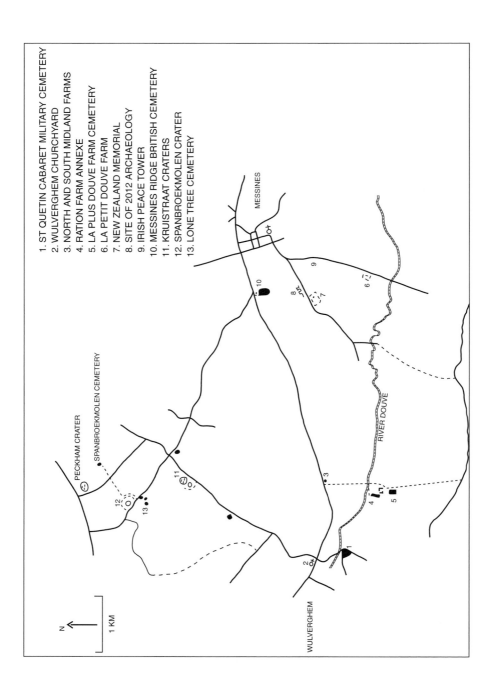

1. ST QUETIN CABARET MILITARY CEMETERY
2. WULVERGHEM CHURCHYARD
3. NORTH AND SOUTH MIDLAND FARMS
4. RATION FARM ANNEXE
5. LA PLUS DOUVE FARM CEMETERY
6. LA PETIT DOUVE FARM
7. NEW ZEALAND MEMORIAL
8. SITE OF 2012 ARCHAEOLOGY
9. IRISH PEACE TOWER
10. MESSINES RIDGE BRITISH CEMETERY
11. KRUISTRAAT CRATERS
12. SPANBROEKMOLEN CRATER
13. LONE TREE CEMETERY

MESSINES

PECKHAM CRATER

SPANBROEKMOLEN CEMETERY

RIVER DOUVE

WULVERGHEM

N

1 KM

September 1918 when the area was recaptured from the Germans after their spring offensive in April. There are 316 British burials, of which eighty are men from the 36th (Ulster) Division, with sixty-eight Canadian, sixty-four New Zealand, seven Australian, two German and five whose unit is not known.

The graves from early 1915 are largely men from the 1/5th and 1/6th Battalions South Staffordshire Regiment, but among them is that of a soldier who fell at Messines in 1914. Private J.W. Bremner (I-G-11) died with the 2nd Battalion Royal Scots on 16th November 1914, but the position of his grave and the history of the cemetery suggests that his body was found on the battlefield many months later and buried here by the Staffordshire Territorials. Among the Canadian graves in Plot I Row C is a row of eighteen men of the 1st Battalion Canadian Infantry, all of whom died on 13th October 1915 while holding the line opposite Petit Douve Farm. Their battalion *War Diary* records a typical episode in the day to day activity of trench warfare in this sector – and the fate of these eighteen men:

> Brigade made a demonstration consisting of artillery bombardment and feint attack with smoke bombs. Heavy retaliation by enemy artillery caused casualties. Killed, 18, wounded, 26. Trenches suffered considerable damage. Behaviour of troops admirable, though many of them had not been under serious shell-fire before.[1]

Two long-serving officers are elsewhere in the cemetery. Major D.D.H. Campbell MC (II-J-5) was killed in action with 112th Brigade Royal Field Artillery in the opening phase of Messines on 7th June 1917, aged thirty-three. The son of a lieutenant colonel, he had previously fought in the Mohmand Campaign in 1908 with the Native Mountain Artillery, and served with the Burma Police in 1913–14. He was the sixth generation of his family to see military service. Lieutenant-Quartermaster J. Bowyer MC (II-E-8) was killed two days later on 9th June, aged fifty. An old soldier who had been commissioned from the ranks, Bowyer was an original member of the 11th Battalion Lancashire Fusiliers, having been their quartermaster since the formation of the unit in 1914. He was awarded the Military Cross for bravery near Le Sars on the Somme in 1916.

The eighty graves of men from the 36th (Ulster) Division in Plot I date from when the formation left the Somme after their blooding at Thiepval on 1st July 1916; the Ulstermen suffered over 5,500 casualties that day. Many of those buried here had survived these operations only

British soldiers put out a fire in a billet behind the lines in 1915.

to be killed in a 'quiet' sector. Among them was the adjutant of the 10th Battalion Royal Irish Rifles, Captain J.E. Sugden DSO (I-D-13). Sugden had been commissioned in 1914, promoted adjutant by the Somme, and awarded his Distinguished Service Order for bravery at Thiepval. He was killed by a shell on 28th September 1916, aged thirty-eight.

Leaving the cemetery gates, turn left and take the minor road leading to Wulverghem. This will soon bring you into the centre of the village and to a crossroads with the church opposite. Cross the road to the churchyard, where there are a number of war graves. It is entered by some steps and a gate.

Wulverghem (now Wulvergem) is a small village west of Messines Ridge which remained behind British lines for most of the war, until the area was swept up in the German offensive in April 1918. It was used as a billet for troops going to and from the line in the Petit Douve sector, and many of the cellars were taken over as dugouts. Artillery units also established gun sites around the village, in the many hidden valleys out of view of the German trenches, and they, too, had their billets here. Gradually, through constant shell-fire, the village was destroyed, and had to be completely rebuilt after the war. A few burials were made in the churchyard in 1914–15, but once a proper advanced dressing station was set up at St Quentin Cabaret, the main military cemetery was established there.

Bruce Bairnsfather, creator of the 'Old Bill' cartoons, came to Wulverghem in late 1914 with the 1st Battalion Royal Warwickshire Regiment:

> The village street is one long ruin. On either side of the road all the houses are merely a collection of broken tiles and shattered bricks and framework. Huge shell holes puncture the street. The church . . . was a large reddish-grey stone building, pretty old, and surrounded by a graveyard. Shell holes everywhere; the old grey grave stones and slabs cracked and sticking about at odd angles.
>
> Not a soul about anywhere. Wulverghem lay there, empty, wrecked and deserted.[2]

Bruce Bairnsfather.

Bairnsfather did some of his earliest drawings at Wulverghem, with many of them painted onto the whitewashed walls of farm buildings in the village. Sadly none of these survived the war.

WULVERGHEM CHURCHYARD consists of one plot of Special Memorials to soldiers who are known to be buried here but the exact location of their graves is now lost; the church and churchyard were heavily shelled in April 1918. Only two headstones mark original graves – those of two unknown soldiers of the 1/9th Battalion London Regiment (Queen Victoria's Rifles). The thirty-two Special Memorials commemorate a variety of units which served in the Wulverghem area between October 1914 and April 1915. Among them is Squadron Sergeant Major H.W. Baker (B-2) of the 11th Hussars, who was killed on the Messines Ridge on 30th October 1914, aged thirty-six. A typical 'old sweat', he had twenty years' service in the army. Even by this early stage of the war cavalry troopers like Baker were no longer on horseback and had dismounted to fight as infantry.

Leaving the churchyard by the same gate where you came in, turn left on the main road and follow it in the direction of Messines. The road soon bends and climbs uphill. In the uncultivated field on the left there are signs of shell-holes in the grass. Continue on this road until it reaches a set of buildings, with a white farmhouse on the right.

The farms to the left and right of this road were known as North and

South Midland Farms respectively on British trench maps, presumably acquiring their names from when the 46th (North Midland) and 48th (South Midland) Divisions were in this sector in early 1915. There are good views towards the Messines Ridge, with the trees surrounding Spanbroekmolen mine crater on the left and Messines itself straight ahead. The importance of this high ground and the way in which it clearly dominated the battlefield are quite apparent.

At the white building on your right (South Midland Farm), and by a CWGC sign for Ration Farm Cemetery, take the minor road going downhill into the Douve valley. Follow this until it reaches a small bridge. **Stop**.

This is the Douve River. Using the accompanying trench map, it is possible to plot the whole extent of the line in this sector, as all the farms destroyed during the war were rebuilt and the ground itself has changed little. It gives a good impression of how a battalion operated in the Salient during the quiet times between major actions. In the far distance La Petite Douve Farm is visible on the slopes of Messines Ridge – this marks the German front line. Short of that the British trenches can be plotted using the map. Here the positions would be held by one or two companies of whichever battalion was in the line at a given date. A second company would be in reserve between Fort Hambury and Fort Stewart, with advanced company headquarters in Stinking Farm. The officer commanding the front-line company would be in La Plus Douve or Ration Farm (now just ahead of you), as would be the ration parties, signallers, runners and the reserve company. Telephone lines, which needed constant attention during periods of heavy shelling, would link

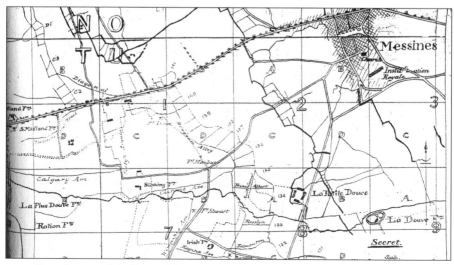

Trench map of the Douve Valley, Messines sector, 1915.

up all these positions and allow communication. Further back at St Quentin Cabaret (also visible from the bridge) was battalion headquarters, where the commanding officer, second in command, adjutant and medical officer had a dugout in the cellar. The battalion cookers were also located there, and at night fatigue parties would bring up tea and stew to Ration Farm, and then, via communication trenches such as Calgary Avenue, to the men in the front line. Such arrangements would continue for days at a time, with companies rotating back and forth between reserve and forward positions until another battalion relieved them and they would move back, usually via Wulverghem, to a village or rest camp well out of shell range. This was just one sector on one part of the Western Front, but this routine was repeated many times over all along the line from Ypres to the Somme and beyond.

Continue on the track to a CWGC sign and take the grass path on the right to the cemetery.

RATION FARM ANNEXE (LA PLUS DOUVE) CEMETERY

The cemetery was started in January 1915 close to the farm complex known on trench maps as La Plus Douve Farm, and remained in use for a further three years until January 1918. No further graves were added after this date; all local burials were then made at La Plus Douve Cemetery nearby. It contains 186 British burials, twelve Australian, four New Zealand, one German prisoner, and one whose unit could not be identified. It was started by the 2nd Battalion Manchester Regiment, and Private H. Bates (I-A-8) was the first burial on 11th January 1915. Most graves are from the 1915–16 period, with a few in 1917 and the last being made by Australian units in January 1918. The cemetery is dominated by Irish regiments, largely battalions of the 36th (Ulster) Division from August–September 1916 after their heavy losses at Thiepval on 1st July 1916. There are also some men of the 2nd Battalion Leinster Regiment, 24th Division, who were here in early 1916. Among these are two drummers: M. Morrissey (II-C-17), who died on 5th April 1916, and A. Murphy (II-C-13), who was killed on 17th April 1916. Indeed there are many 24th Division graves in the cemetery, including a large plot of 9th Battalion Royal Sussex Regiment men who died on 17th June 1916 when the Germans gassed the British trenches using phosgene gas, causing heavy casualties. The last soldier to be interred in the cemetery was Private V.T. Stone MM (III-B-19) of the 12th Battalion Australian Imperial Force, who is recorded as having drowned on 16th January 1918 – possibly in the Douve river?

Leave the cemetery by the path, and at the end **turn right**. Go through the farmyard and take the track to the cemetery on the right.

251

LA PLUS DOUVE FARM CEMETERY

The Douve river ran through two large farms – La Plus Douve and La Petite Douve. The latter was the scene of a large Canadian trench raid in November 1915, and where one of the Messines mines was discovered by the Germans in 1916. You have just passed through La Plus Douve; La Petite Douve is further down the valley and will be seen later. This cemetery, which complemented the one you have just come from, was started in April 1915 by units of the 48th (South Midland) Division, and stayed in use until May 1918, latterly by the Germans who captured the ground in April 1918. It has 101 British, eighty-eight Canadian, eighty-six Australian, sixty-one New Zealand and nine German graves.

The Canadian graves date from 1915 and are all 1st Division men who held this sector after the fighting near Kitchener's Wood and St Julien, during Second Ypres. Elsewhere is an Englishman who had emigrated to America, Private R. Knight Cuthbert of the 2nd King Edward's Horse, one of several men from this unit buried here, who was forty-seven when he was killed on 7th July 1915. The inscription on his headstone reads, 'From America he came on homeland's duty call'. New Zealand graves date from the Messines offensive in 1917, and the Australians from February and March 1918.

Leaving the cemetery, turn right and continue on the track up the tree-lined avenue. At the end it meets a road; here turn left and follow. Further along on the crest are good views. From here you can see, left to right: Kemmel Hill, Spanbroekmolen, Wytschaete Wood, Wytschaete, Messines Ridge, the New Zealand Memorial and Messines itself (distinguished by the church tower). Continue. Further along, between two farms and just before a bend to the right, there is a track to the left going downhill towards Messines. **Stop here** before following this track.

There are good views towards Messines and the area of operations of the New Zealand Division (see map). The NZ Division was one of the most disciplined and highly respected fighting formations in the British Expeditionary Force, and many of its men had fought at Gallipoli in 1915 and near High Wood on the Somme in 1916. Messines Ridge was to prove one of their most successful operations, despite what appeared to be almost impossible odds and terrain. No mines were used on their immediate divisional front – the one at La Petite Douve having been discovered by the Germans in 1916 – and the slopes of the ridge were particularly steep, making movement up them difficult. The Germans had constructed a strong defence line around Messines itself, with many concrete bunkers. However, following a very well planned and executed preliminary bombardment, and the construction of assembly trenches in No Man's Land, therefore reducing the distance men had to advance, the

British tank on the Messines Ridge in 1917.

attack went well. The explosion of the Ontario mine on the left flank (25th Division front) signalled the advance, and the New Zealanders left their trenches. There was no creeping barrage to protect them as they crossed No Man's Land, but a fixed 18-pounder bombardment of the German front line neutralised the garrison as the Kiwis advanced. They soon reached the enemy positions, and as the shell-fire lifted from the German trenches they dashed in at the point of the bayonet. The ground was soon swept up and within forty minutes the New Zealanders were in Messines itself, clearing dugouts and taking prisoners. On their left the 25th Division had come forward and taken its objectives, the 3rd (Australian) Division doing the same on the right. Messines Ridge had been captured. All this was achieved with minimal casualties for a Great War battle, and the ridge was held against counter-attacks.

Follow the track downhill. In wet weather it can be boggy or flooded, and it might be necessary to walk along the edge of a field in several places. The track brings you down to another bridge over the Douve river. Stop here and look east, towards a farm building astride the Ypres–Armentières road.

This is La Petite Douve Farm, a bastion in the German lines which overlooked the British trenches in the Douve valley. In November 1915 the 7th Battalion Canadian Infantry had organised a large trench raid on the position, but it had remained in enemy hands. When plans for the Battle of Messines were being formulated in 1916, the farm was selected as a suitable target for one of the offensive mines, and men of the 171st Tunnelling Company Royal Engineers were allocated to prepare the mine. In August 1916 German sappers, who were counter-mining at the same time, broke into the main shaft and attempted to remove the 35-ton charge. But the REs were aware of their activities and exploded a camouflet, a mine which exploded underground with the blast going outwards rather than upwards, killing the enemy miners. Several days later the Germans retaliated with a 6,000lb charge, which severely damaged the tunnel and killed some of the men from the 171st. The tunnelling officers in command were then in favour of blowing the mine. However, they were overruled; La Petite Douve was deliberately abandoned and the course of the Douve river directed into the tunnel, flooding the workings of both sides and bringing mining activity in the area to an end.

Continue along the track, which soon meets a minor road. Stay on this until you cross a stream. Here, you are on the approximate New Zealand front line for 7th June 1917, with the German lines on the high ground ahead of you; they were just in front of the New Zealand Memorial, and the bunkers, which formed part of it, are just visible on a clear day. It is very obvious from here just how the Germans dominated the British positions in the Douve valley. Stay on this road and follow it uphill. Further along on the left is a small wayside shrine; stop here and look back across the ground you have just walked. It gives a good impression of the German view down into the valley. One of the front-line bunkers is visible in a nearby field on your right.

A little further up the slope is the NEW ZEALAND MEMORIAL. This large Portland stone memorial, commemorating the capture of the ridge in June 1917, was unveiled by King Albert of the Belgians on 1st August 1924. It is part of a park, and also in the grounds are two German bunkers which can be easily explored. They, too, afford good views down to the former British lines. An inscription on the memorial records that these Kiwis came 'from the uttermost ends of the earth', and paid a high price. By 1918 New Zealand, with a population of 1,099,449, had raised 128,525 men to fight in the war. Of these 100,440 served overseas, 16,640 were killed or died of wounds, 41,317 were wounded and 530 taken prisoner. This total of nearly 58,500 casualties is over fifty per cent of those who served overseas. On ANZAC Day – 25th April – every year there is a wreath-laying ceremony at the memorial.

Leaving the park, turn left and go partially downhill and then take a track on the left just beyond the CWGC parking area. This is a local path. Follow it past the New Zealand Memorial and round the back of Messines to the Irish Peace Tower site.

New Zealand soldiers who fought at Messines in June 1917.

German front-line trench at Messines in 1917.

Messines in 1914.

The IRISH PEACE TOWER was unveiled by Her Majesty the Queen on 11th November 1998, the eightieth anniversary of the Armistice. It brought together communities from both Northern Ireland and Eire to commemorate the role of Irish troops from all the different Irish regiments and divisions that fought in the conflict. The tower is made of Irish stone and the memorials in the grounds remember units and individuals who served. At the base of the tower is a small room where the names of Irishmen who died in the war are listed.

Leaving the Peace Tower site, carefully cross the main road and take the track almost opposite. Follow this track to where it joins another to your left. **Stop**.

In 2012 there was a major archaeological dig in this area following the construction of a new water pipe around the town. The dig was one of the largest ever undertaken on the Western Front. It was led by head archaeologist Simon Verdeghem, and he and his team unearthed a large amount of material that significantly added to our knowledge of the Great War in Flanders. It is hoped that some of the material found will eventually be displayed in Messines itself. Meanwhile the documentary about the dig, 'WW1 Tunnels of Death', can easily be found online.

Take the track to the left going uphill into the town. It joins a minor road. Follow this to the end and then **turn right** into the square in front of the church.

Messines (now Mesen) church, St Nicholas, was rebuilt in 1928 on similar lines to the original which was destroyed during the war. The church is usually open and the crypt can be accessed to the rear of the building. This crypt was where Adolf Hitler sheltered from British bombardments during the winter of 1914/15 while serving here with the

Germans in occupation of Messines in 1916.

All that remained of Messines in 1919.

16th Bavarian Reserve Infantry Regiment. Hitler was a runner at this time, moving from regimental to battalion headquarters around Messines. The crypt was later used as a casualty reception post but by 1917 was likely to have collapsed under the weight of the rubble above. It is all that remains of the pre-war structure. In the tower of the church, which is also accessible by steps and then a ladder (but is not a visit for the faint-hearted!), are the 'peace bells' placed here by local resident Albert Ghekiere between the 1970s and 1990s in memory of all those who fell in this part of Flanders. They sound at regular intervals with a variety of tunes.

From the church, take *Korte Mooiestraat* into the main square of Messines. There are several memorials here, including a statue at the far end depicting a New Zealand soldier. In the old town hall is a new (2014) Messines Visitors Centre, which replaces the old town museum that was formerly here. It has tourist information on the region and displays of photographs and artefacts about the fighting around Messines during the First World War.

From the town hall steps walk up to the main road and here turn right, in the direction of Ypres. At the next crossroads turn left at the CWGC sign along **Nieuwkerkestraat** and continue to the cemetery on the left.

MESSINES RIDGE BRITISH CEMETERY AND MESSINES RIDGE (NEW ZEALAND) MEMORIAL

The entrance to the cemetery brings you first to the New Zealand Memorial, which commemorates 840 men from the NZ Division who fell near Messines in 1917–18. Like most memorials to the missing, the names are listed by unit and then rank. Among them is one of the oldest NZEF soldiers to die in the war: Private L.G. Chevalier of the 2nd Otago Regiment was killed on 7th June 1917, aged fifty-six. Private H.G. Hood was an Englishman who had emigrated to Canada, joined the CEF in 1914 and was discharged due to wounds. He went to New Zealand for health reasons, but subsequently joined the NZEF and died serving with the 2nd Auckland Regiment on 7th June 1917.

The cemetery was constructed after the war when all the graves were brought in from the area between Messines and Wytschaete. Burials total 986 British, 332 Australian, 115 New Zealand, fifty-six South African, one Canadian and one whose unit is not known. Of these 954 are unknown: almost two-thirds of the total. Many of the graves are soldiers who died in the Messines fighting in June 1917, although an earlier casualty is Lieutenant P.F. Payne-Gallwey (II-F-8). Stationed in India on the outbreak of war, he was posted from the 21st Lancers on attachment to the 9th Lancers, with whom he was killed at Messines on 30th October 1914.

German reserve trench at Messines in 1916.

Leave the cemetery and take the minor road, Kruisstraat, almost directly opposite. Follow this for a while, then go past a farm on the left, and just before a left-hand bend, stop.

To your left, in the distance, are the buildings of Ontario Farm. Another strongpoint in the German lines, it was also selected as a target for one of the Messines mines. The 171st Tunnelling Company blew a charge of 60,000lbs here on 7th June 1917. It was the only one not to produce a crater; instead there was a circular pulpy patch where the ground bubbled for several days afterwards. It was captured by units of the 25th Division that day.

Continue along the road, going straight across at the first crossroads and stopping at the second.

This area was known as Kruisstraat on British maps and was part of the German defences. Major Cropper's 250th Tunnelling Company Royal Engineers blew three 30,000lb mines here on 7th June, enabling the men of the 36th (Ulster) Division to advance. Some years ago one of the mine craters was filled in, but the other two remain and can be reached by taking a detour down the road to the left; they are in the field to the right of this road.

Otherwise continue straight on at this crossroads and follow the road past a farm to a scrub area on the right, at a bend in the road: this is Spanbroekmolen.

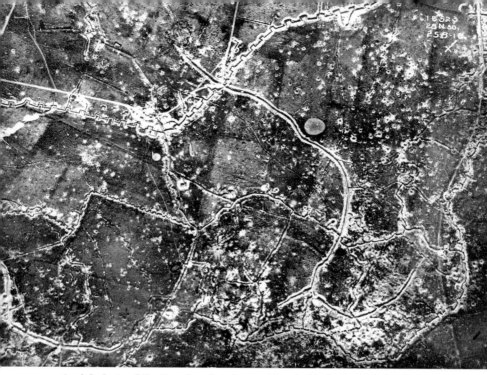

Aerial photo of the Spanbroekmolen position in 1916, showing the German defences here.

Spanbroekmolen was one of the highest German front-line positions on the Messines Ridge. 'Molen' is the Flemish for windmill, and one stood on this spot before the war. The Germans created a particularly strong defensive position around the ruins of the mill, with deep trenches, dugouts, machine-gun and trench mortar positions, and even a sunken light railway, built on wooden rails to disguise the noise. This supplied the forward trenches with ammunition and bombs, and could be used to evacuate the wounded. The British lines opposite Spanbroekmolen bore no comparison, and were typical of many along the Messines Ridge. One battalion, the 1/5th Leicestershires, which was in this sector in April 1915, left a good impression of the positions here (see also map):

Our first sector of trenches consisted of two disconnected lengths of line, called trenches 14 and 15, behind each of which [were] a few shelters, which were neither organised for defence nor even splinter-proof, known as 14S and 15S . . . On the left some 150 yards from the front line a little circular sandbag keep, about 40 yards in diameter and known as SP1, formed a Company Headquarters and fortified post, while a series of holes covered by sheets of iron and called E4 dugouts provided some more accommodation – of a very inferior order, since the slightest movement by day drew fire from the snipers' posts on 'Hill 76'. As this hill, Spanbroekmolen on the map . . . was held by the Boche, our trenches which were on its slopes were overlooked, and we had to be most careful not to expose ourselves anywhere near the front line, for to do so meant immediate death at the hands of his snipers . . . To add to our difficulties our trench parapets, which owing to the wet were entirely above ground, were composed only of sandbags, and were in many places not bullet proof.[3]

By the time the 36th (Ulster) Division arrived in this sector before the Battle of Messines in 1917, little had changed. Major Cropper's 250th Tunnelling Company was by then preparing a huge mine to knock out Spanbroekmolen with 91,000lbs of Ammonal. For the attack on 7th June Zero Hour was set for 3.10am – also the time the mine would detonate. The infantry units taking part were told that, in order to avoid any loss of momentum, if the mine did not explode at exactly that time, they were to advance anyway. On the day the mine blew fifteen seconds late, by which time many men of the 8th Battalion Royal Irish Rifles were already part way across No Man's Land. The debris tumbled down on to the attackers, killing and wounding some in the leading waves.[4] However, the charge had wiped out the main position at Spanbroekmolen and left a huge crater. The remaining garrison offered little resistance to the Irishmen, who were able to capture the position quite easily and move on to Wytschaete and the Messines Ridge itself. The Spanbroekmolen mine crater was given to the Toc-H organisation in the 1920s, and it is now preserved as a memorial to all those who died here in 1917. It is known locally as 'The Pool of Peace'. The crater is large, the flooded part alone being 27 metres deep. In the scrub to the rear of the crater are the remains of a concrete pillbox. There is a walkway to the rear of the site, enabling visitors to walk all the way round.

From the crater entrance, retrace your steps slightly, back towards Kruisstraat. A CWGC sign to the cemetery is seen on the right. Go through the gate and across the fields, following the path to the cemetery.

LONE TREE CEMETERY
This cemetery was started by units of the 36th (Ulster) Division after the Battle of Messines, to bury their dead who had fallen in the advance here;

among them, no doubt, some of the men who had died when the Spanbroekmolen mine went off late. Other graves were added afterwards, as the fighting moved on to beyond Wytschaete. Of the eighty-eight burials, sixty are men from the Royal Irish Rifles, giving it very much a 'comrades' feel.

Return to the road and turn left, passing the mine crater. Further on take a minor road on the left, Spanbroekmolenstraat, and follow it round to the right past some houses. Continue to a lone farm, known as Crow's Nest Farm on trench maps. The track now continues to the left, just past the farm, where it becomes a bridleway; it narrows and is bordered with small trees and a fence. Follow to its conclusion, where it meets a minor road. Turn left, and at the T-junction turn right, taking the road into Wulverghem. This road comes out with the churchyard on your right. At the main road go straight across, and follow this route back to St Quentin Cabaret Cemetery and your vehicle.

Notes

1. 1st Battalion Canadian Infantry *War Diary* 13.10.15, TNA WO95/3760.
2. Bairnsfather, B. *Bullets and Billets* (Grant Richards Ltd 1916) pp.222–5.
3. Hills, J.D. *The Fifth Leicestershire: A Record of the 1/5th Battalion the Leicestershire Regiment TF during the War 1914–1919* (Echo Press 1919) p.25.
4. For further information see MacDonald, L. *They Called It Passchendaele* (Michael Joseph 1978) pp.46–7.

The cost of war.

262

Chapter Fourteen

'Plugstreet Wood' Walk

STARTING POINT: Hyde Park Corner (Royal Berks) Cemetery
GPS: 50°44'14.7"N, 2°52'56.2"E
DISTANCE: 11.7km/7.3 miles

WALK SUMMARY: *A comprehensive walk around the 'Plugstreet Wood' area, visiting all the military cemeteries, going into the wood itself, and following quiet roads and tracks. It is therefore suitable for walkers of all abilities.*

Park your vehicle either outside the cemetery or in a tarmac area beside a nearby café. This café, l'Auberge de Ploegsteert (www.auberge-ploegsteert.be) is well worth a visit as it not only serves drink and excellent food, but also has a lot of interesting Great War memorabilia on display. An alternative is to park outside the 'Plugstreet Experience' (www.plugstreet1418.be), which is a new battlefield visitors centre that opened in 2014. This tells the story of this part of the battlefield, and there are toilets and a small shop here.

Ploegsteert Memorial in the 1930s.

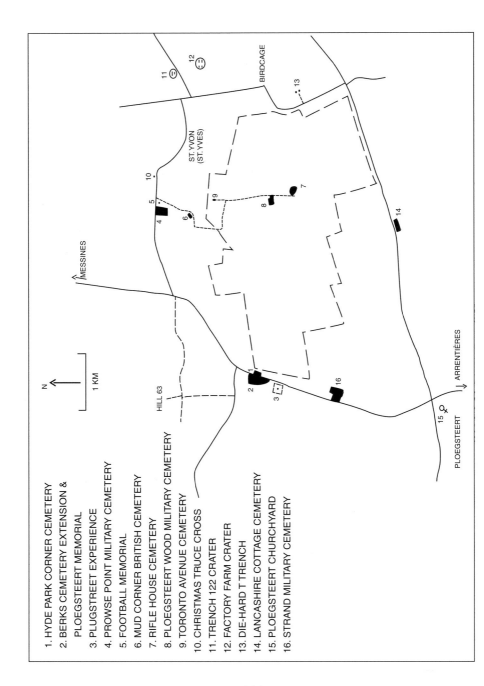

1. HYDE PARK CORNER CEMETERY
2. BERKS CEMETERY EXTENSION &
   PLOEGSTEERT MEMORIAL
3. PLUGSTREET EXPERIENCE
4. PROWSE POINT MILITARY CEMETERY
5. FOOTBALL MEMORIAL
6. MUD CORNER BRITISH CEMETERY
7. RIFLE HOUSE CEMETERY
8. PLOEGSTEERT WOOD MILITARY CEMETERY
9. TORONTO AVENUE CEMETERY
10. CHRISTMAS TRUCE CROSS
11. TRENCH 122 CRATER
12. FACTORY FARM CRATER
13. DIE-HARD T TRENCH
14. LANCASHIRE COTTAGE CEMETERY
15. PLOEGSTEERT CHURCHYARD
16. STRAND MILITARY CEMETERY

Ploegsteert, or 'Plugstreet' as it was known to British troops, was the southernmost sector in the Ypres Salient, and lay close to the French border. It was dominated by high ground north of the village at Hill 63 and by a huge wood, and after the fighting in October 1914 front lines were established east of Plugstreet Wood and trench warfare began in this sector. It was low-lying ground, and the early occupants of the area soon realised that digging here was often impossible and many of the 'trenches' were in fact breastworks: defence lines constructed above ground. By late 1914 Plugstreet Wood was held by 4th Division. Further action took place on 19th December, following which the front lines stabilised and barely moved for much of the next three and a half years. Thereafter Plugstreet was considered a 'quiet' sector, if indeed any part of the Western Front could ever be called quiet. In 1915–16 it was also used to acclimatise many New Army divisions in the business of trench warfare, gaining a reputation as a 'nursery sector' for new units coming to the Western Front. Mining operations began at Plugstreet in 1916, and two mines were blown as part of the Battle of Messines on 7th June 1917, when Australian troops pushed eastwards to La Basse Ville. During the Battle of Lys in April 1918 both Hill 63 and Plugstreet Wood fell in the German advance, being recaptured by units of the 31st Division in September 1918.

HYDE PARK CORNER (ROYAL BERKS) CEMETERY

Hyde Park Corner was a junction on the Ploegsteert road and the cemetery took its name from the 1/4th Battalion Royal Berkshire Regiment, which started it in April 1915 during its first tour of the front-line trenches; the cemetery then remained in use until November 1917. Burials number eighty-one British, four German, one Australian and one Canadian. Lieutenant Roland W. Poulton Palmer (B-11) of the 1/4th Royal Berks, who fell on 4th May 1915, was a well known rugby player whose family were joint owners of the Huntley & Palmer biscuit business based in Reading. Young soldiers abound here: aside from an eighteen year old and six nineteen year olds, there are two even younger. Private F.W. Giles (B-13), also of the 1/4th Royal Berks, was one of the first to be buried at Hyde Park Corner; he was killed on 28th April 1915, aged seventeen. The grave of Rifleman Albert E. French (B-2) has attracted many visitors since a radio programme and booklet featuring his letters home revealed he was a mere sixteen. French died serving with the 18th Battalion King's Royal Rifle Corps (Arts & Crafts Battalion) on 15th April 1916. As a result of public interest, the CWGC consented to add the correct age to his headstone; before, nothing was shown.

Several pairs of brothers died in the Plugstreet sector; and one half of

Aerial photograph showing Ploegsteert Wood and Hyde Park Corner.

such a pair is here, while his brother is buried in Berks Cemetery Extension opposite. The son of James and Sarah Baird of Belfast, Sergeant S. Baird (C-5) was killed on 24th November 1916, aged twenty, while serving with the 2nd Battalion Royal Irish Rifles. The grave of his brother, who died some months later, will be visited shortly.

Cross the road to the military cemetery and memorial opposite.

BERKS CEMETERY EXTENSION

Burials did not begin here until June 1916, when the cemetery was started by units of the 41st Division, newly arrived on the Western Front. It continued to be used until September 1917, by which time there were 295 British, fifty-one Australian, forty-five New Zealand and three Canadian graves. Among them were two unknown British soldiers. The Ploegsteert Memorial was added after the war (see below), and when the cemetery at Rosenberg Chateau, on the slopes of Hill 63, could no longer be maintained due to the wishes of the Belgian landowner, the graves were moved to this cemetery in 1931. This separate plot has the following burials: 171 British, 145 Canadian, 126 Australian and thirty-five New Zealand.[1]

In the original cemetery are several interesting graves. Among them is the elder brother of Sergeant Baird, Rifleman J.C. Baird (O-1), who died on 17th February 1917, aged twenty-two, while serving with the 14th Battalion Royal Irish Rifles. The battalion *War Diary* records that after a British artillery shoot on the German lines on Messines Ridge, 'the enemy retaliated, a number of shells falling in the wood behind our headquarters: one hit a tree beside H.Q. cookhouse and exploded killing Privates Baird and McColl – Capt Gavin's and Capt McKee's servants respectively'.[2]

Two other brothers are also buried here, side by side. Riflemen Leonard Crossley (E-20) and William Crossley (E-21) were from Thirsk. They joined the 21st Battalion King's Royal Rifle Corps (Yeoman's Rifles) together in 1914, crossed to France together and were killed together, possibly by the same shell, after only a few weeks' front-line service, on 30th June 1916. On this day the 21st KRRC troops were in reserve billets between Creslow and Touquet Berthe Farms, and were hit by retaliatory fire after a bombardment earlier in the day.[3]

There are several graves of men who were involved in the mining operations east of Plugstreet Wood and died in 1916 while preparing the Messines mines; particularly noticeable are those from the 3rd Canadian and 171st Tunnelling Companies. Trench mortar batteries had their gun positions in the wood, and many of their casualties were brought here for burial. Among them was Bombardier W.G. Cooling (F-22) of Z/41

Grave of Bombardier W.G. Cooling.

Trench Mortar Battery, who was killed on 12th July 1916 when a round misfired and prematurely detonated as it was leaving the weapon. These divisional trench mortar units were issued with the 2-inch trench howitzer; the rounds they fired, due to their shape and design, were more commonly known as the 'Plum Pudding' or 'Toffee Apple'.

PLOEGSTEERT MEMORIAL

This memorial to the missing records 11,447 British soldiers who fell in the Plugstreet Wood area and between the River Douve and the towns of Estaires and Fournes from 1914 until the end of the war. Many of the names are men who fell in the Battle of the Lys in April 1918. Originally it was proposed that this memorial would be sited in Armentières and be known by that name, but a suitable location could not be found and eventually it was erected here. Designed by Sir Gilbert Ledward, the Ploegsteert Memorial was unveiled by the Duke of Brabant on 7th June 1931, the anniversary of the Battle of Messines. *The Ypres Times*, the journal of the Ypres League, reported that a large crowd came to see the Duke, who had flown into Courtrai for the ceremony.

Among those commemorated here are:

TUNNELLER VC: Sapper William Hackett was a pre-war civilian miner who had worked at the Manvers Main Colleries, Wath-upon-Dearne, near Rotherham. He enlisted on 1st November 1915, aged forty-two, and, like many tunnellers, was in France within a month of joining up. He served with the 254th Tunnelling Company RE and was awarded a posthumous Victoria Cross for bravery in Shaftesbury Avenue mine, near Givenchy, in northern France. Although slightly out of the scope of this book, his VC citation nevertheless gives a good impression of life underground for these miners:

Sapper William Hackett VC.

> For most conspicuous bravery when entombed with four others in a gallery owing to the explosion of an enemy mine. After working for 20 hours a hole was made through fallen earth and broken timbers, and the outside party was met. Sapper Hackett helped three of the men through the hole and could easily have followed, but refused to leave the fourth who had been seriously injured, saying: 'I am a tunneller, I must look after the others first.' Meantime the hole was getting smaller, yet he still refused to leave his injured comrade. Finally the gallery collapsed, and though the rescue party worked desperately for four days, the attempt to reach the two men failed. Sapper Hackett, well knowing the nature of sliding earth, [and] the chances against him, deliberately gave his life for his comrade.[4]

SERVED AS BROWN: Leonard James Pope was one of many soldiers who served under a false name. Born in December 1896, he ran away from home in 1912 and made his way to Ireland, where he joined the Royal Irish Regiment. Aged only sixteen, he produced false papers upping his age by two years and changed his name to Brown. In 1914 Leonard fought at Mons, Le Cateau and First Ypres with the 2nd Battalion, and in 1915 at Neuve Chapelle and Festubert, where he was wounded. He returned to the 2nd Battalion for the Somme in 1916, transferred to the 2nd Leinsters and by 1917 had been wounded a further three times. He applied for a commission and became a Second Lieutenant in the 1st Battalion East Surrey Regiment, serving with that unit in Italy and France. In July 1918 he transferred to 2nd Royal Fusiliers. A few weeks later he was killed near Borre, on 19th August 1918, and was buried there by his comrades, although after the war no grave could be found. By the age of only

Lieutenant L.J. Brown.

twenty-two, Leonard Pope was a veteran soldier of four regiments, four wounds and almost every major battle on the Western Front. For reasons that remain a mystery, his true surname was never revealed to the IWGC and he is recorded on the East Surrey panel as Brown.

THE WRONG MEMORIAL: In the immediate post-war years the Imperial War Graves Commission faced the mammoth task of compiling records of all those who had died in the war, and understandably many mistakes and omissions were made. Indeed, names are still being added to the Menin Gate and Tyne Cot. Some men were also commemorated on the wrong memorial, and one of these was Thomas Henry Bowley. A Regular soldier who had joined the Border Regiment in 1893, Bowley served in the Boer War with the 1st Battalion. By 1914 he was a Company Sergeant Major in the 2nd Battalion, and when war broke out he was offered a commission in the regiment

Lieutenant
Thomas Bowley.

that had been his home for more than twenty years. However, no vacancies were then available for Second Lieutenants in the Border Regiment and he was eventually commissioned in the Leicesters. However, he never served with that regiment, nor wore its badges. Keeping his Border badges, he stayed with the 2nd Battalion until he was killed on Kruiseek Hill on 26th October 1914. Although buried in a makeshift trench with his men, Bowley's grave was lost in later fighting and as this sector of the battlefield was covered by the Menin Gate Memorial, he should have been commemorated there. But when the IWGC looked at its records, he was officially listed as an officer in the 1st Battalion Leicestershire Regiment, which was south of Armèntieres on the day Bowley died. With so many names to commemorate there was no time to double-check all the details and his name was therefore erroneously recorded here at Ploegsteert on the Leicesters' panel.

Leaving Berks Cemetery and the Ploegsteert Memorial, **turn left** onto the main Ypres road and continue to a junction by a café on the left. This was Hyde Park Corner, a major road junction. There is an information panel on the grass area ahead. Here **turn left** down a secondary road. The wooded embankment of Hill 63 is then on your right. Just up on the right

Hyde Park Corner in 1919.

is a signposted footpath going up the side of the hill. Follow it through the trees towards the crest of Hill 63 and where this path meets a track, **stop**.

Hill 63 was a high point south of the Messines Ridge which dominated the terrain west of Plugstreet Wood. It fell into British hands in 1914, and remained behind their lines until captured by the Germans in April 1918. It was retaken by the 31st Division in September 1918. On the western side was Rosenberg Chateau, an advanced dressing station where a military cemetery was established (see above), and on the southern slopes huge dugouts and tunnels were constructed by Australian Engineers at the 'Catacombs'. To the east was La Hutte Chateau, used as a headquarters by the 1st Cavalry Brigade in November 1914, but in ruins by 1915. However, due to its commanding position, there were several observation posts here and even today the view from the crest of Hill 63 is considerable.

A good account of the April 1918 period is given by Major R.T. Rees, who was in the defences on Hill 63 at this time with the 8th Battalion Loyal North Lancashires. Having served in Plugstreet Wood during 1916–17, Rees knew the ground well, but he soon found himself in a precarious position as Messines fell on his left flank, Armentières was known to have been captured on the right, and Plugstreet Wood was rapidly being infiltrated in front of his battalion. A telephone conversation with his commanding officer, telling Rees to hold at all costs, was suddenly cut short when the dugout occupied by this officer and the two other battalion commanders in the brigade, as well as their adjutants, was suddenly over-run by the Germans. Rees found himself the only senior field officer left on Hill 63. As the Germans swarmed forward, Rees went to consider the situation:

> I was standing with my Adjutant on the Messines road, and as we had no trenches to hold on to, I told him that I thought we might justifiably regard the position as untenable.[5]

Hill 63 was captured by the Germans, and Major Rees and his men were forced into the Douve valley, under heavy fire from German machine-guns. Several days later Rees was wounded by a shell at Ravelsberg, losing a hand. He returned to his civilian occupation as a schoolmaster at Dulwich College.

Follow the track on Hill 63 eastwards and down the slopes to the main Ypres road. Cross and follow a minor road signposted with a large CWGC sign indicating several cemeteries. Plugstreet Wood is clearly visible to your right. Continue to the first military cemetery.

PROWSE POINT MILITARY CEMETERY

Prowse Point was a feature on British maps named after Brigadier General C.B. 'Bertie' Prowse DSO; it was one of several sites on the Western Front named after this brave and charismatic soldier. Prowse was a Regular army officer, and served at Plugstreet in December 1914 as a Captain in the 1st Battalion Somerset Light Infantry; later he rose to command the battalion and by 1916 was Brigadier General of the brigade in which the 1st SLI served. Mortally wounded on the Somme on 1st July 1916, he is buried at Louvencourt. The cemetery here was started by the 2nd Battalion Royal Dublin Fusiliers and the 1st Battalion Royal Warwickshire Regiment (both from 4th Division) in November 1914, and stayed in regular use until April 1918, with a few graves added during the September 1918 fighting. Burials total 159 British, forty-two New Zealand, thirteen Australian, twelve German prisoners and one Canadian. Among them is one unknown British soldier.

Bruce Bairnsfather, creator of the 'Old Bill' cartoons, was an officer in the 1st Royal Warwicks, and the cemetery contains many of this unit's dead in Plot I. The only Canadian grave is that of Private W. Davis (I-F-14) of the 10th Battalion Canadian Infantry, who was killed on 25th February 1915, during the unit's first tour of the trenches; indeed, he was their first combat casualty. Having only been in France for a few weeks, many Canadian battalions were on attachment to British formations at this time for instructional purposes. A small group of men from the 2nd Royal Berkshires are in Plot III, continuing that regiment's connection with the Plugstreet area. Among them are Regimental Sergeant Major J. Campbell (III-A-4) and Sergeant W.A. Connor DCM (III-B-7); both were killed on 15th October 1917 when shells fell on the front-line positions opposite Warneton. RSM Campbell was a holder of the 1914 (Mons) Star and had been Mentioned in Dispatches. In addition to his DCM, Connor had been

Soldiers of the Rifle Brigade in Ploegsteert Wood in the winter of 1914/15.

awarded the French Croix de Guerre. The New Zealand burials include several from the Maori Pioneer Battalion, amongst them an officer, Second Lieutenant A.P. Kaipara (III-A-26), who died on 4th August 1917.

In recent years the area around Ploegsteert has seen an increasing amount of battlefield archaeology, during which the bodies of several soldiers have been found. Three recent reburials are here, two from the same unit and the same action. Privates Harry Wilkinson (I-A-7) and

Christmas card and two images of men of the 2nd Essex Regiment taken in the trenches near Ploegsteert in early 1915.

273

Three further images of men of the 2nd Essex Regiment near Ploegsteert in 1915.

Richard Lancaster (III-C-1B) died with the 2nd Lancashire Fusiliers on 10th November 1914. Harry's remains were found in a field near the wood in 2001, and Richard's a few years later. Both were identified following work by the local archaeology group. Private Alan J. Mather (III-C-1AA) was killed in the Battle of Messines on 8th June 1917 while serving with the 33rd Australian Infantry; he was found in 2008 and reburied here in 2010. With the work continuing, no doubt there will be other burials.

Next to the cemetery is a new memorial site created for the Great War Centenary. It includes a memorial to the Christmas Truce in 1914 and two sets of trenches, along with a First World War bunker. A casual visitor looking at this site will quickly believe that a game of football took place in this area on Christmas Day 1914; while there was indeed a truce here, there is no evidence at all for a kick about, let alone a game of football. Such memorials often say more about modern views of the war, rather than reflecting the past. The trenches, while interesting, do not represent any aspect of the system that was once here: both are located behind the British front line, for example. The bunker, while original, was removed from another site near Ploegsteert and moved to this site in 2015.

Leaving the cemetery/memorial site, continue along the road for a short distance, then take the **first right-hand turning**, following a track down to another military cemetery.

MUD CORNER BRITISH CEMETERY
Those who walk these routes outside of the summer months will realise how apt the name Mud Corner was – and is – for this junction on the north edge of Plugstreet Wood. The cemetery was started on 7th June 1917, the opening day of Messines, and continued in use until the end of that year. New Zealand graves dominate with fifty-three burials; in addition there are thirty-one Australians and one British soldier, who is unknown. The NZEF graves include many Gallipoli veterans, among them three older men: Private E. Breach (II-C-6) of the 2nd Wellington Regiment was fifty-four when he died on 26th July 1917; Privates D. Cowie (II-A-1) and A. McKenzie (II-A-9) of the Auckland Regiment were forty-three and forty-seven respectively when they were killed in June 1917. McKenzie had been at Gallipoli, and was a veteran of the Boer War.

Returning to the metalled track, continue in the direction of the wood; the track soon goes left and then later turns left again into the wood itself, and brings you out on the main ride through Plugstreet Wood.

This ride is a new one and was not here during the war, but it runs parallel to another ride, which was; known as Hunters Avenue by the British troops who served in the wood, it was lined with duckboards and corduroy tracks, easing the frequent problems of mud. All the other rides and breastworks were given similar names, often reflecting the units that passed through here. For example, Strand, Charing Cross, Oxford Circus, Rotten Row, London Avenue, Fleet Street and Bunhill Row all date from when the 1/5th Battalion London Regiment (London Rifle Brigade) served at Plugstreet in the winter of 1914/15. This unit was a pre-war Territorial battalion raised in April 1908, and its London headquarters were in Bunhill Row, thus one of the names. Henry Williamson, in later life to achieve fame as author of *Tarka the Otter* and the series of fictional novels *A Chronicle of Ancient Sunlight*, served with the London Rifle Brigade (LRB) in the wood at this time. The brigade was attached to Regular battalions of the 4th Division and its men were largely employed on fatigue duties, repairing and expanding the network of defences in and around Plugstreet.

Others who knew Hunters Avenue were future Prime Minister Anthony Eden, then a young subaltern in the 21st KRRC (Yeoman's Rifles), on his first visit to the front line, and also Roland Leighton, fiancé of Vera Brittain, and immortalised in her *Testament of Youth*. Leighton spent several months in Plugstreet Wood with the 1/7th Battalion Worcestershire Regiment, prior to meeting his death on the Somme in late 1915. He wrote the following poem, *Villanelle*, in April 1915 while in this sector:

Violets from Plug Street Wood
Sweet, I send you overseas.
(It is strange that they should be blue,
Blue, when his soaked blood was red,
For they grew around his head;
It is strange they should be blue.)

Violets from Plug Street Wood –
Think what they have meant to me –
Life and Hope and Love and You
(And did you not see them grow
Where his mangled body lay,
Hiding horror from the day;
Sweetest, it was better so.)

Violets from overseas,
To your dear, far, forgetting land
These I send in memory,
Knowing You will understand.

There are three military cemeteries along Hunters Avenue, and it is suggested you walk to the furthest first and then come back, as there is sadly no through route in the wood; from here, follow the ride south to the end where it meets the military cemetery.

RIFLE HOUSE CEMETERY

Deep in the heart of Plugstreet Wood, this quiet and secluded cemetery was started by the 1st Battalion Rifle Brigade of 4th Division in November 1914. These early graves are now in Plot IV Rows E–J. There are 229 British burials and one Canadian; among them are two unknown soldiers. A very young soldier among the 1st Rifle Brigade casualties is Rifleman Reuben Barnett (IV-E-10), who died on 19th December 1914, aged fifteen. From Stoke Newington, he is ranked among the youngest soldiers to die at Ypres. Again continuing the Royal Berkshire Regiment connection, early officer losses from the 5th Battalion are found here. They died during their first tour of the front line. The 11th Cheshires are also well represented from when they first came to Plugstreet, between November 1915 and January 1916. Ironically, the unit returned to the wood in April 1918 during the Lys offensive.

Returning to the main avenue go north; another cemetery is on the left.

PLOEGSTEERT WOOD MILITARY CEMETERY

The headstones in this cemetery are arranged in an irregular fashion, reflecting the layout as and when burials were made. There are four distinct regimental plots – 'comrade cemeteries'. Plot II was the 'SLI Cemetery' containing thirty-two graves of men from Bertie Prowse's 1st Battalion Somerset Light Infantry, with a further ten in Plot I; among them are five officers and a Company Sergeant Major. Nearby is the brave medical officer of the 1st SLI, Lieutenant J.R. Waddy MC (I-B-3), who survived the 1914 actions only to be killed on 17th March 1915. Plot III has sixteen men from the 1/5th Battalion Gloucestershire Regiment who fell in May 1915, twelve from the 8th Loyal North Lancs and twenty-eight Canadians, their presence once giving it the name 'Canadian Cemetery, Strand'. Plot IV is the 'Bucks Cemetery', and commemorates twenty men of the Bucks Battalion Oxfordshire & Buckinghamshire Light Infantry, who died in April 1915. The cemetery remained in use between 1916 and 1917, the last burial being from the New Zealand Division in August. Total burials are therefore: 118 British, twenty-eight Canadian, eighteen New Zealand, and one Australian. Among them are two unknowns.

Again returning to the main avenue, follow it to the far end where it reaches another small cemetery.

TORONTO AVENUE CEMETERY

Despite having a Canadian name (after a trench that ran near the Moated Farm north of the wood), all seventy-eight graves are Diggers from the 9th Brigade, 3rd (Australian) Division, who were killed in the Battle of Messines between the 7th and 10th June 1917. The four battalions in this brigade were all recruited in the New South Wales area. Most were killed at Factory Farm, east of Plugstreet Wood.

Leaving the cemetery, turn right at the main ride junction, and follow the same route as you came in by, out past Mud Corner and back to Prowse Point. When the track meets the minor road, **turn right** and follow to the first bend in the road. **Stop**, and look north-east.

Here, you are only 100 yards from the site of the British front line in December 1914. Bruce Bairnsfather served here with the 1st Royal Warwicks on Christmas Day 1914, and his unit was one of many to be involved in a truce with the Germans. He later wrote:

> . . . a complete Bosche figure suddenly appeared on the parapet, and looked about itself. This complaint became infectious . . . This was the signal for more Bosche anatomy to be disclosed . . . until, in less time than it takes to tell, half a dozen or so of each of the belligerents were outside their trenches and were advancing towards each other in No Man's Land.
>
> It all felt most curious . . . Here they were – the actual, practical soldiers of the German Army. There was not an atom of hate on either side that day . . . It was just like the interval between the rounds in a friendly boxing match.[6]

Close by is a memorial to the Christmas Truce; it actually records an event staged by a re-enactment group to commemorate the truce and overlooks the fields where these events took place in December 1914.

Continue to the next bend. This is the hamlet of St Yves, and just past it on the right was the site of the St Yves Post Office mentioned by Bairnsfather in his book, *Bullets and Billets*. It was in these buildings at St Yves that the genesis of the famous 'Old Bill' cartoons lay, with Bairnsfather often painting them on the walls. By 1918 all traces of the original hamlet had gone. A recent memorial on the wall of one of the buildings records this fact.

Staying on the minor road, follow it until it becomes sunken and joins another. Here **turn right** and then **first left**. Head for the group of trees a few hundred yards further up, to the left of the road.

Although this is private ground, it can often be entered. Within the trees is a large mine crater, from one of several mines blown here on 7th

In 1955 one of the unused mines from the Battle of Messines exploded during a thunderstorm near Ploegsteert Wood. Local villagers are shown standing in the crater. (*John Giles archive*)

June 1917 during the Battle of Messines. On that day nineteen mines were blown between Hill 60 and Plugstreet, creating the largest ever man-made explosion to that date; it was heard as far away as London and Dublin. This is Trench 122 crater, worked on by men of the 3rd Canadian Tunnelling Company, and a charge of 20,000lbs of Ammonal was used. Just to the south another crater can be seen; this is Factory Farm crater and was created by a mine dug by the same unit. Here, on 7th June, a charge of 40,000lbs of Ammonal blew a hole 228 feet across.

The craters were attacked by men of the 3rd (Australian) Division, then led by John Monash, who later rose to command the whole Australian Corps in 1918. Units of the 9th Brigade took these positions at Trench 122 and Factory Farm; their dead were buried at Toronto Avenue Cemetery in Plugstreet Wood (see above). The Australian official historian recorded:

> The mine explosions and the tremendous barrage caused the great assault in its early stages to be easier than any in which Australians had been involved. The local German garrison . . . was entirely unstrung. The mines blew vast craters . . . and each shattered or buried beneath its heaped-up rim the garrison of some 150 yards of trench.[7]

German soldiers in a flooded trench near Ploegsteert.

Leaving the craters, return along the same road to a T-junction. Here **turn left** and follow this route running parallel to the eastern edge of the wood; further along on the right is a small memorial to Harry Wilkinson, who was found in this field in 2001. Later it goes to the right where a minor road joins it from the left. **Stop**.

This was the site of the Birdcage. It was in this sector that the London Rifle Brigade spent the winter of 1914/15. Men used to the city streets of London found conditions here at that time very difficult:

When the Regiment moved into Ploegsteert there was a good deal of frost, and many of the men suffered from it, particularly in their feet. Immediately afterwards rain set in and continued almost without a break during the winter, which was one of the wettest for some time. No small amount of pluck was required to step into trenches which generally had two feet or more of icy cold water in them, on a dark night, knowing that boots and puttees would be soaking wet for two, three or four days.[8]

Continue, following the road by the tree line. A couple of hundred yards past the last bend, a farm can be seen in the field to the left. **Stop.**

These farm buildings are on the site of what Henry Williamson knew as 'The Diehard T-trench' when he served at Plugstreet with the LRB in 1914. He recalled in his fictionalised memoirs:

The Diehard T-trench, of 'unsavoury reputation' as the current phrase went, was a bad, water-logged trench on the left of the battalion front. Before the October fighting, it had been a draining ditch of the arable field now part of No Man's Land. It lay parallel to, and just behind a quick-hedge bordering a lane fifty or sixty yards away from the eastern edge of the wood. Not only was it a natural drain, but as it projected into a salient in the German lines, it was enfiladed both down the stem and along the cross of the T.

Saturday Night Soldiers: men of the London Rifle Brigade in 1914.

281

Everywhere it could be shot straight down from the various points in the opposing trench. A fixed rifle dominated one part of it; at least two snipers had two other places 'set'. [Here] . . . two men had been shot, one behind the other, one shorter than the other, by the same bullet, apparently, passing through the head of the first and the neck of the second.[9]

Continue. At the crossroads, in the hamlet of Le Gheer, turn right and follow a better road along the southern edge of the wood for over a kilometre to a military cemetery.

LANCASHIRE COTTAGE CEMETERY

Named after a farm building on the opposite side of the road, the cemetery was started by the 1st Battalion East Lancashire Regiment and the 1st Battalion Hampshire Regiment of 4th Division in November 1914. It remained in use for front-line burials up to March 1916 and on a few occasions in later years. After the Germans captured the area in April 1918, they established a military cemetery of their own to the rear of this one, but these graves were removed after the war. Today Lancashire Cottage contains 229 British graves, along with twenty-three Australians, thirteen German prisoners and two Canadians. Special Memorials exist to two men, and there are three unknowns.

The original plot is dominated by the 1st East Lancs, with eighty-four graves. The 1st Hampshires have fifty-six. Both these battalions had been at Le Cateau and on the Aisne before coming to Plugstreet. The 1st East Lancs buried eight of their original officers in this cemetery, among them Captain G. Clayhills DSO (I-B-7). Clayhills had been with the regiment since 1899, serving in the Boer War with a mounted infantry unit and being awarded a DSO for bravery, along with two Mentions in Dispatches. The 1st Hampshires section is dominated by the losses suffered on 19th December 1914. In Plot I are several LRB casualties, and the youngest soldier at Lancashire Cottage is Bugler M. Dudley (II-D-7) of 15th Battalion Canadian Infantry (48th Highlanders), who died on 29th September 1915, aged seventeen.

Leave by the main gate and rejoin the road, turning left in the direction of Plugstreet village. It is reached after a further kilometre or so. At the roundabout in the centre of the village walk over to the church, behind which are several war graves.

Captain G. Clayhills DSO.

Ploegsteert village in 1914.

The entrance to Ploegsteert in 1915.

PLOEGSTEERT CHURCHYARD

The 1st Hampshires buried their other rank casualties in Lancashire Cottage Cemetery, but the officers were brought here for burial. Five of them are in this churchyard, including Major G.H. Parker (A-6), who was killed on 19th December 1914; he had been commanding the battalion since September, and was a veteran of the Boer War. Two other 1914 casualties were laid to rest here, the next burials being made by the Canadians, who added a further two in 1915. One of them was Lieutenant H.B. Boggs, who was the first officer to be killed with the 7th Battalion Canadian Infantry.

Return to the roundabout. From here take the main road north, using the pavement and the cycle path, where necessary. Many new houses and other buildings have obscured the view to the wood. Further on, another military cemetery is reached on the right.

STRAND MILITARY CEMETERY

The Strand was a long trench which led into Plugstreet Wood. An advanced dressing station was started near the section of the trench which ran close to the current location of the cemetery, and two soldiers who died of wounds were buried there in October 1914. No further burials were made until April 1917, when a proper military cemetery was established in what are now Plots I–VI; this was used until July 1917. Of

The road near The Strand in 1919.

the 351 graves, 232 are men from units in Monash's 3rd (Australian) Division which held this sector at that time. Plots VII–X were made after the war by concentrating graves from a wide area between Wytschaete and Armentières. In total there are now 725 British burials, 284 Australian, eighty-seven New Zealand, twenty-six Canadian, four German prisoners and one South African. Of these, 356 are unknown and there are nineteen Special Memorials.

Of the British burials, many are Regular soldiers who died in 1914. Private J. Harrington (IX-F-8) of the 2nd Leinsters was killed during the Christmas Truce on 25th December 1914 in the trenches at L'Epinette. The first Canadian officer to die on the battlefield in the Great War was Lieutenant Duncan Peter Bell-Irving (X-H-9) of the 2nd Field Company Canadian Engineers. The Canadians had only been in France for a few days at this time, and Bell-Irving was attached to a British unit when he was killed by shell-fire on 26th February 1915.

Continuing along the main road, return to Hyde Park Corner (Royal Berks) Cemetery and your vehicle.

Notes

1. For further information see Spagnoly, A. *Salient Points* (Leo Cooper 1996).
2. 14th Battalion Royal Irish Rifles *War Diary*, 17.2.17, TNA WO95/2511.
3. 21st Battalion King's Royal Rifle Corps *War Diary*, 30.6.16, TNA WO95/2643.
4. Anon. 'Sapper Hackett VC' in *The Ypres Times* Vol 1, No 29, October 1923, p.251.
5. Rees, R.T. *A Schoolmaster At War* (Haycock Press c.1930) p.110.
6. Bairnsfather, B. *Bullets and Billets* (Grant Richards Ltd 1916) pp.91–2.
7. Bean, C.E.W. *The Australian Imperial Force in France 1917* (Angus & Robertson 1943) pp.593–4.
8. Anon. *The History of the London Rifle Brigade 1859–1919* (Constable 1921) pp.74–5.
9. Williamson, H. *A Fox Under My Cloak* (MacDonald & Co 1985) p.34.

Acknowledgements

The genesis of *Walking Ypres* began a long time ago now and for some early help I would like to take this opportunity to thank my former teachers at Holy Trinity School, Crawley, for taking me to the Salient all those years ago: the late Roger Bastable and Les Coates (himself the author of two superb books on the Great War) have a lot to answer for!

Those who have walked Ypres with me over the years include: the late Stephen Clarke, Geoff Goodyear, Marc Hope, Tony and Joan Poucher, the late Terry Russell, Peter Smith, Frank and Lou Stockdale, Pam Waugh, Andrew Whittington, and not forgetting of course the old 'Sussex Pals': Geoff Bridger, the late Brian Fullagar, Clive Metcalfe, Julian Sykes and Terry Whippy.

Dozens of others helped with a multitude of tasks, among them: the Commonwealth War Graves Commission office Ypres, Ron Jack who obtained a copy of Talbot Papineau's service record for me, Andy Moss, the staff of the Public Record Office, Tony Scala, Rob Schaefer and the late Klaus Späth for the loan of several German photographs, and Mike Stockbridge.

Having organised battlefield tours to the Ypres Salient for tens of thousands of people since 1997 with Leger Holidays, this had brought me into contact with many good work colleagues from office staff to our fantastic teams of drivers, many of them keen battlefield enthusiasts. And not forgetting the passengers – many have become good friends.

In the Ypres area itself the locals have always been kind and helpful. Over the years I have been lucky to find many good friends in Flanders and would like to thank just a few of them here: Niek and family at the superb Hooge Crater Museum, Henk and family formerly of the Hotel Sultan, the late Albert Beke who worked in the Ypres Salient Museum, Charlotte Cardoen Descamps and her family of Varlet Farm, Burt Heyvaert, Jacky Platteeuw, Aurel Sercu, Simon Verdegem and Johan Vandewalle. Two special people have been friends for many, many years and it is always a pleasure to see them: Jacques Ryckebosche and Genevra Charsley.

Unless otherwise stated, all photographs and maps are from the author's archives. As with my previous books, I have tried to include a large number of previously unpublished, or rarely published, photographs which, judging by the reaction of the readership, is warmly welcome. John Giles' aerial photographs are used with the kind permission of his wife, Margery. Extracts from the works of Henry Williamson are reproduced courtesy of the H.W. Literary Estate.

Abbreviations

Ranks:

2/Lt	Second Lieutenant
A/Bmdr	Acting Bombardier
Brig-Gen	Brigadier-General
Capt	Captain
Col	Colonel
Cpl	Corporal
CQMS	Company Quarter Master Sergeant
CRA	Commander Royal Artillery
CSM	Company Sergeant Major
Dmr	Drummer
L/Cpl	Lance Corporal
L/Sgt	Lance Sergeant
Lieut	Lieutenant
Lt-Col	Lieutenant-Colonel
Lt-Gen	Lieutenant-General
OC	Officer Commanding
Pnr	Pioneer
Pte	Private
RSM	Regimental Sergeant Major
Sgt	Sergeant

Medals and awards:

DCM	Distinguished Conduct Medal
DSO	Distinguished Service Order
MC	Military Cross
MM	Military Medal
VC	Victoria Cross

General:

ADS	Advanced Dressing Station
AIF	Australian Imperial Force
ASC	Army Service Corps
Bn	Battalion
Bty	Battery
CWGC	Commonwealth War Graves Commission
KOYLI	King's Own Yorkshire Light Infantry

KRRC	King's Royal Rifle Corps
NZEF	New Zealand Expeditionary Force
RAMC	Royal Army Medical Corps
RAP	Regimental Aid Post
RE	Royal Engineers
RFA	Royal Field Artillery
RFC	Royal Flying Corps
RGA	Royal Garrison Artillery
RHA	Royal Horse Artillery
RND	Royal Naval Division
RWF	Royal Welsh Fusiliers

Grave Location in Cemeteries:

(B-22)	Row B Grave 22
(I-C-17)	Plot 1 Row C Grave 17

Further Reading

The fighting at Ypres has prompted a wealth of publications, many of which are mentioned in the chapter notes at the end of each walk. Other useful books include:

Anon. *Ypres and The Battles of Ypres* (Michelin Tyre Company 1919, reprinted)
Now reprinted, this book is widely available again. Probably the first battlefield guide to the Ypres Salient, it is a remarkable document in its own right and the photographs give a good impression of the state of the battlefield just after the war.

Barton, P. *Passchendaele 1917* (Constable 2007)
A large, landscape-format book, this excellent account of the Third Battle of Ypres is enhanced by the use of panoramic photographs taken during the war. It offers a real insight into the wartime landscape.

Brice, B. *The Battle Book of Ypres* (John Murray 1927; Pen & Sword 2014)
Now reprinted, this book is easily available. Although far from complete, it lists by location many battle sites within the Salient, relating incidents and actions which took place there. A useful gazetteer.

Coombes, R. *Before Endeavours Fade* (After The Battle – many reprints)
Rightly considered as the 'bible' to the Western Front, the late Rose Coombes' love of the Ypres Salient is clearly apparent from the section dealing with the battlefields in Flanders. No library is complete without this book.

Giles, J. *The Ypres Salient Then and Now* (After The Battle 1986)
Originally published in the 1970s, this was one of the books that helped to renew interest in the Great War, inspiring many pilgrims to visit Ypres, this author among them.

Fox, C. et al. *Arras To Cambrai: The Kitchener Battalions of the Royal Berkshire Regiment 1917* (University of Reading 1997)
This is part of a series of four books chronicling the history of the New Army battalions of the Royal Berkshire Regiment in the Great War. A superb example of how research into a particular battalion, or regiment, can be made relevant and of interest to a wider audience. Highly recommended.

Liddle, P. (Ed.) *Passchendaele In Perspective* (Leo Cooper 1997)
A collection of essays by various authors with a particular knowledge or research interest in the Third Battle of Ypres. This mammoth book covers everything from tactics and generalship, to what equipment the soldiers used and the battlefields today.

McCarthy, C. *Passchendaele: The Day by Day Account* (Arms & Armour Press 1995)
Similar to his previous volume on the Somme, this book relies heavily on the Official History, and is a useful diary of the conduct of the campaign, and what each division was up to and when. Profusely illustrated with IWM photographs, but sadly the maps are generally poor.

MacDonald, L. *They Called It Passchendaele* (Michael Joseph 1978)
Another of the books that helped rekindle interest in the Great War, it remains as impressive today as when it was first published almost forty years ago. It conveys a view of the battle from the men who were there, veterans who are sadly no longer with us.

Powell, A. *A Deep Cry: A Literary Pilgrimage to the Battlefields and Cemeteries of the First World War Soldier Poets Killed in Northern France and Flanders* (Palladour Books 1993)
A superb and well researched book giving biographies of sixty-six soldier poets who died on the Western Front, with extracts from their letters, diaries and poems. Many of these either served at Ypres or died in the Salient.

Schaefer, R. & Doyle, P. *Fritz & Tommy: Across The Barbed Wire* (History Press 2015)
An important book in our understanding of the Great War, telling it from both sides. It includes much material relating to Flanders and is highly recommended.

Scott, M. *The Ypres Salient: A Guide to the Cemeteries and Memorials of the Salient* (Gliddon Books 1992)
Despite its many faults and omissions, this publication remains the only comprehensive study detailing every military cemetery within the Ypres Salient. Although out of print, it is still widely available from several sources.

Westlake, R. *British Battalions in France & Belgium 1914 & British Battalions in France & Belgium 1915* (Leo Cooper 1997, 1998)
The first volume covers the whole period from the outbreak of war to the end of 1914, but those with an interest in First Ypres will find this a most useful reference book. The second covers January to June 1915, so Second Ypres is well covered. Every battalion which took part in the fighting is listed, together with a summarised account of their movements.

Index

Bedford House 117–19, 137
Bluff, The 117, 121, 122, 123, 124–5, 133–4, 136
Boesinghe 70–1
Bridge No. 10 21–2
Brombeek 144

Cemeteries and Memorials to the Missing:
1/DCLI Cemetery, The Bluff 124–5
Artillery Wood Cemetery 72–3
Bard Cottage Cemetery 67–8
Bedford House Cemetery 117–21
Berks Cemetery Extension 266–7
Birr Cross Roads Cemetery 84–6
Blauwepoort Farm Cemetery 115–16
Brandhoek Military Cemetery 173–5
Brandhoek New Military Cemetery 172–3
Brandhoek New Military Cemetery No. 3 170–2
Cement House Cemetery 138–41
Chester Farm Cemetery 136–7
Croonaert Chapel Cemetery 242–3
Dragoon Camp Cemetery 74
Duhallow ADS Cemetery 61–2
Essex Farm Cemetery 62–7
Hagle Dump Cemetery 177–8
Hedge Row Trench Cemetery 124
Hooge Crater Cemetery 94–5
Hop Store Cemetery 186–7
Hospital Farm Cemetery 181–2
Hyde Park Corner (Royal Berks) Cemetery 265–6
Irish House Cemetery 235–8
Kemmel Chateau Cemetery 221–4, 239
Kemmel Churchyard 224
La Plus Douve Farm Cemetery 252

Lancashire Cottage Cemetery 282
Langemarck German Cemetery 145–9
Lijssenthoek Military Cemetery 202–7
Locre Churchyard 211–12
Locre Hospice Cemetery 213–15
Lone Tree Cemetery 261–2
Maple Copse Cemetery 113–14
Menin Gate Memorial 31–6
Menin Road South Cemetery 39–42
Messines Ridge British Cemetery 258
Mud Corner British Cemetery 275
Oak Dump Cemetery 134
Oxford Road Cemetery 50–2
Passchendaele New British Cemetery 165–6
Ploegsteert Churchyard 283
Ploegsteert Memorial 267–70
Ploegsteert Wood Military Cemetery 277
Poperinghe New Military Cemetery 200–2
Potijze Burial Ground 53
Potijze Chateau Grounds Cemetery 46–7
Potijze Chateau Lawn Cemetery 47–8
Potijze Chateau Wood Cemetery 48–9
Prowse Point Military Cemetery 272–5
Ramparts Cemetery 25
Ration Farm Annexe (La Plus Douve) Cemetery 251
RE Grave 89
Rifle House Cemetery 277
Ruisseau Farm Cemetery 141–2
St Charles de Potijze French Cemetery 49–50

St Quentin Cabaret Military
  Cemetery 245–7
Sanctuary Wood British Cemetery 82
Spoilbank Cemetery 134–6
Strand Military Cemetery 284–5
Talana Farm Cemetery 77
Toronto Avenue Cemetery 278
Transport Farm (Railway Dugouts)
  Cemetery 103–6, 115
Tuileries British Cemetery 111–12
Tyne Cot Cemetery & Memorial
  154–62
Vlamertinghe Military Cemetery
  183–5
Wieltje Farm Cemetery 52–3
Woods Cemetery 125
Wulverghem Churchyard 249
Wytschaete Military Cemetery 227,
  229
Ypres Reservoir Cemetery 19–21
Ypres Town Cemetery 54–7
Cloth Hall 13–15
Croonaert Wood 238, 240–2, 243

Diehard T-Trench 281–2
Dirty Bucket Camp 178–80
Douve River 245, 250, 252, 253

Essex Farm 62–7

Factory Farm Crater 279

Grand Bois 238, 240

Hellfire Corner 42–4
Hill 60 105, 106, 107, 108, 111, 112,
  116, 117, 124, 125, 127–33
Hill 62 101–2
Hill 63 265, 266, 270, 271
Hollandscheschuur Farm 238, 239, 240
Hooge Chateau 95
Hooge Crater Café & Museum 92–4
Hussar Farm 44–5

Irish Peace Tower 256

Kemmel 212, 213, 218, 219, 220,
  225, 226, 231
Kemmel Hill 211, 212, 213, 215–18

Langemarck 138–51
Le Gheer 282
Lettenberg Bunkers 224
Lille Gate 25–7
Locre 208, 210, 211, 226
Locre Hospice 213

Maedelstade Farm 231, 232
Maple Copse 113
Memorial Museum Passchendaele
  152–4
Menin Gate 29–31, 37–9
Messines 252–62

Observatory Ridge 113
Ontario Farm 259
Oxford Road 49–50

Passchendaele 152–69
People:
  Ackroyd VC, Capt H. 85–6, 100
  Bairnsfather, Bruce 249, 272, 278
  Baker, Herbert 156
  Barrett VC, Pte T. 67
  Battenberg, Prince Maurice 55
  Beatty-Pownall, Lt-Col. G.E. 205
  Bedson, Spr W.H. 222–4, 239
  Bell-Irving, Lt D.P. 285
  Bent VC, Lt-Col. P.E. 159–60
  Blomfield, Sir Reginald 18, 40–1,
    54–5
  Blunden, Edmund 45–6, 182–3
  Blythe, Colin 52
  Boardman, Lt-Col. T.H. 173
  Bonham-Carter, Capt G. 183
  Bowley, Lt T. 269–70
  Brown, Capt J.E.G. 112
  Brown, Lt L.J. 269
  Bugden VC, Pte P.J. 94–5
  Bye VC, Sgt R.J. 72
  Carlill, Pte A. 148

Carlos, Lt E.S. 136
Chapman, Capt G.M. 46–7
Chavasse VC, Capt N. 91, 172–3
Chester-Master, Lt-Col. R.C. 213
Chisenhale-Marsh, Capt A.H. 206
Clamp VC, Cpl W. 160
Clarke, Lt-Col. J. 174
Clayhills, Capt G. 282
Colyer-Ferguson VC, Capt T.R. 41–2
Congreve VC, Mjr W. 88
Cooper VC, Sgt E. 149–51
Croshaw, Lt-Col. O.M. 119
Crossley, Rfn L. 266
Crossley, Rfn W. 266
De Coteau, Pte A. 165
De Gunzberg, Baron A. 109
Dix, Lt-Col. S.H. 159
Du Maurier, Lt-Col. G.L.B. 222
Dwyer VC, Pte E. 128
Eddy, 2/Lt C. 161
Evans, Elas ('Hedd Wyn') 73
Fazakerley-Westby, Capt. G. 124–5
Fitzclarence VC, Brig-Gen. C. 34
French, Rfn A.E. 265
Garstin, Lt C. 140
Glubb, Sir John 108
Gordon, Brig-Gen. A.F. 205
Gordon-Lennox, Lord B.C. 109
Grenfell VC, Capt. F.O. 183
Hackett VC, Spr W. 268
Haggard, Capt. R.L. 166
Haig, Sir Douglas 42
Hallowes VC, Lt R. 96–7, 121
Heyworth, Brig-Gen. F.J. 174
Humphreys, Mjr G.G.P. 224
Jeffries VC, Capt. C. 157, 168
Knott, Capt. J.L. 20
Knowles, Capt. J. 140
Ledwidge, Francis 73
Leighton, Roland 276
Lockley, Pte L.H. 148
Lodge, Raymond 86
Lutyens, Edwin 156
McCrae, John 58, 64

McGee VC, Sgt L. 157–8
MacLachlain, Brig-Gen. R.C. 213
Marillier DCM, 2/Lt F.C.J. 34
Maxwell VC, Brig-Gen. F.A. 20–1
Mercer, Brig-Gen. M.S. 205
Mitford, Mjr Hon. C.B.O. 183
Moorhouse, Lt-Col. H. 161
Moorhouse, Capt. R. 161
Neave, Mjr A. 56
Papineau, Mjr T.M. 33, 34, 162–4, 166
Parnell, Lt H.F. 110
Parry, Harold 184–5
Patch, Harry 142–3, 149
Philby, Mjr H.P. 186–7
Playfair, Lt L. 182
Plumer, Lord 32, 50
Poulton Palmer, Lt R.W. 265
Prowse, Brig-Gen. C.B. 272
Rae, Lt T.K.H. 83
Redmond MP, Mjr Willie 211, 214, 215
Rees, Mjr R.T. 271
Riddell, Brig-Gen. J.F. 158–9
Rising, Mjr R. 110
Robertson VC, Capt. C. 51–2
Robertson VC, Pte J.P. 158
Robinson, Lt-Col. H.T.K. 133
St George, 2/Lt H.A. 110
Sargeaunt, Lt-Col. A.F. 174
Scott, Lt-Col. A. de C. 111
Seaman VC, Cpl E. 160–1
Service, Robert 105
Shedden, Capt. G. 56
Skinner VC, CSM J. 143–4
Snow, Mjr-Gen. Sir T. D'O. 45
Spindler, Staff Nurse Nellie 206–7
Steere, Lt J. 111
Strudwick, Valentine 66–7
Talbot, Lt Gilbert 82
Tubb VC, Mjr F.H. 205–6
Voss, Werner 148
Waddy, Lt J.R. 277
West MM, L/Cpl H. 35–6
Wilkinson, Pte Harry 273, 281, 282

Williamson, Henry 186, 276, 280
Wilson, Lt-Col. G.C. 111
Worsley, Lord 55
Youens VC, 2/Lt F. 106
Young, Lt A.C. 159
Petit Bois 232, 234, 235, 238, 239, 243
Petit Douve Farm 247, 250, 253–4
Ploegsteert 265, 281, 282, 283
Ploegsteert Wood 265, 267, 271, 275–8, 279, 284
Plugstreet Experience 263
Poperinghe 190–207
Potijze 44–50
Prowse Point 272–3

Railway Wood 87–8
Rosenberg Chateau 266

St George's Memorial Church 18
St Martin's Cathedral 15–17
St Yves 278
Sanctuary Wood Trench Museum 78–82
Scherpenberg 225
Skindles 200
Spanbroekmolen 259–62

Talbot House 193, 198–200
Trench 122 Crater 279

Units:
    2 Dragoon Guards 47
    6 Dragoon Guards 229
    10 Hussars 183
    11 Hussars 249
    19 Hussars 183
    1 King Edward's Horse 65–6
    9 Lancers 183, 206, 258
    21 Lancers 258
    Royal Horse Guards 110, 111
    1 Life Guards 110

    2/Auckland Regiment NZEF 258
    7/Australian Imperial Force 205, 206

12/Australian Imperial Force 251
33/Australian Imperial Force 275
34/Australian Imperial Force 157, 168
40/Australian Imperial Force 157
53/Australian Imperial Force 119
2/Border Regiment 269–70
8/Buffs 124, 136
1/Canadian Infantry 247
2/Canadian Infantry 125
7/Canadian Infantry 253
13/Canadian Infantry 80
15/Canadian Infantry 282
21/Canadian Infantry 121
25/Canadian Infantry 211
26/Canadian Infantry 211
28/Canadian Infantry 97
31/Canadian Infantry 210, 237
42/Canadian Infantry 175
49/Canadian Infantry 165
60/Canadian Infantry 105, 114
72/Canadian Infantry 164
85/Canadian Infantry 167–8
4/Canadian Mounted Rifles 102
1/9 Argyll & Sutherland Highlanders 174
1/Cheshire Regiment 111, 112
2/Cheshire Regiment 136
9/Cheshire Regiment 243
2/Coldstream Guards 141
1/Dorsetshire Regiment 115–16
6/Duke of Cornwall's Light Infantry 15, 17, 82, 84
2/Duke of Wellington 124
10/Duke of Wellington 13
2/Durham Light Infantry 92
6/Durham Light Infantry 211
8/Durham Light Infantry 106
13/Durham Light Infantry 106
1/East Lancashire Regiment 282
1/East Surrey Regiment 128
7/East Yorkshire Regiment 120
2/Essex Regiment 63, 273–4
1/Gloucestershire Regiment 99, 110

2/Gloucestershire Regiment 120
1/Gordon Highlanders 236–7
2/Grenadier Guards 109, 110
3/Grenadier Guards 111
1/Hampshire Regiment 283
2/Hampshire Regiment 48
15/Hampshire Regiment 47
1/10 King's Liverpool Regiment
  (Liverpool Scottish) 88, 89–91,
  172–3, 184, 212
17/King's Liverpool Regiment 100
2/King's Own Royal Lancaster
  Regiment 44
1/King's Own Scottish Borderers
  143–4
1/4 King's Own Yorkshire Light
  Infantry 161–2
12/King's Own Yorkshire Light
  Infantry 52
1/King's Royal Rifle Corps 55, 101
11/King's Royal Rifle Corps 53,
  149
13/King's Royal Rifle Corps 213
17/King's Royal Rifle Corps 184,
  265
21/King's Royal Rifle Corps 267,
  276
2/Lancashire Fusiliers 275
11/Lancashire Fusiliers 247
19/Lancashire Fusiliers 217
1/5 Leicestershire Regiment 107,
  113, 125–6, 261
9/Leicestershire Regiment 159
2/Leinster Regiment 92–3, 251,
  285
4/Lincolnshire Regiment 220
1/5 London Regiment (LRB) 276,
  280–1
1/7 London Regiment 134
1/9 London Regiment (QVR) 124–
  5, 127, 130, 249
1/19 London Regiment (St Pancras)
  120
1/28 London Regiment 166
1/4 Loyal North Lancashire
  Regiment 148

8/Loyal North Lancashire Regiment
  271, 277
2/Manchester Regiment 122, 251
2/Middlesex Regiment 96–7
4/Middlesex Regiment 91–2, 121,
  140
1/8 Middlesex Regiment 47–8
16/Middlesex Regiment 161
1/Norfolk Regiment 136
2/Northamptonshire Regiment 41–2
9/Northumberland Fusiliers 20, 77
12/13 Northumberland Fusiliers 159
2/Otago Regiment NZEF 258
Princess Patrica's Canadian Light
  Infantry 162–4, 166, 178
1/Rifle Brigade 77, 277
7/Rifle Brigade 82
1/4 Royal Berkshire Regiment 265
3/Royal Fusiliers 222
11/Royal Fusiliers 180
2/Royal Inniskilling Fusiliers 160
8/Royal Inniskilling Fusiliers 173
9/Royal Irish Fusiliers 172
2/Royal Irish Regiment 173
6/Royal Irish Regiment 215
2/Royal Irish Rifles 218, 236, 266
8/Royal Irish Rifles 261
10/Royal Irish Rifles 248
11/Royal Irish Rifles 236, 237
14/Royal Irish Rifles 267
2/Royal Scots 222, 247
2/Royal Sussex Regiment 34
9/Royal Sussex Regiment 251
11/Royal Sussex Regiment 45–6,
  180
13/Royal Sussex Regiment 35–6,
  133–4
1/Royal Warwickshire Regiment
  272, 278
10/Royal Welsh Fusiliers 135
15/Royal Welsh Fusiliers 74
1/Royal West Kent Regiment 112
8/Royal West Kent Regiment 183
10/Royal West Kent Regiment 177–8
4/Seaforth Highlanders 148
1/6 Sherwood Foresters 136

1/8 Sherwood Foresters 222
16/Sherwood Foresters 172
1/Somerset Light Infantry 272, 277
2/South Lancashire Regiment 86
1/5 South Staffordshire Regiment
247
1/6 South Staffordshire Regiment
247
10/South Wales Borderers, 120
2/Suffolk Regiment 122–3, 135
1/Welsh Guards 72, 175
11/West Yorkshire Regiment 128
2/York & Lancaster Regiment 186
7/York & Lancaster Regiment 133
1/4 Yorkshire Regiment 106
6/Yorkshire Regiment 160

153 Field Company RE 137
171 Tunnelling Company RE 127,
253, 267
175 Tunnelling Company RE 91–2
177 Tunnelling Company RE 89
250 Tunnelling Company RE 222–
3, 231, 232, 234, 235, 244, 259,
261
254 Tunnelling Company RE 268

Z/41 TMB RGA 267
112 Brigade RFA 13, 112–13, 247
180 Siege Battery RGA 134

232 Brigade RFA 173
296 Brigade RFA 20
298 Brigade RFA 135

44 Casualty Clearing Station
RAMC 206, 207
113 Field Ambulance RAMC 172

2 Field Company Canadian
Engineers 285

Varlet Farm 166
Vlamertinghe Mill 185

White Chateau 42
Wieltje 50–3
Wipers Times 27
Wulverghem 245, 248, 250
Wytschaete 227–9, 239, 243, 244

Y Wood 86–7
Yorkshire Trench 75–6, 141
Ypres Barracks 23–4
Ypres Prison 18–19
Ypres Station 22–3
Ypres Water Tower 21

Zillebeke Lake 106–7
Zouave Wood 83–4